FIVE ARCHES

AND

'PHILOCTETES' AND OTHER POEMS

BY THE SAME AUTHOR

LONGINUS AND ENGLISH CRITICISM
THE LONELY TOWER
THE HARVEST OF TRAGEDY
THE APPLE AND THE SPECTROSCOPE
SCIENCE IN WRITING
PLAYS AND POEMS OF JOHN MILLINGTON SYNGE
PASSAGES FOR DIVINE READING
RUDYARD KIPLING
POEMS 1964
THE BIBLE AS LITERATURE
THE LIVING IMAGE
LAST ESSAYS

FIVE ARCHES

A Sketch for an Autobiography

and

'Philoctetes' and Other Poems

T. R. Henn

with illustrations by Alan Freer

COLIN SMYTHE
Gerrards Cross, 1980

Copyright © 1980 Estate of T. R. Henn

First published in 1980 by Colin Smythe Ltd., Gerrards Cross, Buckinghamshire

British Library Cataloguing in Publication Data

Henn, Thomas Rice
    Five arches: a sketch for an autobiography, and 'Philoctetes' and other poems
    1. Henn, Thomas Rice
    2. Critics – Ireland – Biography
    3. Poets, Irish – 20th century – Biography
    I. Title
    821'.9'14   PN75.H/

ISBN 0–901072–92–3

Printed in Great Britain

Set by Watford Typesetters Ltd.

Reproduced from copy supplied
printed and bound in Great Britain
by Billing and Sons Limited
Guildford, London, Oxford, Worcester

'I leave both faith and pride
To young upstanding men
Climbing the mountain-side,
That under bursting dawn
They may drop a fly;
Being of that metal made
Till it was broken by
This sedentary trade.'

       W. B. YEATS, 'The Tower'

CONTENTS

Page

Five Arches

Foreword		11
Acknowledgements		11
I	Sligo and Clare	13
II	The River	27
III	'We too had many pretty toys. . . .'	53
IV	Preparatory School	62
V	'The Troubles'	76
VI	Cambridge	86
VII	Indian Interlude	101
VIII	Return to Cambridge	110
IX	'Mere arithmetician'	130
X	Invasion and After	156
XI	Italy, 1944–5	173
XII	Cambridge Post War	185
XIII	Fall of the House	202

Philoctetes and Other Poems

Foreword	223
Philoctetes	229
Threnody in Time of Civil War	230
To Wilton House	235
Christmas Eve, 1940	237
Reflections before Jericho	238
On Cattistock Hill	239
March Moon	240
Return to the Daye House	241
Fragments of a Testament	244
Antiphon: After Battle	248
The River	251
Buddha and the Fish	256
Shooting a Bat	257

	Page
Ebb Tide	259
Sluice-Gate	260
Accomplice	261
The Tower Revisited	262
Ode pour l'Election	263
Prelude for 1962	265
Dark Journey, 1919	267
Two Pictures	271
29 December 1964	272
Urbs Beata Jerusalem	274
On a Dying Lady	277
First Anniversary	279
In the Beginning	280
For Shotaro Oshima	283
Living Images	284
The Harrowing of Hell	286
Burning of a House	289
Waterfall	291
Nine O'Clock	293
Convalescent	294
Wave	295
Apocalypse	296
Attentions	300
Notes to the poems	303
Appendix: Genealogy	313
Index	317

ILLUSTRATIONS
by
Alan Freer

	Page
Five Arches	10
'The Big River'	26
The Waterfall	33
The Shore Wood	56
The Central Arch, St. Catharine's College . . .	112
Standing Stones	155
Thoor Ballylee	193
Ben Bulben	201
A Mountain Lake, near Delphi	208
Paradise aflame	213
Graveyard Hill	219

ACKNOWLEDGEMENTS

The prose passage on pp. 36–40 was once broadcast on the old Third Programme of the BBC in the series called 'The Making of a Poem': I am grateful for permission to reproduce it here. I acknowledge a debt to Macmillan Publishers and to Michael B. Yeats and Anne Yeats for permission to use a number of quotations from W. B. Yeats's works, and to Macmillan also to use a quotation from Kipling; to Jonathan Cape Ltd. for the quotation from 'The Stand-To' by C. Day-Lewis; to the Society of Authors as the literary representative of the Estate of A. E. Housman and Jonathan Cape Ltd. publishers of A. E. Housman's *Collected Poems;* to Curtis Brown Ltd. on behalf of John Child-Villiers and Valentine Lamb as literary executors of Lord Dunsany for permission to publish the poem by Lord Dunsany; and to Kathleen Raine for permission to use the two quotations, in the last chapter, from her *Collected Poems*. The remaining verses of mine in *Five Arches,* mainly concerning Ireland and Italy, originally appeared in my *Shooting a Bat,* published in 1962 by the Golden Head Press.

T. R. Henn

*

The publisher wishes to thank Edward Malins for his work in preparing the typescript for publication, and John Andrew, Tom Henn's Literary Executor, for his advice and assistance.

FOREWORD

... *'till, flowing through a bridge of five low arches, it mingles with the brackish waters of the Shannon estuary.'*

This is a quotation from a forgotten book, *Wild Sports in Ireland*; largely written at my home by a former Trinity Hall man, 'John Bickerdyke'. Some of it concerns the River, once part of our estates, on which I spent some of the happiest years of my boyhood; growing to know it and to love it, and to revisit its many pools in dreams, in distress and in time of war.

It is not large, or famous, or a particularly good fishing river. The centre arch was destroyed, broken down with crowbars so as to make it impassable except on foot, at the time of the Irish Troubles; but it was quickly rebuilt. On one side the sea-wall below it has been allowed to lapse into ruin, like so many things in Ireland, and the river itself has become almost too overgrown to fish; but the bridge is much as I remember it. The divisions of this book do not correspond strictly to the five arches: but, with some memory of Tennyson's image in *Ulysses,* this seemed as good a title as another.[1]

It has been said that an autobiography begins at every fresh chapter: perhaps that is why I have found it difficult to make a beginning. Life, like the tragedies of which I have written, may perhaps be imaged by a revolving wheel. Every so often some external event – the appearance of a ghost, the outbreak of a war, love, or the resurrection of a past sin, will set the wheel spinning with a new impetus; till, that force exhausted, it seems to slow down; sometimes even sticking on the dead-point, like a model engine with insufficient head of steam. So the cycle goes on; seen, in retrospect, in some arbitrary pattern in time, such as I have tried to present in this book.

[1] I had not read, when I chose it, Richard Church's *Over the Bridge*: nor J. B. C. Grundy's *Five Windows*.

Perhaps the better image is from Yeats: 'Events come upon us like waves.' It is no more possible to analyse the quality of past events than to catch, even in the iridescence of oils such as the paintings of the poet's brother, the quality of light and air in an Atlantic breaker bursting in foam on a reef at Spanish Point or Mullaghmore. But when one has read much poetry, and written a little, there is the further problem of the manner in which one's reading colours the past; less colouring it, perhaps, than certifying, confirming it into a pattern, as if in some progressive and ordered revelation, or a jagged and intermittent puzzle that will one day close up (like the disparate experiences of metaphysical poetry) to reveal some subjective intuition of truth. In this analysis of the past one can never be wholly honest. Some of the emotions that have gathered round vital parts in my life I have tried to set out in verse; here, I have tried to do no more than recall a story that may throw some light on a culture that died between 1916 and 1921, a peculiar and perhaps ambivalent relationship to 'country' and to wild things, some little experience of wars, and a life that has been a happy one.

Cambridge
Osborne

I

SLIGO AND CLARE

The town of Sligo has achieved some fame as the home or at least the nursing-mother of Yeats. It was, and perhaps remains, a small provincial Irish town, redeemed from sordidness by the two mountains that are in constant sight, Ben Bulben and Knocknarea, and the lesser height of Cairns's Hill; the first two frequent in Yeats' poetry, the third the subject of a superb impressionistic landscape by his brother. At the time of my birth and childhood the houses had not spread far along the road to Ballisodare and Dublin, and the square ugly house in which I was born stood almost on the outskirts, in its own grounds, and was called, perhaps in some excess of Victorian patriotism, Albert House. For a small boy there were many delightful things about it. The garden was large, raised well above the road, and held a tiny wood at one end, where slivers of bark could be peeled from birch trees and lighted for their exquisite burning smell; the edges of the strip curl up and crackle as the thin blue smoke rises. Clumps of red-hot pokers made excellent butts at which to shoot arrows; behind, by climbing a stone wall, I reached a large windy field in which kites could be flown. Indeed, I think we have lost much by substituting model aircraft for kites, in which there is something mysterious, fearful, erratic; the initial control of the plunging powerful thing, the final steady flight, the sending to it of 'messengers' cut from circular pieces of cardboard, along the string. And to make a kite, out of split garden bamboos, string, paper and paste is in itself a joy.

Along one side of the walled garden lay a deep sunken lane, leading to the yard and the coach-house. Once a year, on St John's Eve, my Mother bought large quantities of boiled sweets which we children repacked, all day long, in paper 'screws'.

When dusk fell, the lane was filled with one or more large bonfires, and a mob of children and young men, from the nearby little streets. In the light of the fires the youths would run up the lane and leap through the fires in honour of St John, while we flung packages of sweets to the children.[1] Next day we would see boughs of furze fastened over the lintels of the cottage doors, to discourage the fairy people if they came to alight on them. There were other customs, as of the Wren Boys,[2] who appeared throughout St Stephen's Day; youths with masked or blackened faces, in groups of five or six, with rough music accompanying. Their badge of office was a sizeable gorse-bush, trimmed with ribands, in which was a dead wren; the party stood outside the hall-door and sang lugubriously:

> The wren, the wren, the King of all Birds,
> On Stephenses Day was cot in the furze.
> Though he be little, his family's great –
> So up, Your Honour, an' give us a thrate.
> And if your thrate be of the best
> In Heaven we pray your soul may rest . . .

Local ingenuity then added a personal couplet:

> On Cairnses Hill we cot the wren,
> And now we bring it to Misther Henn.

Some sort of 'thrate' would be produced; biscuits, tea, pennies, and the group went its way with blessings. We were always exposed to beggars, of every kind; some with music, usually the fiddle, more often elderly women, with black shawls over their heads; slum children who ran beside the trap or outside car; the ubiquitous truculent tinkers with their caravans and dogs.

The little town, in the period of my childhood, was mainly Protestant, with two large churches; the social gap being complete, or nearly so, between Protestant and Catholic; and

---

[1] The same ritual is described in Honor Tracy's *The Straight and Narrow Path*, viewed by an English anthropologist from a tree overlooking a convent garden. The Mother Superior exhorts her nuns to gird up their habits and jump through the fires.

[2] Their folk-lore is mysterious and complicated in origin. See E. A. Armstrong's *The Folklore of Birds*.

surrounded, at distances varying from a mile or two to ten or more, by a group of the 'big houses'. Of some of these Yeats has written in verse or prose: in particular, of Lissadell, where as a ragged boy he used to go, and be given better clothes and shoes than those he wore.[1] There were many others: Hazelwood, Markree, Cooper's Hill, Annaghmore of the O'Haras: my eldest sister, remarkable for her beauty and sweetness, married one of that family, and I was a babe-in-arms at her wedding.

The small port, laid out in long stone quays on the south side of the short river that flows out of Lough Gill, was then thriving and busy; a coastal trade of small ships, and others that took cattle and pigs to Liverpool and elsewhere. I do not know whether troops were ever embarked, or what Kipling's authority was for the snatch of a marching song that he quotes somewhere (it sounds promising):

We crave your condescension to tell us what you know
Of marching with the Mulligan Guards to Sligo Port below.

The estuary of the port, with a big rise and fall of tide, so that the larger boats could only use the springs, was of infinite delight to a boy, who did not know that the quays would one day be the setting of Yeats' last pamphlet, *On the Boiler*. Indeed, I do not remember his Boiler; only a maze of rusting anchors, mooring chains and railway wagons at the end of the quay. There was always occupation there; steamers to watch loading, cargo swung on the derricks (later I was sometimes allowed to work the donkey-engines); a corn mill where maize was ground, and one could watch the huge steel piston-rod sliding quietly between the high and low pressure cylinders, to make vivid, in later years, Kipling's description of the engine-room in *MacAndrew's Hymn*. Sometimes my father took me on a trip on a harbour tug, down to Rosses' Point, and the statue of The Metal Man at the entrance to the channel, that you may see in J. B. Yeats' illustration to his brother's *Reveries Over Childhood and Youth*. We would go down the winding channel, marked by seaweed-covered cairns of stone surmounted by poles carrying black triangular perches, on which sat many cormorants and

---

[1] I would have hesitated over this, since Yeats' people were respectable middle-class as George Moore noted maliciously; but my informant was Maeve de Markiewicz, the daughter of the Countess, once my schoolmate.

shags, Synge's 'black hags that do be flying on the sea'; till the white sands opened, left and right, to Ballisodare Bay and Rosses' Point. For a boy of seven or so to be allowed to take the wheel of the fussy black smoking tug was sheer ecstasy.

But the harbour yielded other things. At certain times of the year it was invaded with young pollack, known as "bullagogues', perhaps eight or ten inches long; these could be readily caught from the piers with a small rod and line, baiting with fragments of peeled shrimp, and taken home with pride to be eaten. And here I must record, with unending gratitude, my Father's firm conviction that a small boy should live dangerously (my Mother at any rate thought the slimy piers, with twenty foot of tide beneath, no safe playground). This attitude of my Father's remained constant; a wholly lethal gun at the age of nine, a full-sized one (but both after meticulous drilling) at eleven; and allowed to sail a boat alone, on one of the more dangerous estuaries of the kingdom, at the age of twelve. Perhaps this tolerance came from memories of his own boyhood in Clare, and perhaps from an ancient prophecy of that county that the sea would never drown anyone of our name.

My Father plays such a large part in my childhood and afterwards that I must try to picture him here. I was born of his later middle age, the eldest of my three sisters being some twenty years older; my brother, next to me, ten years. So it happened that, with my Mother much busied with the household and the older children, I was a great deal with him. He had been to Radley, a good runner and oarsman; then, after the family pattern, a classical scholar of Trinity College, Dublin; then the Inner Temple, the Bar, and a return to Admiralty practice in Dublin. A marriage that was early, or at least before he was established in practice, took him to a Resident Magistracy, first at Ballina and then at Sligo. He was the second son; but his brother, who, after marrying a rich woman, spent all his fortune and much of hers on a series of yachting adventures while in the Royal Navy, for he challenged three times, unsuccessfully, for America's Cup with a steel ninety-tonner called *Galatea*;[1] died childless, and my father inherited the family place about 1902. But it was heavily encumbered with jointures and settlements;

---

[1] Her opponent was *Mayflower*: both were heavily canvassed, plank-on-edge cutters of the old type. The new bulb-and-fin hulls were just coming in; the next challenger was Lipton's *Shamrock*.

my grandfather's large family took their shares; and my Father continued his career. He retired in 1913, and died of cancer two years later.

He was of less than middle height, with twinkling blue eyes and a face weather-beaten from an open-air life; for though he was a lawyer, he had to drive long distances in all sorts of weather, by horse and trap, to his Courts. There was always a coachman, except when my Mother drove him to Quarter-Sessions and the like; for he had no skill with horses, and I think mistrusted them. In a boat he was superb; experienced, quick and fearless (he had steered big yachts in races on the Clyde), and from him I took my love of the water and my first lessons in seamanship. He had been, perhaps, one of the best shots in Ireland, and I do not know that his record of thirty-nine snipe with forty-one cartridges has been bettered. One of my earliest recollections was of being allowed to clean and oil the fore-end of his gun when he came in, wet and tired, from shooting. He was an excellent fisherman, both in fresh and salt water, making and inventing his own gear, and tying his own flies. At Sligo, a long low room, a sort of pent-house added on after the square plastered house had been built, served as his study; a second door opened on to the stable-yard, so that the RIC Sergeants and Court Clerks who came often to see him could have access directly. There, at a great black desk, which was afterwards to become of importance to me, he wrote up his cases and judgements. On one wall the fishing-rods, all old-fashioned spliced greenhearts, hung on nails. The bookshelves contained his law library, many Greek and Latin Classics, and – rather strange and exciting to a small boy – books of the 'eighties on the physics and hydrostatics of the time; for he had a strong mechanical bent as well as being a classics prizeman.

He was fifty-three when I was born. As I grew older there were expeditions with him; to the Harbour at Sligo; to the shores of Lough Gill where we sometimes took out a rowing-boat, or sailed a model yacht; occasionally to the exquisite lake that lies under Ben Bulben, called Glencar. Drumcliff's fame as the burial place of the greatest poet since Shakespeare was far in the future; but on the steep rocky ledges of that numinous mountain I was shown wild goats and, once, an eagle. I did not then know the story, that Yeats makes much of, of the fiery riders that pass nightly between Ben Bulben and Knocknarea; the legend aligned, nostalgically or ironically – this was Yeats' method – with memories of the Gore-Booth girls and the meets of harriers in the open country at the foot of the mountains:

> Saddle and ride, I heard a man say,
> Out of Ben Bulben and Knocknarea,
> *What says the Clock of the Great Clock Tower?*
> All those tragic characters ride
> Yet turn from Rosses' crawling tide,
> The meet's upon the mountain side.
> *A slow low note and an iron bell.*

My Father was quick-tempered, precise in his law judgements and writing, intolerant of fools; with the gift and quality of being able to get on terms, instantly and without effort, with all types of men: particularly fishermen, sailors and the peasantry of the West. He was, I think, a good lawyer. Many generations of legal ancestry had provided an immense fund of anecdotes, both about the old Munster Circuit and his own experiences on the Bench. One story, which he was fond of telling against himself, concerned his first appearance in Sligo: he had just been posted there from Ballina. In the train going to Petty Sessions he found himself in the company of some cattle-jobbers: he was hidden behind his paper, and found after a time that they were discussing him.

'Yerra, Mick, what d'ye think of that new Stipendiary they've appointed at Sligo?'
'Sure an' I wouldn't know, John. I'd be thinking M— (naming his predecessor) was betther."
'An' why would that be, now?'
'Well, the other day there was a class of a cousin of mine had a process against him for rates; and I got up to say a word for him in Court, An' that fella Henn was on the Bench.
"Are ye a barrister?" says he.
"I am not," says I.
"Are ye a solicitor?" says he.
"I am not," says I.
"Then go to hell an' blazes," says he. Yerra, he's a coarse-minded man.'

Sligo and Clare

There was another incident of which I just remember the domestic aftermath. An important fishery case was to be tried in Sligo the next day. Late that night after supper there was a knock at the back door; two masked men came into the kitchen, each with a sack slung over his shoulder. Without a word they swung the sacks off their shoulders and poured them on the floor; several dozens of live lobsters, unpinioned or 'nicked', which were the bribe for the next day's proceedings. The family came in to find the cook and the maids in hysterics, the candles overturned, and the black lobsters snapping angrily on the stone floor of the old-fashioned kitchen. It was some time before the household recovered, but it was not possible to return the bribe.

My Father had a slight stammer, which apparently descended to me, and which, until I learned to box, caused me a good deal of misery at school; but he spoke well in court, and was an accomplished and witty teller of stories. I remember his pausing, at the vast dinner-parties of the time, in the act of carving a joint, while he related some story, oblivious to the hovering maids and my Mother's angry glances. He used to go into great rages over the slackness, unpunctuality and what he called the 'blackguardism' that he met; before he died he often said that the only hope for Ireland was to see a German fleet come up the Shannon, re-colonize the country, and teach the people habits of cleanliness and industry. He could not foresee that within half a century his home would be sold for a tiny fraction of its value to be the summer playground of a wealthy German. (When Siemens-Schückert built the Shannon Barrage after the Treaty, and I went sometimes to speak with the workmen on the site, their comments on Irish labour were unprintable.) The workmen at Paradise, the family home in Co. Clare, used to irritate him, and he attempted to secure some measure of honesty and efficiency by employing Protestant stewards, preferably of Northern or Scottish stock.

It was then that I first became conscious of the religious problem. Sligo at that time carried a large Protestant population, and, as Sean O'Casey has written in his memoirs, their habits and hygiene differed widely from those of the Catholics. The further one went south, the thinner became the 'Prodestants' (the hard 'd' is significant); in Clare, the attendance at our church under the most favourable conditions was perhaps a score for an area of some twenty square miles. (These were gradually eliminated from 1916 onwards, and the church itself demolished in the 1950s.) Even in Sligo the Southern Irishmen were looked upon as semi-barbaric; before my Father retired to Paradise a deputation of citizens called upon him, begging him not to leave civilization and commit himself to 'thim savages'. And soon after we had moved there there was indeed some evidence; as I drove on a jaunting car to my first term at the preparatory school my Father leaned across and covered my eyes, so that I should not see the pool of blood on the limestone road. A postman had been murdered, shot from behind a hedge, early that morning; the motives were said to have been purely personal.

This 'violence on the roads' was traditional, the source of endless stories and ballads. Synge's *Danny*, set in North-West Mayo, is convincing in its realistic brutality. I remember a verse from a poem by my brother:

> They drink their pints in Ennis town,
> Their pints of porter, strong and brown:
> Then wipe their lips and boast how they
> Shot Shaun O'Dwyer, out Darragh way.

There were times and places when one did not sit between an unshuttered window and the light.

> 'Augusta Gregory seated at her great ormolu table,
> Her eightieth winter approaching: "Yesterday he threatened my life.
> I told him that nightly I sat from six to seven at this table
> The blinds drawn up." '
> W. B. Yeats, 'Beautiful Lofty Things'

At coffee on the terrace on a summer evening one might hear a casual shot, a rabbit being poached somewhere in the 'back woods'; the usual jest was to say, 'There goes another landlord'. My Father had a story of a curate preaching to a congregation in Clare Island, Co Mayo, then as remote a parish as one could find: 'Boys, what makes ye bad members of holy Church an' back in y'r dues? Drink! What puts y'r wife in rags an' leaves y'r children in starvation? Drink! What leaves ye back in the rent? Drink! What makes ye shoot at y'r landlord – AND MISS HIM? Drink!' But any shooting was a complicated and, as usual, slightly ambivalent affair; it might have some of the characteristics of a religious act, or the assertion of freedom against tyranny, or an ancient feud, or some more sensible object such as the hope of obtaining the dead man's land. My Mother and Father were married in 1881, when agrarian troubles were at one of their peak periods.

My Mother told me how in those days she would walk out along one of the roads, to meet my Father driving home in the evening from one of his courts; and how a group of loafers outside a public house would call out to the bride, 'O, Mrs Henn, 'tis all right; we aren't going to shoot your husband *yet*!' And my Father used to talk of a friend of his, also a Resident Magistrate, who was stopped on a lonely road while walking the horse and trap (he was driving alone) slowly up a hill. A man came out from a hedge, reined back the horse, and put up against his chest the muzzle of an old-fashioned .45 revolver. He pulled the trigger; the cartridge in the first chamber misfired. Now there are two ways of cocking such a revolver for the next shot; one by bringing back the hammer with the thumb, the other by pressing on the fore- or trigger-finger, which raised the hammer and fired it with one pull. The would-be murderer chose the second course, and continued to pull on the trigger. Such an action requires a good deal of muscular strength, as well as a well-oiled weapon. After some seconds of futile sawing, his nerve broke; he flung down the revolver and bolted across a field. The magistrate went to the trap, took out from under the seat a Winchester rifle which he always had with him, and shot him dead as he ran.[1]

But my Mother never ceased to be anxious, and particularly mistrusted the sea and my Father's love of it. She was a big, powerfully-built woman, her hair white even in my earliest memory; gay, vigorous, impatient of books or art, and therefore the opposite, or perhaps the complement, of my Father. She had been brought up as a member of a large family, running wild in Co Clare; her father, Colonel Gore, was an MFH and she was said to have been a fine and daring horsewoman, as well as having had, as a girl, countless suitors. Her family were all big vigorous people, of no intellectual pretensions; bringing to my Father's side something to counteract some three centuries of

---

[1] For a sober picture of violence in the mid-nineteenth century. Trench's *Memoirs of a Land Agent* is worth reading.

law and scholarship. (There is a reference in 1708 in a poem – perhaps by Swift, but more probably spurious: *The Counter Scuffle:* Whereunto is Added a Duel between two Connaught Doctors: with an Elegy on the Lord Chief Justice Henn's Connaught Pig.') She was, I think, a bad manager where money was concerned, impulsive, generous, unmethodical; of great spirit and kindness. It was certainly due to her courage and gaiety, and the respect of the people for her, that Paradise was one of the few big houses in the County that was not burnt in 'The Troubles'. Long afterwards we thought how much better if it had been so killed, rather than left to linger on like a dying animal.[1]

Of the rest of the family, my eldest sister married young, in Sligo; the second took the chance of the First War to become a VAD, for I think she had been frustrated at home; the third married a Major of Gunners, who had been badly gassed in 1917. My brother I saw little until we were both well on in years. First of all he was at his public school, then an Exhibitioner of Magdalene; a figure of awe, bringing his friends from school and from Cambridge to stay at Paradise. He took his degree just in time to join up in 1914. He had always intended to go into the Egyptian Civil Service, and did so when the war ended; eventually commanding the Alexandria Police before becoming Chief Constable of Gloucestershire. He was a superb shot, an indifferent fisherman; and keeping, like myself, to my Father's side of the family, was good in a boat but bad with horses. He also wrote excellent light verse. But I saw very little of him till he came back to Gloucestershire in 1935.

Some twenty miles to the north-west of Sligo is a small fishing village called Mullaghmore; a tiny harbour, a long stone breakwater, and a sandy bay open to the Atlantic; then a row of white lodges, a public house or two, and little else.[2] There the family took its seaside holiday each year, before we moved to Clare; I can just remember travelling in a long waggonette, drawn by two horses. We ran wild among the dunes and pinewoods; and, though I was too young for this, fished and sailed. My Father had originated the sport of spinning for the big pollack that

[1] My last chapter describes its burning on 6 October 1971.

[2] One of the Mountbatten estates, an incongruous Gothic building called Classibawn, lies just outside the village.

haunted the kelp-strewn reefs; when the country-folk saw him going down in the evening they would come to meet him with sacks and donkey-carts to be given his catch. Just before he retired, I had a memorable week alone with him there. Most of the time was stormy, and we had to keep inshore, but once as a special treat he took me far out in one of the fishing-boats of that coast, trolling for pollack. They were big, able whaler-type boats, the 'Greencastle Yawls', rigged with two sprit-sails and a jib, and by custom ballasted, no doubt for some good reason, with broken tombstones. That day I made my acquaintance with the big pollack of the outer reefs, running from fifteen to twenty-five pounds, whose first rush down to the kelp is as violent as that of a salmon. They were so voracious that, as a fish was played up to the side of the boat, another would often come up and bite at the tail of the rubber eel hanging from its companion's mouth. Once when a fish came to the side, there was a whirl and a snap, and the line went slack: a small shark had bitten off all but the head. Towards the afternoon the weather changed, and we had to run for home under double reefs. I had great joy in the immense waves and the big boat reeling along down to her gunwhales: I remember my Father smiling and saying to one of the boatmen: 'He doesn't know yet what the danger is.'

As time went on we moved more often to Paradise for part of the summer, and in winter for two ar three weeks round Christmas, my Father following when his Courts allowed; in winter for the shooting, and to dry and air the big house, subject to the strong and steady process of decay of that rain-sodden climate. Finally, in 1913, we moved there from Sligo for good.

My education up till then had been varied. There had been several governesses, one a German Fräulein Wolff, I remember the family's ribald amusement at seeing her make me do physical drill to the time of a mouth-organ on which she played 'Deutschland über Alles'. For a time just before we left Sligo I went to the local grammar school, but was never old enough to play games there. After we moved there was an interregnum of six or seven months before it was time to go to a preparatory school. The interval was bridged by the village schoolmaster who came up to the house several hours a week in the evenings, well primed with whiskey, to teach me with skill a rather antiquated brand of mathematics.

In that uncertain climate one was much indoors; whole days of driving rain came from the western weather. There was an infinity of things to do in the schoolroom or in the Carpenter's Shop that was in the outer courtyard, built on stilts over part of the long turf-house. We had two model steam-engines, with their delightful smell of methylated spirit, hot metal and oil. With the aid of a blowlamp, which must have been highly dangerous, they could be made to achieve incredible revolutions. A number of tattered magazines, called 'Japan's Fight for Freedom', had roused an excitement in all naval things; for a time it was thought that I might go into the Service. Model battleships were to be made out of cardboard and glue, and bombarded with real gunpowder charges out of guns made from garden bamboo, the pith bored out with a red-hot skewer, and a touch-hole made above the knot. The excitement was greater because the guns were apt to burst after a few rounds, but their life could be prolonged by lapping them with brass snare-wire. There were various home-made boats, often called after the America's Cup yachts: and in particular a greatly-loved cutter that my Father had given me.

The appeal of model yachts is a curious one. Years later I paid a call on Jack Yeats, and noticed a magnificent model schooner some four feet long, on a high shelf in the studio. He showed me a number of photographs he had taken of models under sail, the camera held low to the water to give the illusion of size. But this particular yacht had been the object of a family quarrel, and when the poet came to visit his brother he used to look at the yacht and shake his head in sorrowful reproach. I remembered Shelley and his sailing of paper boats, Shelley who in many things was Yeats's early master, and wondered if one could find some link.

On such wet days I read, widely and erratically on my own account, and picked up a considerable amount of miscellaneous verse. I found that anything I liked – and my preference was for strongly-marked rhythms – would 'stick' if I read it over twice. So large quantities of Scott, Macaulay's *Lays of Ancient Rome,* much of Kipling, some of Byron and Moore, were committed to memory. For prose, we had been brought up on a comparatively few books, to which I returned again and again. Kingsley's *The Water Babies* was especially loved (in the edition with the original illustrations) and I can still recall the thrill of horror at the scene where the Wicked Otter prowls round the lobster-pot with Tom inside. Perhaps it was that the book touched so nearly on things that we knew of water and sea and moorland; was there not an image of Tom going down the fell-side 'like a salmon over the falls at Ballisodare', where I had landed my first salmon at the age of nine? I know that the contemporary allusions to Professor Owen and Darwinism passed far over my head. Then there was Kingsley's *Gods and Heroes*: Lamb's *Tales from Shakespeare*, Richard Jefferies's *The Amateur Poacher* from which I drew some knowledge of woodcraft, and perhaps something of Jefferies's ambivalent attitude towards the death of bird and beast; best of all, perhaps, James Stephens's *The Crock of Gold*. For the rest it was a strange miscellany; Wood-Martin's *Traces of the Elder Faiths of Ireland* (his wife had been my Godmother, but died, on my birthday, almost before I knew her); Pope's *Homer*; Somerville and Ross's *Experiences of an Irish RM*; Mary Johnson's novels of the American Civil War; all the Badminton Library volumes, and the two-volume *Encyclopaedia of Sport*; a history of Winchester, of which my grandfather and great-grandfather had been Scholars; and mysterious law books in great quantities. By the time I went to my preparatory school I had small Latin and no Greek: I spoke reasonable German (but then dropped it for five years), some French, and had perhaps more mathematics than was usual. I had no games, but I could sail a boat, harness a horse, throw a fair line, and shoot very straight.

It was during those last six or eight months of freedom that I came to explore the resources of the country round about the house; at first under my Father's tutelage. It was he who brought me to the River, and to some of the mountain lakes; but after a little while I was left to my own devices, for the garden and the orchard, the clearing and the managing of the woods took much of his time. He grew sweet-peas for exhibition; there was a vinery, a begonia house, and a mixed greenhouse that supplied plants for the house. It must have been about this time that my Father decided that two small boys, turned loose all day with a gun, rods or boats, or exploring the wild mountain country behind the estate, with mires and quaking bogs, were less likely to get into serious trouble than one. So there appeared, I do not know how, the son of one of the nearby tenants, who attached himself as bodyguard, co-conspirator and friend; his name was Jimmy, but he was always known as The ADC. He was a little older than I, physically tougher, but afraid of boats and water. I remember that he loved shooting, but was impatient of fishing. He would appear each morning in the inner courtyard, ready for whatever expedition the day held. These were often laborious, and sometimes dangerous. There was a lake some ten miles away over rough roads – it lay, somewhat improbably, on the top of a hill – called Effernan. The sides were boggy and dangerous, but there was an ancient gun-punt, pensioned off as too rotten for the Big River, which we took out to fish from. She leaked and wallowed like a log. At one end of the lake was a *cranógue,* a tiny island that had once served the Lake Dwellers. A submerged causeway, that could be held by a determined man against wolves or human raiders, connected it to the shore; one could still see fragments, the bog-oak piles on which they had built their huts. Jimmy's aunt lived two or three miles away from Paradise, and made dresses for my sisters; I can remember enormous teas with hot soda bread, at her cottage in the middle of Cooga Bog. We had much happiness together. There were no young people of my age on our side of the County, and, because of the complete isolation imposed by 'The Troubles', I do not think that I spoke to a girl till I was twenty.

'The Big River'

II

THE RIVER

i

The River in Summer

Only one man, I think, has written of a river with complete love and understanding; and he made the 'river' of his dreams, which he had known in boyhood, when he came to it on retirement.[1] It is because our own River (and its companion, the Big River, as we called the Shannon Estuary on which Paradise looked out) played so large a part in my education between the ages of ten and eighteen that I write of it here. For its seasons were tied to mine; the Easter holidays, with the fishing newly-opened and the hawthorn in bloom; the summer holidays in thirsty August, with the inch-rain days to bring the occasional flood, that ended all too soon with the return to school in September. One of my duties when I was home was to take and register the rainfall each morning, pouring it into a graduated glass from the blue copper-funnelled receiver that stood on the front lawn. And this had the advantage that one knew early what the state of the River would be, fed from the mosses of the hills and 'mountain'. At other times, in the reputedly 'best' months of May and June, I did not know it at all.

The River was two miles or so away by the main road. In the earlier days I had a donkey for transport, and rode her to the bridge, carrying a fishing-rod slung like a lance across my shoulders, and a slab of bread and bacon for the day's provisions.

---

[1] J. E. C. Jukes, *Loved River*. But since then I have read Neville Nuttall's *Proud River*—in Natal.

A mile from where the avenue turned off the main road, you came to the straggling village, with its one street and five public-houses, crossing a bridge over a lesser stream. The Townland, and consequently the house, had been called originally Ballinagard, a good name; in the Irish 'The Ford-Mouth' or 'The Ford of the Rocks'. So many of the names are beautiful, and ring like chimes in memory: a lake called Gort Glas, 'the green meadow'; the townland of Laválley; Ballydinéen; Lough Lomáun; Sorrel Island – this for a village; Cahircón. But legend had it that in the Seventeenth Century a visiting Bishop, coming round the drive in front of the house and seeing the sudden panorama of estuary, islands, woods and shrubberies, sheltered and set off by the great Turret Hill rising behind to screen it from the westerly gales, exclaimed: 'O, what a perfect paradise!' Paradise it remained, the subject of many ribald jests, of some ironic nostalgia, and of a verse in a hymn.

There was a school house on the village green; a whitewashed RIC Barracks burnt down in 'The Troubles'; very senselessly, for the Royal Irish Constabulary were a fine and popular race of men, tolerant and peaceable, and good at mending bicycles. Occasionally they turned up at winter shoots, at some of which the guns had to be placed (quite illegally) on the main road, and volunteered to act as beaters; much to the consternation of a certain visiting undergraduate from Magdalene, who had no game licence. Further on, one passed a fine ruined Norman tower or, more accurately, a 'Square House' – there are many such in the West – standing on a little plateau fenced with thornbushes, on to which the cattle would have been driven for security during the innumerable raids. One corner of the high walls ended in a narrow neck of masonry which in turn supported a larger block, and this seen from a certain angle on the main road, formed the silhouette of a girl's head, with ivy for her hair. The country-folk said that this commemorated the story of a Norman chief, owner of the castle, whose daughter had eloped with her lover; she had been betrayed by a servant, and her father had overtaken the fugitives and killed them both a mile or so away. At any rate it was certain that the castle was powerfully built. Sometimes we went there for picnics. It was possible to climb far up to the 'neck' of stone. Once, legend said, two village children had climbed higher, and been killed in a fall. Then the village decided to pull down the neck, and

The River

brought many horses and ropes for the attempt. They could not stir it; because, it was said, the mortar of the masonry had been mixed with blood.

It was just such a tower as this that Yeats bought for thirty pounds, and rebuilt for his bride, at Ballylee a few miles from Gort, to give him images from the waters that run below, and later plunge into the cleft of a limestone fault:

> Under my window-ledge the waters race,
> Otters below and moorhens on the top,
> Run for a mile undimmed in Heaven's face
> Then darkening through 'dark' Raftery's 'cellar' drop,
> Run underground, rise in a rocky place
> In Coole demesne, and there to finish up
> Spread to a lake and drop into a hole.
> What's water but the generated soul?

But I did not know Yeats then, still less Plotinus or Porphyry, who answers the last question. Only at school, in the dusty classrooms, I remembered verses from some forgotten book – was it Stoddart's *Angling Songs*? – that seemed to fit the great pool with the Ossianic name of Glenavarra, higher up the river:

> Just there, where the waters dark and cool,
> Linger a moment in yonder pool
>   The dainty trout are at play.
> And now and then one leaps in sight
> With sides a-glow in the golden light
>   Of the long sweet summer's day.

On the way to the River I would be greeted by many friends, some of them my Father's tenantry; if they were in the fields, the proper greeting was to say 'God bless the work!', the proper reply 'And you too'. Then came the forge, where I spent many happy hours, with horses to be shod; blowing the vast lumbering bellows for Sullivan the Smith, watching the miracle of the glowing shoes cut and shaped from the bars that lay racked on the rafters; the smell of burnt horse-hoof and wet slack, leather apron and quenched iron. Are not all smiths powerful and mysterious people? In Africa they can inflict curses and spells from which there is no escape. Then came the Chapel; my grandfather had given the land for it in the middle of last century, and the front pew was still kept for the family, in case they should one day see the light. Then the five-arched bridge, and the River.

It is not easy to explain the excitement, always recreated anew, that it produced in a boy's mind; as still, in memory, it does. Indeed, the sight of a lake, the crossing of a casual river on some journey, still brings back something of the magic; so that one must stop on the bridge and watch the water for a moving fish. Like all mountain rivers, dependent on rain, it was wholly erratic in character. As a further complication, the four lower pools were tidal; and according to the height of it – which somehow one never really bothered to predict – those pools might be useless, or profitable. If the tide had newly left them, there would be redshank and sandpipers, perhaps a curlew or an oystercatcher, probing among the mud and stones; the seaweed smelt fresh, and crackled underfoot. In the Easter holidays the blackthorn on the banks would be in flower, adding yet another scent.

Each pool had its special character, partly generated from family legend, partly out of memories of one's own past failure or success; partly from its own quality of stream or bank or bed which might alter a little from year to year. In any event, wherever one chose to start, there was a ritual to be observed. The cast taken out of an old tobacco-box, and put to soak in a pool; the long Castle Connell rod – infinitely clumsy to modern notions – to be spliced with wax-end made up of many strands of shoe-makers' thread spun together by hand, like a bowstring; the line run through the rings. Then height and colour of water, light and wind and season, had all to be considered before the last act of mounting the flies; for this was before the time of eyed hooks, and it was not easy to change afterwards. Besides, had not The Master said that to see a man changing his flies was the worst possible sign of the day? So to the ecstatic moment of the first cast: the line lengthening and the greenheart rod falling into its peculiar slow rhythm; watching for the flash of silver as the little trout came up. Little they were; a pound fish might well be the prize of a week; and it was, I think, customary to throw back the first fish of the day, unless he were very sizeable. (So does one avoid *hubris.*) But all omens are important: a single magpie on the road to the river, a grey heron fishing at one's favourite throw, these might be enough to spoil the day.

If luck did not come at once, she might be tempted by apparent unconcern, the ritual rejection of expectation, like Yeats's heron:

> And may be I shall catch a trout
> If but I do not seem to care.

Soon one left the tidal pools and their marshy banks, backed by the low sea-walls; struggled through endless hedges of bramble and blackthorn; fishing upwards, pool after pool, as the river wound through its valley towards the next single-arched bridge at the head of Glenavarra. Half-way up there was a long slow tree-lined pool, with bracken-covered slopes on either side; shut in, and usually windless; far out of sight of any cottage. Its smooth deep water always seemed numinous, in a wholly irrational way; and I never came down to it without thinking of the verse quoted by Walter Peard (from Byron) of a fairy funeral procession, coffin and all, gliding over a dark pool:

'Loud Wul-wulleh' (what a word!) 'warns his distant ear.'

But indeed no numen ever showed itself there; only at one pool of the Upper River, for so we called the part that wound into the mountain above the Klondagad waterfall, many miles further up. Because the incident seems to be of a pattern with others, and has no possible explanation, it is worth recollection; and you may read its duplicate, almost exactly, in John Buchan's *Memory Hold the Door*.

It was a hot August afternoon in 1915; the time, two o'clock or thereabouts: I can date the episode fairly closely, because my brother had just been posted as wounded and missing with the Munster Fusiliers at Gallipoli. I came to a pool where the river, after splitting into streams round a substantial rocky island covered with furze, met again; at the head of one pool was a small waterfall, on the left a low cliff. The water was shrunken, the day windless, and I had done little since the morning; the only hope of a fish was in the rapid broken water at the head of the pool. I waded in a yard or two, and threw upstream. Suddenly as I stood and watched the flies come down, an overpowering fear attacked me, utterly cold in quality, and terrible because of its irrationality in that sunlit lonely place. I remember that I dashed out of the water, up and out of the hollow and ran and ran, sweat-sodden, till after a mile or so I came within sight of a cottage. There was nothing following me.

Several times afterwards I went and stood at the base of the same pool to see if the experience would repeat tiself; it never did. It was not till long after that I read of John Buchan's experience, also fishing, and in such a hollow, in the Scottish Lowlands; and then, in a correspondence in a journal, of several parallel happenings all in Scotland. In Plutarch there is an account of the Temple of Fear, that was always kept locked except when someone took sanctuary in it.

Yet there was little of the numinous or tales of the supernatural in that part of the world. The River ran below an ancient ruined church and churchyard at Klondagad; a pleasant place, ivy-covered, not far from the great waterfall that divided the Upper and Lower Rivers. It was a place with its own characteristic and powerful *numen*, separating two worlds: a barrier that the salmon and sea-trout – the Leapers – could never scale to reach the hazel-glens and the moorlands for their spawning, but where the young eels fought their way upwards over the wet rock.[1]

In the churchyard I searched in vain for a traditional rhymed Epitaph on a kinsman's grave:

> Here on his back lies Tom Ross-Lewin,
> A man beloved by all who knew him:
> Who in his youth was a chatty lad;
> He now lies mute in Klondagad.

The ancient raths, ruined castles and fairy rings carried no legends with them. I suspect that these were far more common in the north of the County, where the great limestone area called The Burren was full of remains of early Christian settlements; and in the districts round Kiltartan, where Yeats and Lady Gregory collected their folk-lore and fairy legends.[2] Paradise itself was not haunted: the Coach that comes for the dying person was supposed to appear, as part of the establishment, but was not seen by the family, and only heard by the servants. It

---

[1] See 'Waterfall', p. 291

[2] See *Visions and Beliefs of the West of Ireland* (2nd edition Colin Smythe 1970); and D. A. MacManus's *The Middle Kingdom* ((1959, and Colin Smythe 1973).

arrived at Cambridge, passing my house, in 1934 (the evidence was from the wife of a friend, who lived in the same road, but who was quite unaware of the tradition); but that must have been a mistake in the card-index system, since one of my uncles, a Colonel of Gunners, had died that night at Camberley, not Cambridge. A large and beautiful house, on the Big River six or seven miles to the south, was said to be under a curse, that the oldest son should never inherit; a wise woman from the hills had cursed it because its builder had brought stones from a ruined Abbey on an island in the Shannon. I have never brought myself to deny the power of curses or of blessings.[1] This particular curse appeared to be on the point of being broken in 1914, when the new inheritor went to France with the Irish Guards, and was hit by a high-explosive shell. The house – it was unburnt in 'The Troubles' – is now, I believe, a training college for Roman Catholic missionaries.

Waterfall, from Bickerdyke's *Wild Sports of Ireland*

[1] Lord Dunsany's *The Curse of the Wise Woman* describes such an incident: as well as a boyhood not unlike my own.

ii

The River in Winter

The year was divided by the seasons, by events at school, and by what was going on at home, so that three rhythms were superimposed. September meant the last floods in the River, the sea-trout running, and perhaps an occasional expedition on the 'mountain' after the few snipe that did not migrate to breed. But more strongly it recalled the smells of school, of disinfectant and new books, the sound of footballs being kicked about on a crisp October afternoon, the white fives-courts, and the inexpressibly satisfying wrist-drive as the gloved hand met the ball. At home there would be various land – or time – marks; the first full moon in October would bring in the flights of foreign snipe from Scandinavia, the woodcock a little later; boats would be laid up for the season; apples by the cartload gathered and stored from the great orchard; all these would be noted in my Father's letters, leading up to the Christmas holidays.

In that westerly climate of high temperature and higher rainfall, gales and floods were common, ice or hail comparatively rare. A wet Christmas would mean day after day indoors, browsing in a good though Victorian library; perhaps carpentering in the workshop in the outer courtyard; and such days were unlike the spring and summer, when wet days heralded a flood in the River, and must be profitably spent making fishing gear and tying flies. I looked eagerly for hard weather, frost with hail preferably; for that drove the woodcock in from the open country to the laurel and rhododendron coverts where the thick varnished leaves, especially of the holly, kept the ground underneath moist and warm, so that the long sensitive bills with the nerve-riddled overshot tips could probe for worms and larvae. The tiny stiff 'pin-feather' on each elbow was carefully saved as a trophy; we were told that artists used them for painting miniatures. Indeed the woodcock still seems to me the most mysterious and exciting of birds; unpredictable in his coming and going; flitting in the dusk through his own airways in the thickest woods; rising up disturbed from cover with a characteristic and unmistakable rattle of wings; with the delicate mottled plumage that blends so perfectly with dead leaves or bracken, so that one

The River

may walk many times within sight of a fallen bird without discovering it. Yet often enough a good dog will refuse to retrieve a woodcock, perhaps misliking the harsh scent.

Next in importance came the snipe, moved mysteriously, like the woodcock and women, by the moon. A mile westward from the house there were thousands of acres of snipe-ground that one might walk, returning drenched in the evening; for however skilful the walking – and one knew by long practice whether the ground in front would bear one's weight, relying all the while on touch, for the eyes had to watch the ground a score of yards ahead – it was certain that sooner or later one would go over the knees in sphagnum moss, which was pleasant and springy, or quaking bog, which was not. It was said to be healthy, this wet wilderness, peaty water and iodine, kind to the feet. I remember that my sisters collected quantities of sphagnum at the beginning of the First World War, for medical swabs and pads. There were multitudes of these bogs, sometimes small, lying in the hollows of valleys, cultivation edging up to them as men wrested the rushy sour land into little black potato fields, or small patches of late-harvested stunted oats. But as one went westward up into 'the mountain' the stretches of bog became vast, interspersed with streams and, sometimes, a little lake hidden in the hill-foldings. One such was the pivot of our beat, the point where one turned back for home; it bore a musical and mysterious name, Lough Lomáun. It was utterly lonely, and, to me, numinous; at one end, a mire of coarse grass and quaking bog, on which it was unwise to walk. You come upon it suddenly, climbing a little hill, taking cover in a sunken ditch as you peer over the ridge; for though it is unlikely that you will get a shot at them, there may be anything on the water; a sord of mallard, a couple of teal, even a wild goose. There will surely be a heron fishing, but this is far from the River, and there is no need to try to shoot him. But the lake renewed its being each time one edged over the crest for some reason that I do not understand; and it has remained 'the image of my last content'.

According to moon and weather the snipe came and went; in the full of the moon mainly on the 'red ground', as we called the heather and turf bog itself; in the moon's dark, scattered in the rushy fields and beside 'the little streams that wandered everywhere'. After a night of storm and wind, which had presumably made them ill at ease in feeding, they might be nearly unapproachable, rising a gun-shot or more out of reach; a dull calm night, and they might lie well. But a first frost that crisped the ground noisily with small ice made them wild again.

The River itself was generally in flood, unfordable. Below the Five Arches it meandered through its own estuary, between sea-walls, served by a sluice system that kept the tides from what were called the 'corcass' lands; big fields intersected by dykes and cut into irregular shapes by subsidiary winding creeks, reclaimed, in the eighteenth century, from the banks of clean grey mud. It was all meadow and pasture-land, thrusting richly out of the alluvial soil; a hundred years before it had grown corn, as the occasional ruined granary beside a stone quay testified. Now it was under hay and cattle, tending always to return to reeds and rushes if the fields were neglected.

In and out of such creeks the tide swept restlessly with a huge rise and fall. Countless sea-birds and waders followed its ebbing, to feed on the shell- and fish-life of the water-edge. In hard weather duck of all kinds, and occasional geese, would come in from the Big River. Besides the snipe, that lay by ones and twos in rushy corners, seeming to haunt the same spots year after year so that each was remembered as a record of triumph or defeat, occasional teal or mallard might be found as one peered cautiously over the sea-walls. Once, on a bitter morning the ice froze in the twenty minutes or so of slack water at high tide, to explode with great crackings as the water fell from under it. In a fog everything became mysterious, the wild-fowl curiously large and black, coming and going like ghosts with sudden swerving cries of alarm.

iii

It was very quiet in that frosty dawn. Somewhere just beyond the great sea-wall, with the narrow path on top of it, there was a pack of widgeon. They were talking to each other: with high soft whistles, and faint discontented flutterings in the water, as they came in on top of the tide. There were some mallard, too, not far away: one could hear the faint quacks, a more domestic and discordant note. The flood-tide came up: along the edge of the marram grass it crept, and lifted the thin layer of ice forming among the clean scum that had been floated off the mud. On the landward side, in the dyke whose dead reeds shifted a little as the leakage of the sluice went by, one could hear a faint patter: a moorhen, perhaps, in the crisp grass at the edge of the meadow.

Under the hand, the lockwork and trigger guard burnt as with fire: it was a relief to shift it to the walnut of the grip, and feel the wood kindly and alive with linseed. The wildfowl came in steadily, and through the edge of the false dawn little eddies of fog twisted above the bents of grass: the speech of the birds grew louder, and one fancied little querulous notes in it: complaints thrown to and fro, or answered sympathetically, or disregarded, as the mood of the speaker required. It was nearly high water; for a few minutes the spring tide would hang in standing water, and the rim of ice would form out over the shallows, and hide the dead gulls that had come in, their plumage oil-sodden, to wash to and fro. From somewhere to landward there was the crowing of a cock.

No one knows who wrote that ballad and fixed the moment so exactly, with such knowledge of the cold and tension of dawn:

> O cocks are crowing on merry middle earth,
> I wot the wildfowls are boding day . . .

Every now and again there starts up, through imagery and epithets which are in the main conventional, this sudden certainty of phrase, this consciousness of the thing lived. Clerk Saunders was a ghost: the fatal seventh brother had (though the rest were, through dramatic stages, moved to pity) stabbed him sleeping in Margaret's arms. Now he comes to reclaim his troth: he stands at the shot-window: in grave-clothes, perhaps. He comforts Margaret, who in those few short stanzas has turned from girl to woman, and from woman to mother, with a bitter intensity of hatred against the father who has tried to comfort her. She will die, as she knows, 'in strong travailling'; but the ghost of her lover reassures her. He gets his troth, 'stroken' on a crystal wand – what better symbol? – and the rhythm quickens with his relief:

> I thank ye, Margaret; I thank ye, Margaret;
> And ay I thank ye heartilie;
> Gin ever the dead come for the quick,
> Be sure, true love, I'll come for ye.

Then into that poem, miraculously, to give the sense of that tenseness and cold of dawn:

> I wot the wildfowls are boding day.

The air grows a little thinner. There is no dapple or complexity in the movement of the light; merely a shading of heaviness, and the first water shows a few feet away, the eddies of fog swirling above it. For a moment the soft whistling of the widgeon is stilled; they are listening. The thrill of excitement, which communicates itself so instantly in the open, seems to unite us for a moment in the expectancy of fear. For the coming of the dawn can be something tense and terrible; whether that sun lifting palpable, foot by foot, over an Indian mere, or the light breaking over the green hollow seas that seem level with the tiny boat in the Atlantic.

> West and away the wheels of darkness roll
> Day's beamy banner up the East is borne . . .

There was nothing of Housman's bitter crescendo in this coming of the light: only a flexing of muscles in readiness. The sentinel birds on the edge of the pack of widgeon were waiting too. So Spenser:

> And he that 'points the Sentinell his Roome
> Doth licence him depart at sound of Morning Drum.

The watch is relieved: the signal is that tremendous thud of the drum, so exciting as the herald of death or life:

> But hark! my pulse, like a soft drum,
> Beats my approach, tells Thee I come.

In the silence that followed one can hear the blood throbbing across the temples: some deep lust of the hunter awakes for the moment, and forgets the cold. A moment more, and the black shapes, curiously large, would stand out on the water; there would be a single vital instant as they rose in swift noisy motion.

I suppose that the hour of death and of dawn are always in some inexorable association; as if the symbol-counters of life and death must at that moment change: as if, indeed, there were no more than a fixed number of either in the sum-total of the vitality or blood of the world. For the dawn is the hour of the attack, and as such has come into our consciousness, dulled though it was in the space between wars; it is the hour of all sacrifice; it is, perhaps, the hour when all wild life has the faculties acutely sensitized, and those of civilized man are lowest. Yet, I think, it is the hour when one fears death least, for the imagination, by which alone we have 'created death' is less in play:

> Nor dread nor hope attend
> A dying animal.
> A man awaits his end
> Dreading and hoping all.

Yet death seems such a little thing, if the imagination does not drive it with the strong ghosts of time and history: the sudden convulsion of the muscles:

> A sudden or a bloody end
> Gunshot or running noose –

The greatest are perhaps those who have watched it, and allowed their minds to play upon it, and let their thoughts link image upon image, and then, at the last, risen to religious exaltation, the tension of high breeding in the pun or jest:

> When my physicians by their love are growne
>   Cosmographers, and I their mappe, who lie
> Flat on this bed, that by them may be shown
> That this is my South-West discoverie.
> *Per fretum febris,* by these Straits to die.
>
> I joye that in these Straits I see my West;
>   For, though those currents yield return to none,
> What shall my West hurt me? As West and East
>   In all flat Maps (and I am one) are one,
>   So death doth touch the Resurrection.

They have waited long enough, out there in the slack water; the thin frosted stalks of grass form a screen, and as I look the widgeon seem vast, black, and very silent. Inch by inch the gun stock moves to the shoulder. Suddenly the sentinel birds on the outskirts of the pack raise their heads, and with that movement seem to spring. In their upward thrust there is the splendid athleticism and grace of fear that seems to belong to all wild life. The whole dawn is a tumult of cries: pentecostal, borne on wings. A redshank who has been resting on some point nearby complains with them. Over the barrels, not so much seen as felt, I am aware of a single moment of exaltation, and of power over these symbols of strength and mystery. They go out, into the lift of the darkness: the barrels drop, unfired.

iv

In summer when the trout-stream had shrunk in a spell of drought and its stones grew slimy with green weed, I turned to the Big River and its resources. Three hundred yards and five hundred feet below Paradise was the boathouse, with a sort of miniature hard; a flagstaff on which the Green Ensign was supposed to be flown when the family were in residence, or when anyone remembered to send it up on the wind-rattling halyards; seats of split pine logs; a little creek formed by the river that ran at the bottom of the orchard, and round the west end of the garden. There the remains of a Falmouth Quay Punt, a cutter of seven tons or so, lay rotting; she had been sailed from Plymouth by two of my uncles, then junior dons at Trinity Hall, and in the voyage run through a south-westerly gale in the Atlantic. Now the tides flowed quietly in and out of her, and left their grey mud on the moulded lead pigs of her ballast. Embedded in the mud at the mouth of the creek, beyond the perch that was the sea-mark for the entrance, were parts of the ribs and keel of a 'Galway Hooker', which, it was said, had once served as a sort of auxiliary yacht for expeditions down the River and out to sea. (Why do these dark Homeric ribs of ships always look so sinister?) She belonged to that breed of bluff-bowed heavily-built cutters, of twenty to forty tons, much used before the time of road-lorries to carry all kinds of goods, flour, coal and cattle, round the little harbours of the West. Richard Murphy has salvaged the last of them and refitted her: described in his poem called *The Last Galway Hooker*. Below, a couple of boats were always moored in summer; one of these my brother's, the Grey Boat, a narrow, fast and dangerous centre-boarder, with bamboo spars and an immense standing lug. Sometimes there would be a big pram-bowed lighter used by the islanders to ferry sheep or cattle across; their horses were swum behind the island craft, the curious 'gandola'. This is a long narrow boat, flat-bottomed, curving upwards at bow and stern; fitted to slide joyfully at low tide down the long hard banks of mud, and be pushed up laboriously, with oars jammed athwartships to act as levers, on the other side. There were a dozen islands within sight of the house, the largest inhabited by three to six families each; keeping much to themselves, and, by long inter-marriage, regarded by the mainlanders as 'quare'. But all their stores had to be procured from the mainland, and cattle sold there, and they had to go, whatever the wind and tide

– 'To feastings, and to christenings, and to Mass'

– with a long muddy walk after they had moored their boats.

The Big River was full of fish; but its water, forty miles from Loop Head and the Atlantic, was muddy, and thick with green crabs, so that bait fishing was useless. On a summer's evening at high tide you could dangle a string, with a piece of bacon-rind on the end and weighted with a stone, over the side of the creek, and pull out crabs continuously. In hot weather huge shoals of big mullet could be seen near the islands, swirling and playing within an oar's length of the boat, but they were uncatchable. It was said that long ago the islanders worked several nets, and caught abundance of fish; common sloth and lack of initiative had long killed that, as so often with the fisheries of the western coasts. But up to the time of my Father's death we always kept a seine net in repair, and fished for the house and village perhaps twice a month. 'Hauling', as it was called, involved a good deal of staff-work and co-operation; for a boy it was an immensely exciting process.

The summer usually saw some sort of house-party in being; young women and young men, often friends of my brother's from Cambridge. The first essential was to raise at least four strong men and, luckily enough, a small boy to hold the boat and do odd jobs. The next was a supply of old gym shoes to prevent cut feet from mussels, and the oldest possible clothes, shorts and a ragged sweater, so that there were no buttons to catch in the meshes of the net. Tides had to be carefully calculated, for fishing was only possible for less than two hours on either side of dead low water springs, when the 'banks' were exposed. Then the net had to be spread out on the quay, tested, mended: it was perhaps a hundred yards long, tapering at the ends with a deep purse in the middle. Each flank ended in a wooden pole, weighted at the bottom with sheet lead; these poles having attached to them bridles like those of a kite. To the bridles, in turn, were bent very long coir ropes, semi-buoyant, known as 'swangs'; the inboard end of one was bent to a thwart in the stern of the boat.

The net was piled most carefully, so that it would run out without check, on a smoothed wooden platform at the stern, for any nail or splinter is fatal; the boat was slid down the mudbank, and launched into the tide. Some area was selected, perhaps a mile away, often near the mouth of a small channel. One man, preferably the toughest, was put ashore with one end of the 'swang' knotted round his chest. Then the boat was rowed quickly out at right angles to the shore, paying out rope, net, then rope again: to turn gradually into a half-circle, with two oarsmen one side, one on the other, dragging the extended net. The shore-man for his part trudged along, sometimes half-way up to his knees in the grey salt-smelling mud, dragging his end of the rope. At a signal the boat turned towards the shore, gradually converting the semi-circle to a horse-shoe; finally it landed. At this stage speed became vital. Two men rushed to each rope, and started to haul quickly and evenly, keeping the large cork, that marked the middle of the 'purse', in the centre of the diminishing horse-shoe. First the ropes came in, then the wooden poles; then the cork and lead-lines were 'handed'[1] in together. We watched anxiously as the circle closed, for now the purse could be seen to be alive with fish – or, if the haul was a bad one, with a mass of squirming grating crabs; or even, on one bitterly cold day, a moderate-sized blackthorn bush. Disentangling a net from anything of that kind is sheer hell; larger crabs come into the same category; and there was an occasional conger-eel; a menace, though an edible one. Sometimes the shout

---

[1] This is the image that Yeats uses in the epigram 'Three Movements': 'Romantic fish swam in nets coming to the hand'.

would go up 'There's a round fish!' – a bass or pollack or mullet, as distinct from the plaice or sole. It was long odds that the 'round' fish would jump the cork-line of the net before they could be drawn in; the leader chose a place, and the rest followed like sheep. It was said that they could be checkmated by sprinkling straw or hay on the surface within the net circle; I never saw it tried.

Finally the purse of the net with its struggling mass was heaved into shallow water and left to lie there; the boat was backed down and the net fed back on to its platform, cork and land-lines together; the fish taken out and flung into the boat. Three or four hours' work might result in two or three hundred fish – plaice, soles, flounders; enough to keep a large household for several days, and to make a distribution among the tenants and in the village.

But the net rotted in the 'bad times' after the Master's death; and this fishing required much co-operation. There were still things to do alone.

Southward from the boathouse, along the Shore Wood, there was a line of very low cliffs out of which seeped small springs, rust-stained from the iron in the black-brown shale. The tide came well up to them. One of the sights was a very old oak-tree, with two-thirds of its roots in the air because of the crumbling of the edge; it was said that the family would cease to be when that tree fell. Further on, the wood ended in a magnificent cluster of Scotch firs where I used to wait for wood-pigeons flighting in the dusk of winter evenings. Then came more low cliffs lined by thickets of whitethorn and sloes. A large dome-shaped rock, known as the Coffin Rock because the islanders used to bring in their dead by that landing and rested the coffin there, was the start of a line of low reefs that ran far into the water. Among the sea-weed that covered them on a flood-tide quantities of prawns could be caught. Any morning, after the ebb-tide had swirled the grey waters down to Loop Head and the Atlantic, I could potter about the foreshore, gathering cockles, catching prawns, investigating the life of the tide.[1]

Beyond the rocks of the foreshore and showing only at lowest springs was a separate reef, still carrying a stump that had once been a sea-mark when my uncle's big yachts, *Galatea* and

---

[1] See 'Ebb Tide' on p. 259.

Gertrude, used to come up the river. If one stripped to shorts and gym shoes, and chose carefully the moment of the tide, it was possible to half-swim, half-wade to this reef. For such an expedition I carried a short wooden cudgel, made fast to the wrist with a thong; and a bamboo garden cane on the end of which was lashed, with brass snare-wire, a large cod-hook. On the reef itself there were half a dozen known holes: deep ledges under rocks, pools under boulders. A hasty exploration with the hooked bamboo might reveal a large squirming body, making a sound that we thought of traditionally as 'barking', but was really only the splashing of the conger eel in the shallow water of his lair. Then one of two things happened: either the resentful eel, three or four feet long and thicker than one's thigh, came out to the attack; or one stuck the hook into him somewhere and dragged him out protesting. Then came a battle, in some few inches of water, with the furious writhing beast; aiming with the club for the head or the lymphatic heart, near the tail. The tides allowed twenty minutes or less on the reef; with luck, there was time to kill just three of the eels, and to tow them home across the flowing channel. The country people welcomed them, both for soup and as strong meat for fast-days. Between the tide and the upper ground came first the *portheens,* muddy land pitted with pools of small brown sand-shrimps, with odd clumps of reeds. Behind these were the sloping sea-walls that ran for miles north and south, holding the tide back, draining the water out through sluices from the rich 'corcass' lands. So long as the sluices and the walls held, there were cattle, hay and timber along the banks. Now the tide flows in and out over them, for our jealous people would not co-operate with one another in repair. The Paradise corcass went early, as I described in 'Sluice Gate'.[1]

In after years I have thought much over a chronicle which on the surface appears to be one of killing. I do not think of it as wanton, though the strange paradox, that one may love wild creatures and yet take their lives, becomes more pronounced, more disquieting, as one grows older. We were miles from a town, and everything we killed was eaten in the household, or given away for food. I was often confronted with an order from my Mother to 'go out and shoot some rabbit for the pot; there's

---

[1] See p. 260.

nothing in the house'. This, in summer time when the cover was heavy, involved patient stalking, either in the late evening or the early morning; preferably with a .22 rifle or with a shot-gun. I can still feel the ecstasy of the early morning dew on one's feet, for whenever possible during the holidays I went barefoot, because one moved so much more silently and securely; on warm summer nights, keeping close to the ground in a long stalk, it was possible to smell the rabbits. Such a stalk, with a primitive home-made bow and arrow, once resulted – luckiest of flukes – in a kill.

In all this we had been most strictly brought up. If a schoolboy is to be entrusted with any weapon at the age of eight – as I was – the rules of safety must be instilled – beaten in if necessary – from the first. (I thought of this when I found eighty-three men, casualties in hospital at Udine, in 1945, after the battle was over; all caused by 'playing with' captured enemy weapons and grenades.) Under my Father's training it became a crime to wound or to cause unnecessary suffering; my brother and I both shot with fully-choked guns, in which a clean kill or a clean miss was normal. When ammunition was unobtainable, and it was always scarce because of the cost, I learnt to snare rabbits for food, going the rounds of the snares in the very early morning. It was then that I conceived an intense hatred of the hooded carrion crows that haunted the foreshores; I would find rabbits with their eyes pecked out in the snares. Afterwards I realized how well the unknown author of the ballad of 'The Twa Corbies' knew his stuff; how the birds would go first for the eyes of the dead knight lying in the heather:

> Ye'll sit on his white hause-bane,
> And I'll pike out his bonny blue e'en.
> Wi' ae lock of his gowden hair
> We'll theek our nest when it grows bare.

Certain birds thus became enemies, unlike the birds we shot for food. The grey scald-crows, magpies, hawks; the wood-pigeons that periodically devastated the garden and would rise in clouds from the gooseberry-plot on a summer's evening; the black-backed gulls that attacked dying sheep, and in winter would sometimes swoop down and carry away a fallen snipe before the dog could reach it. Weasels (which were really stoats) and, worst of all, domestic cats that had gone wild, were enemies also; jays I never saw till I came to England, though we prized their feathers for salmon flies. Not till long afterwards did I see the opposite viewpoint, when one of my pupils, an ex-RAF pilot who had been shot down over Germany, said to me: 'You know, it's always wrong to bring down anything that flies. You're putting them in the wrong place. Everything's so lovely in the air, always.'

v

I did not then know the epigram from Blake's *Milton*, which perhaps crystallizes one side of the conflict; a conflict unrealized in youth, but growing stronger in old age:

War and Hunting, the two Fountains of the River of Life,
Are become Fountains of Death and of corroding Hell.

During my Father's lifetime he had tried to preserve game in Paradise: I was forbidden the main woods till after the Christmas Shoots had taken place, even for rabbiting. Afterwards the pheasants died out rapidly; the main road ran through the outside woods, and without keepers the demesne was too vulnerable. But about 1916 another hunting-ground was thrown open to me. Seven or eight miles away there was an estate called Cragbrien: a big ugly square house, rapidly falling into ruin, but with the servants' quarters intact and maintained on the other side of the courtyard. As a house it was badly sited, almost on the edge of a great marsh, intersected by water-meadows and dykes, but there were some woods and much 'crag' land, limestone outcrop with valleys of sweet grass; thorn thickets, briars, bracken, everywhere. The top-soil was so shallow that there were only three or four rabbit-burrows on the whole estate, and so the rabbits had acquired the habit of lying out all the year round in the thickets.

The owner of the place – no one had lived in the big house for many years – was a prisoner of war in Germany, and I was told that I could shoot there as I liked. It was a long bicycle ride from Paradise, but the shoot held even more variety and excitement than my home-ground. There were still many pheasants, for the owner's gamekeeper continued to rear them in what was left of the walled garden. The keeper himself, John Markham, was a

The River

great character. He must have been over forty even then: his father, a venerable slow-spoken white-haired old man, was full of stories of 'the gentry' and of the Blood family who had once lived there. His son addressed him scrupulously as 'Sir', asking his advice with great ceremony on all matters of the chase.

John himself was a great talker, and I think a great liar; cheerful, optimistic, swarthy-looking, using the strangely French-sounding expletive 'By Gar!' He was a good shot, knew his country well, and was a great retailer of scandal about the neighbouring 'gentry' as well as the people of the countryside. He treated me, young as I was, as an honoured guest; whenever I came there was a table laid in the great decayed drawing-room with Regency mouldings and peeling wall-paper, and the boards rotting at the corners of the room. A pot of tea would be borne in for me to drink with the sandwiches I had brought. There were miscellaneous dogs, usually spaniels which John swore were of unexampled intelligence, blood and training; they were invariably wild, and paid not the slightest attention to him. (All spaniels, engaging as they are, are apt to become foolish and headstrong unless they are worked perpetually; I found that after having two springers at Cambridge.) As we worked the wild brakes for the rabbits that never went to ground, there were occasional woodcock to be met, and in the vast wet 'currachs'[1] or water meadows, endless snipe. But the wonder of the days at Cragbrien was the evening flight. If the floods were at the right height, pools of water – 'flashes' as John called them – would lie here and there in the vast water-meadows. As the light waned we would go out and stand beside them, a few hundred yards apart: at first taking cover in the reed-beds, later, as the light fell, standing boldly in the open, facing the western glow, until it was too dark to swing the muzzles at some imagined thickening of the cloud. One was utterly alone, but all around was small subtle movement; splashings and callings of the moorhens, the crackle of marshland as the water, backed up by the disant tide, rose over it: the *krraak* of a solitary heron startled from his night pool: the quick swish of wings of snipe dropping in to feed, so unlike their springtime drumming. Then anything might

---

[1] Not to be confused with the 'curragh' which is the lath-and-canvas craft of the Atlantic sea-board, famous in Synge's writings and in Jack Yeats's paintings.

happen as the duck started to come; the quick wing-beats of mallard, by twos and threes, often unseen, so that one stayed frozen, hoping that they would circle nearer; the tiny black flashes that were teal alighting, noiseless, dropping like meteorites from space. Once there was a great roar, like a tube train in a tunnel, that was a company of widgeon, many of them, low and terrifying with massed wing-beats. We shot little, as I remember; at most three or four mallard a night; it was the loneliness, the sounds, the excitement of what might come out of the dark, that fascinated me.

Then there was the long ride home by an uncertain acetylene lamp; game and cartridge bags on shoulder, and the gun slung over all: loaded (dangerously) but giving some confidence on the dark roads. For at the crossroads, or outside lonely pubs, stood little groups of men (this was after the Rebellion) who might be exchanging the endless gossip of the countryside, or might not. A gun and cartridges could have been a temptation, and my Mother was apt to be in a fret of anxiety till I returned; it was a relief to turn in at the lodge-gates, and to smell the wet rhododendrons, laurels and pine-needles that seemed so pungent in the night air.

vi

This flighting at nightfall had a peculiar mystery of its own; with often a strong fear of the thick woods, the 'wanted' men of the IRA on the run; the semi-illicit possession of a gun; the movement of unexpected birds, so curiously different in sound from anything I knew by day. Pigeons ravaged the crops and the garden, and were good food; and waiting for them at night had its own special place in the events of winter. A narrow path through trees and choked with undergrowth and johnswort led along the top of the sea-wall to the corner of the Shore Wood; the last few hundred yards were the low shale cliffs of which I have spoken, the stunted oak-trees growing along and over them. Then the cliff rose a little as the wood ended in a clump of gaunt Scotch firs, the most exciting and mysterious of trees. At their feet were rhododendron thickets, into whose flanks I would crouch; or flatten against the great trunks of the firs with their brown brittle scales.

The time to go there on the winter evenings is an hour or so before sunset; you must see the whole dark come down, and tea will be kept before the turf and log fire in the library. The pigeons drift in, singly or in twos and threes, from feeding on the ivy-berries along the shore; their crops are packed to bursting with the small hard black fruit. Generally you will hear the wings only, for the boughs are thick at the tops of the firs. Then you must keep utterly still for a minute or more; for when he has alighted the pigeon will scrutinize every yard of ground all round his perch, and will detect the movement of a finger, the glint on a lifted gun-barrel. It is best if the night is wild and stormy, for then there is much natural movement and sound in the undergrowth. After two minutes you may raise your head, very carefully, and search the boughs for the black silhouette; and that moment is dangerous, for the pigeon will often shift till he is satisfied with his roosting perch, and after each move he watches the ground again. If he is to your right, facing what remains of the western twilight, you may throw up the gun quickly and take him as he rises, wings rattling. If he is to your left, and the west wind is strong, he will certainly fall in the tide below the cliff if you let him fly, and so be lost; shift the trigger-finger to the left barrel with fours in it and raise the gun inch by inch, till you see the perched silhouette over the rib.

The sea-birds are moving along the edge of the tide outside; across the Shore Field beyond the wood you may see a pack of green plover, flighting inland for the night, in their superb acrobatics.[1] They will pass on either side of our Burial Ground on the hill; its screen of young firs bent eastward by the wind, the rhododendrons and briars round it; and tomorrow you may shoot a woodcock there, and your shot may have the nature of a salute.

vii

The episodes that bring youthful disillusionment are no less bitter for their wholly ridiculous character. I can remember two at this stage. The first was on a long bicycle-ride to the West to see my Grandmother and an Aunt who had had much to do with us when we were children; and combining the visit, I think, with some sort of fishing expedition. The roads were appalling, with

---

[1] Wasn't it T. H. White in *England Have my Bones* who noted that the green plover is the only bird that does stunt-flying for the sheer love of it?

limestone mud and patches of unrolled metal so that punctures were frequent. On a steep hill I met a youth a year or two older than I, looking hopelessly at punctures in both wheels. He had nothing to mend them with. In a burst of charity I lent him tyre-levers and a repair outfit; he expressed eternal gratitude. Then, since we were apparently on friendly terms, and I was pressed for time, I asked him to put the tools when he had finished in a recess behind a big stone, unmistakable, in the wall of the roadside. When I returned some hours later there was of course nothing there.

The second episode was my own fault, an act of *hubris* and haste. I think it was in 1917 that my Mother, under extreme financial stress, sold a fair quantity of timber in the woods, mainly larch and fir. A small sawmill was set up near the Gate Lodge, to cut the timber into planking on the spot, for even unseasoned timber was at a premium in wartime. All felling of timber is cruel and desolating, perhaps most of all when one is young, and the woods had grown for me into a special character from the personalities of those who planted them. I think now of 'Kilcash':

> What shall we do for timber?
> The last of the woods is down.

Nearly forty years later I saw the huge sawmills, some of the biggest in the world, at Salem in Oregon, the great trunks flung about by mechanical claws, stripped of their bark by hydraulic jets, fed to the bandsaws that were sharpened every hour, night and day, in the lofts overhead; the plywood layers peeled off rotating logs by razor-edged blades; the machines that compressed even the sawdust into logs for burning; and I thought of the little sawmill that had unselved[1] our woods.

One effect of our remoteness from town, and a steady but not yet rigorous shortage of money, was the training, rough and ready though it was, in a number of manual skills. All gear that had to do with boats we took as a matter of course; scraping, painting, splicing, net-mending. Later in my teens, when Paradise was being kept together precariously, there was much to be done on the place, farm and fences and shrubberies, though only of

---

[1] See G. M. Hopkins's 'Binsey Poplars'.

course in the holidays or vacations. Woodwork I loved; but I have always been impatient of those who praise the aesthetic or rhythmical beauty of land work, the chopping of wood or the scything of corn, with no first-hand knowledge of the labour. I know of few worse jobs than binding by hand sheaves of oats with plenty of thistles in them under a hot September sun; by hand, that is, forming the binder out of straw, and fastening it with a curious twist of the thumb before the sheaf goes to the stooks; or the slow monotonous drag of the cross-cut saw, hour after hour. Last year, at a fishing lodge, I found the ghillies cutting wood in the yard on a wet afternoon. I took one end of the saw for a while, for there is no luck unless the 'stranger' sets a hand to whatever work is going on. This is particularly important if butter is being churned in a cottage. And one said: 'It's easy seen it isn't the first time you've handled a cross-cut.'

I had long wished for a boat, light and small enough to take on a donkey-cart to one of the many lakes within a ten-mile radius. There was nothing suitable in the boat-house, except a thirty-year-old well-loved dinghy, the White Punt that had been my Father's, and it was unthinkable that she should be left out on a mountain lake. An ancient Berthon boat hanging in a loft had its canvas rotted, and woodworm was in the spidery ribs. I decided to beg some planking from the sawmills and build myself a simple flat-bottomed boat. True, the wood was sappy and unseasoned, but I wanted desperately to have the boat quickly, to use it that summer. With vague memories of diagrams in *The Boy's Own Paper* – or was it in a book called *Things to Make*? – I started in, saving my meagre pocket-money for nails. Behind it there was, I think, a recollection of a delightful book on the Norfolk Broads, written I suppose in about 1870, part instructive natural history, part sailing, called *The Swan and Her Crew* – a sort of catamaran vessel built largely and improbably from the remains of a dismantled greenhouse.

My own boat, over which I toiled incessantly for many weeks in every hour of daylight, was a complete fiasco. She was too narrow and high-sided for her length, for I had not realized the problems of stability in a small flat-bottomed craft. The newly-sawn wood was much too thick and heavy, and split and warped even in the making. When finished, she looked tolerable, and I brought her down to the creek to be launched. She promptly sank, the seams leaking under the pressure; when these were caulked, nothing would induce her to float upright with a passenger on board. With two, the seams started to open again. I remember an agony of bad temper and frustration as I sat and watched my useless handiwork. It was my first bitter lesson in that kind, for I had prided myself on my skill with tools.

III

'WE TOO HAD MANY PRETTY TOYS WHEN YOUNG...'
(W. B. Yeats)

i

Except for the various holiday visits to Paradise, I saw little of the life of an Irish country house until my Father settled there on his retirement in 1913. Even now it is seen through the memory of a boy of twelve or thirteen; companionless and very naturally debarred from the grown-up pursuits and talk. It was a self-contained and quasi-feudal world employing eight or ten men, for the garden, the woods, and the home farm half a mile away. Horses provided the transport for every occasion; the coach-house held a strange assortment of vehicles – traps, a lumbering carriage, and the inevitable Irish side-cars. There was even a wickerwork bath-chair arrangement, pony-drawn, just like the one used by the famous Mrs Knox in Somerville and Ross, that had belonged to my Grandmother. A coachman and a yard-boy ruled over four or five horses and a vicious squealing jennet – no doubt suffering from the frustrations of its breed – that, shod with leather sandals, drew the big lawn-mower and took the servants to the seemingly incessant Masses on Sundays and holy days.

Across the outer courtyard lay a long building, a dozen feet below ground level. Coal was almost unobtainable; Mary the Cook would say of the odd cartload brought with labour from the tiny port of Clarecastle, 'Sure, that'd be as good for me as pure gold itself.' For three or four days each September relays of carts, piled high with turf, came in from the bog where it had been bought in ricks against the winter. To measure and value the content of such ricks was a complicated mathematical problem, always undertaken by the village schoolmaster. One end of the turf-house had cradles for sawing logs; on the frequent wet days the men on the estate came in to saw and split the fallen timber dragged in from the woods. There one could spend long hours talking to the men and listening to their stories, or exploring the recesses of the carpenter's shop next to it. This was an exciting place; on the piled shelves were all the oddments that a house produces, of the 'sure-an''-it-might-come-in-handy-sometime' variety; as well as the old gear of the yachts'; blocks, binnacle-lamps, thimbles, shackles, wire rope, out of which I made shift to rig my own boat.

The economy of the house was bountiful, erratic, wasteful. The neighbouring village supplied a succession of girls, mostly daughters of the men who worked on the place. These graduated upwards through the hierarchy of scullery, kitchen and pantry. Probably not less than ten sat down to meals each day in the servants' hall. Provisions were bought in vast quantities in the county town of Ennis, eleven miles away; and this was a day's expedition, for the horse had to be rested and fed after the long drive over roads mended incessantly with raw broken stone. Steam-rolling was unknown. Along the roads at intervals of a mile or two were little embrasures, where men sat all day cracking the limestone boulders into the three-inch macadam metal; one was a dwarf, with a great powerful chest and shoulders, who made a point of greeting us and telling us local news. It must have been the dreariest of occupations; and that is the point of Yeats's bitter epigram:

> Parnell came down the road, he said to a cheering man:
> 'Ireland shall get her freedom and you still break stone.'

We took for granted a household economy that seems fantastic now. Paradise had no effective bathroom, and only an erratic cold water system; baths were taken in tin tubs, in the bedrooms, from garden watering-cans drawn from the kitchen range. A copper jug of hot water was brought up, covered with a clean towel, to each bedroom before every meal. There were the usual domestic crises: cooks, especially the superior ones from Dublin, came and went. One departed after a few weeks with an escort of RIC Constables, and twenty-eight empty whisky bottles were found in her room. To the house came an incessant stream of callers to see my Father, who was naturally known as 'The Counsellor'; beggars, blind fiddlers or musicians, tinkers; tenants from remote townlands with every kind of request or family or legal problems. Some wanted 'a stick' for the rafters of a new cottage; others advice over a quarrel with a neighbour; yet others, letters of recommendation for daughters who wanted to become nurses, sons who wanted to go into the 'polis' or the Civil Service.

Besides the horses in the stables, there was always an assortment of dogs: a black Labrador, a clumber spaniel, a terrier or two. These were charming and sometimes of mixed ancestry and ill discipline (again one remembers the type from Somerville and Ross), for woods full of rabbits surrounded the stable-yard, and the dogs would go off together on systematic hunts; the clumber working the bramble brakes, while the retriever 'fielded' adroitly on the other side. Perhaps every country house acquires its saga of dogs. My Father told me of an old pointer of his who, if one missed the first few shots of the day, would go home in disgust. A black retriever bitch, Doreen, used to bring me hedgehogs, rolling them first in loose hay so that the spines should not hurt her mouth. And for a time there was an evil-tempered parrot, who would irritate the dogs to fury by imitating my whistle.

Doreen had an incurable dislike of music, particularly of anything with high notes in it. My Mother, like many good housewives, was constantly losing her keys. They were therefore kept, along with oddments and her spectacles, in a small round wicker basket with a handle. This also held odd copper coins, and when beggars arrived, the basket was produced and they were given money from it. On this particular occasion it was a hot summer day; the house was empty, the family perhaps at a picnic on the shore, A blind fiddler from 'the mountain' arrived, guided by a small boy from whom we heard the story afterwards. The fiddler sat on the hall steps and played, to a house empty of all but the black retriever. After howling for a time in misery she went into the house, got up on the library table, and carried the magic basket in her mouth to the fiddler, saying in effect, 'Take your money and stop this horrible noise!'

That race of shooting dogs died out in the '20s at Paradise. At Cambridge I owned a succession of them, for in the autumn and early winter I could usually arrange my work so as to have

Saturdays 'off', and shoot in the Fens. We had first spaniels, then retrievers, as well as smaller dogs. When the end came for each, I had taken to heart Axel Munthe's advice[1] never to send a dog to a vet: it is far better to take him into the garden, give him a bone, and shoot him through the head yourself. But this, though I know it is right, I have always found a peculiarly disintegrating experience from which it takes some days to recover.

[1] *The Story of San Michele.*

The Shore Wood

Because the distances in Clare were considerable, and most of our friends and relatives lived in the northern side of the country, visits were long affairs, except for occasional formal tea-calls in the afternoons. From these I would always try to bolt into the woods, for visitors meant an appearance in tidy clothes, and a wasted afternoon. My sisters used to go on long visits for hunt balls and the like. In the summer and during the university vacations the house was always full of young people, cousins, or friends of my brother or my sisters. Naturally enough a small boy was out of it, and certainly a great nuisance. One episode from such a house-party must have remained in my mind, for forty years later it came back in a poem, 'Shooting a Bat', perhaps out of shame that I had killed for wantonness or exhibitionism.[1]

Of the political side I then realized little. My Father was a Conservative in thinking as well as in name. Lloyd George and his plans were anathema; so was the growing Home Rule movement under Redmond. I think that his sympathy lay with the North and Carson's arming of Ulster. It was said that Carson had learnt his law in my Grandfather's court; I know that he was good to me when I was a young man at Cambridge. The Labour movement in Dublin under Larkin was a remote example of 'blackguardism'; associated with the land troubles, shootings, and other inevitable consequences of Home Rule. These, so the talk went, would be the spread of universal corruption and bribery, an accentuation of the hereditary sloth of the West; government by publicans and the 'gombeen men'.[2] However much we might curse Dublin Castle and all its bureaucratic ineptitudes, however we might mock the slow-wittedness of the English, there was a certainty that without English government the country would decay.

Of that corruption the stories were many, and often true: as of AE's discovery, through the Irish Agricultural Organization Society, that sixty per cent of the seeds used by Irish farmers were useless. Half a century later they would be paralleled by the infinite ingenuity expended in circumventing the orders of their own Free State, such as those dealing with tubercular testing of cattle, and other agricultural orders.

[1] See p. 257.
[2] Yeats's poem *The Curse of Cromwell,* and the last verse of *The Statues,* are relevant.

The remarkable Irish literary events in the Edwardian period seemed to leave little impression on the household. My brother had brought back from Cambridge many modern books – Shaw, Wells, Synge, Moore. But Dublin was a full day's journey from us, and the town house at 48 Merrion Street, kept up for the Dublin season in my Grandfather's time, had long since been sold. Forty miles to the north Lady Gregory's Coole Park was reaching its fame as the Urbino of Ireland – 'That grammar-school of courtesies' – yet we never visited it. I suspect that our particular circle, Conservative and Unionist, was shocked by the association of certain figures of the Irish Literary Revival with revolution. And there was indeed much scandal attaching to them, for many reasons; notably for their support of the Boers in the war in which many of the Irish gentry had been killed, for the stories about George Moore and his publicly announced conversion in 1903 to Protestantism, for the work of Maud Gonne and of the Countess Markiewicz in attempting

> – To hurl the little streets upon the great,
> Had they but courage equal to desire.

All this was, I suppose, natural enough. We had no great family tradition of politics, though my Grandfather had once been asked to stand as Member for Clare, and I have a cutting from a local paper of the late '70s:

> And who will we have then?
> *Says the Shan Van Vocht.*
> And who will we have then?
> *Says the Shan Van Vocht.*
> We'll put Calcutt in the Den[1]
> But for a while, and then
> We'll change him for Tom Henn
> *Says the Shan Van Vocht.*

A great-uncle, a QC with the rhythmical name of Jonathan Henn, had defended Daniel O'Connell. He was said to have lived during many of his early years at the Bar entirely on his whist-playing while on circuit; and when a solicitor at long last brought him his first brief, Jonathan Henn – still in bed at noon – threw his boots at the solicitor's head, suspecting a practical

---

[1] The British Parliament.

joke. Of the uncles on my Father's side, the eldest had been in the Navy. Another, bearing my own name and my grandfather's, had been killed in the Afghan war holding the Pass at Maiwand with the 'Last Eleven'; there is a tablet to him in St Patrick's, and a window in Rochester Cathedral. In a mood of braggadocio that yet seemed clean enough in the exaltation of September 1940 that memory came alive again; of the epic situation, which is the one against the many, or that of an old man and two boys against the Roman army of *Cymbeline*:

'Behind the dead horses, in the white Afghan sun,'

for it was said that the enemy so honoured the valour of the dead Bombay Sappers that they buried the bodies in a garden without mutilating them. Another uncle was a Colonel of Gunners, one a barrister, another a Bishop. There was some tradition of scholarship, but not of literature; and perhaps some of the books that my brother brought back with him from Cambridge were suspect. I remember that they included Wells, Wilde, Shaw.

Of the contemporary writers, in the great period of Irish letters, I heard nothing except of Synge, who had indeed written of the Aran Islands, of Wicklow and West Kerry. His speech and idiom still seem to me authentic, except in parts of *Deirdre,* the more so since I have edited the plays. His attitude to the peasantry combines a characteristic blend of dispassionate analysis and impassioned sympathy; his knowledge of the humour and squalor of peasants and tinkers; the very smell of wet frieze and turf smoke and the filthy byres beside, the rutted lanes, rushy fields, and the endless depression of rain. Out of that resigned misery and depression he could make high or low comedy that has always a bitter flavour and, twice, high tragedy. His pictures of the relationship of the people to their priests seemed to have that fine ironic ambivalence that we knew. There were the meticulous-casual observances of Stations and Masses; the little shrines in each cottage, as in O'Casey's Dublin tenements, surrounded by the anatomical holy pictures of Sacred Hearts transfixed with swords, or the crude china images of saints that crowded the draper's shop in the village. On the tiny farms the big handsome women who were old at thirty, because of child-bearing and child-illness and the sodden labours of the farm, moved heavily in black, clumsy men's boots, unlaced; the men working casually in the fields, or walking the cattle long miles to the fairs. Sickness of all kinds was prevalent, much of it tuberculosis from damp and bad sanitation. Several times I went with our country doctor, sometime an Irish rugger international, on his rounds; we drove up remote lanes in a ramshackle Model T Ford which I learnt to handle. Once a child ran down a steep bank from a cottage, and the car met it full in the chest. Fortunately the doctor was driving. We stopped and dashed out, imagining in horror what we would find. But there was no body; the high spidery vehicle had provided ample clearance and the child was back unhurt in its house. On those sick visits I saw something of the lives of the people in sickness – it was usually tuberculosis – and the hopelessness of it, made light, momentarily, by their resignation, like that of Maurya in Synge's *Riders to the Sea*: 'No one can be living for ever, and we must be satisfied.'

Disease, melancholia, these were part of the price to be paid for the exquisite scenery in that country of remote homesteads, immense rainfall and chronic rheumatism, perpetual work in mud and damp. I think that few material things have changed their lives more than the ordinary gumboot. It is useful to recognize the characteristic ambivalence; the nostalgic sentiment of a hundred lyrics, good and bad: Eva Gore-Booth's *Breffny,* Brett Young's *Lochanilaun,* Allingham's *Erne,* Yeats's *Innisfree,* the poem that he himself hated so greatly.[1] I am still conscious of the dualism, when the exquisite beauty of heather under wind, the massed fuchsia bushes, the smell of bruised myrtle, the mountain lake discovered suddenly in a fold in the hills, like David Ross' painting of a loch in Sutherland that hangs over my desk, takes one suddenly by the throat.

It was, I suppose, for some such reason that one's attitude oscillated between two poles. To the north of us in Connemara there was George Moore, the Catholic who had half-turned Protestant, whose life was notorious; the bosom enemy of Yeats –

Old lecher with a love in every wind.

The sentimental pictures of Kathleen-ni-Houlihan, the Shan Van Vocht, were set against the lines of public-houses in the mean

[1] But did he, or anyone else, remember that nine beans are the offerings for the dead in Ovid?

village streets, the aimless gossiping groups at every street-corner in the ugly provincial towns, ugly, in parts, because the builders, with no security of tenure, did not think, as they did in the English village, of the future; the squalor, piety, indolence, decay. It was later that I saw the horribly bogus paganism of the Puck Fair at Killorglin, instituted as a tourist attraction and a pretext for three days of drinking. Of Dublin we knew nothing, nor of Joyce, who, like Synge, was to turn filth into that comedy that met so well the mood of the early twenties. But again the mood changed and much that Irish Catholicism stood for put the Protestant ascendancy to shame. The fishermen and the peasantry rose at times to a fierce proud stoicism that flowered in their speech; the fatalism of the devout Roman Catholic confronted with poverty, sickness, the inexorable fretting of the sea; among the curraghs and the drying-nets and the whitewashed cottages there was something of the exalted bitterness of Pierre Loti's people. It is Kipling in *Captains Courageous* who quotes that snatch of Breton song which remains with me as a touchstone for *Riders to the Sea*:

> La brigantine
> Qui va tourner
> Roule et s'incline
> Pour m'entrainer.
> O Vierge Marie
> Pour moi priez Dieu!
> Adieu, patrie,
> Quebec, adieu!

IV

PREPARATORY SCHOOL

i

I suppose that it is fashionable to run down one's preparatory school; so many first novels start with descriptions of the horribleness of life there. It is hard to say how much of this hatred is subjective, clouded by subsequent retrospection and the desire to account for or justify some adult malaise. Perhaps some of it comes from the first shock of home-sickness which is never quite so bitter again; more, from the troubles of the rapid and critical growth between eleven and fourteen. Nothing seems capable of mitigating the unease, hunger for excitement, shame at one's own brashness, the general 'ignominy of boyhood'. Perhaps, too, schools of this sort necessitate a tightness of physical control that exacerbates the ignominy.

The school to which my parents sent me seems in retrospect of a very mingled web. It has since been described by Lionel Fleming, in his book *Head or Harp*. It was at Fermoy, some four hours' journey from Ennis, and two changes away, but nowadays but seventy miles by car. Fermoy was then a garrison town, and the boredom of school life was lessened by the presence there, for a few weeks early in 1915, of my brother and his regiment; he had a new motor-bicycle, a Levis, and once allowed me to ride it for a few hundred yards! The surrounding country was good, but a little tame by the standards of the West, too prosperous and civilized; and not far away was the River Awbeg, Spenser's Mulla, and the site of his Kilcolman Castle. But I did not know of this.

My Father brought me to the school on a fresh May Day, and the Headmaster showed us round. There was a small swimming bath, with a diving-board, something I had never seen before; I

Preparatory School

jumped on it excitedly while my Father was talking to the headmaster, and then felt suddenly a cold eye upon me, ruthless and appraising. I was left alone, and the unending gnawing homesickness closed in.

The headmaster was a muscular Christian of the more inconsistent type, a former rugger international, a strong preacher, and mildly, a sadist, though I did not get this into perspective or know the word till many years later. The school was organized in terms of a boy scout troop, by patrols. We wore scout uniform continually except when, as punishment for any offence that could be described as 'breaking the Scout Oath', one's shirt was taken away for a time and a scratchy blue jersey substituted: or when the scout shirts themselves had to be washed (too infrequently). The patrol leaders were the equivalent of prefects, and controlled the school in the myriad details that govern a small boy's economy and that lend themselves so neatly to petty tyranny; changing of shoes, going to the lavatory, and so forth. But the scout organization demanded also the unceasing study of the manual in order to acquire more and more 'badges', which, after an oral examination on farming, first aid, or suchlike had been successfully passed, were sewn on one's sleeve. The senior boys were expected to acquire a dozen or more of these. It was all highly theoretical and largely useless, being indoors; I never had to light a fire, or bandage a limb. Odd useless pieces of information still return: if a child has convulsions, put it in a hot bath of a hundred degrees!

One bright spot there was. My Father had told the headmaster that I could shoot; the headmaster prided himself on the school's performance in the competitions of The Preparatory Schools Air Rifle Association. I was promptly taken into the gym and told to lie down on a rough coconut mat. The weapons were powerful .177 BSAs, of great accuracy; the standard range was thirty feet, at targets reduced to represent the open-range ones at 200, 500 and 600 yards. The last, if I remember right, was about the size of a sixpence. After a few shots, and experience of the differing weight and trigger-pull of each rifle, it became fairly easy to make one-hole groups, so long as one were in the mood; my place in the team was assured, giving me, for a new boy, some little standing in the school. Once or twice there were good hours when the headmaster gave me his gun to shoot woodpigeons in the grounds; I can still smell the gun-oil, which was different from that which we used at home. Soccer I played but was useless at, then and afterwards, being large and clumsy; cricket was more fun and I became a reasonable slow bowler. Many hours were spent in the gravelled playground; in winter playing a loathsome game called Fox-Across, in summer learning to catch, by patrols, with composition cricket-balls. This at least was harmless and had some point; less so when the headmaster took it into his head to hit balls at us with a cricket-bat, at all ranges and levels, and beat us if we committed the unforgivable sin of 'funking it'. One result was that for years afterwards I could catch anything at any pace or angle, and developed a reasonable 'ball eye', which stood me in good stead at my public school; particularly when I discovered Eton Fives, and finally became Keeper of the Courts. But there was always with me the longing for the River and the woodland smells. I knew of no other school and supposed this to be typical; one crossed off the days on the calendar, and endured. I remember that I used to teaze out, from the scout khaki shirts or their yellow tassels, little pinches of wool that might serve for the bodies of trout-flies – Rough Olives or Partridge and Yellows – when I got home. A fisherman is always looking for such things, fur or fibre or feather; but I could not have foreseen that one day I would write a book about the making of trout-flies.

The 1914 War broke out during the summer holidays of my second year; it left little mark on my life, except that my brother and my Gore-Hickman cousins – in fact, all the young men among the 'gentry' of the West – joined immediately, having no need or compulsion, for the unreasoning adventure of it:

> Nor law, nor duty, bade me fight,
> Nor public men, nor cheering crowds,
> A lonely impulse of delight
> Drove to this tumult in the clouds.

By 1916 many of them were dead; among them my first cousin, Eric Lovett Henn, just down from Cambridge and about to enter the Diplomatic Service. Some, like that company of the Dublin Fusiliers composed of crack rugby footballers, refused to take commissions and were all killed in the fiasco of Gallipoli. My brother was for three weeks 'wounded and missing' at Suvla Bay with the Seventh Munsters. A deputation from the countryside came to condole with my Father. As they left, one was overheard to say to the coachman: 'Sure, wouldn't it be a great pity an' him to be killed, after the fine expensive education the poor Masther gave him?' We had heard off Loop Head the firing of a cruiser that was exploding mines off the Shannon mouth; and I remember that cock pheasants flew crowing into the trees, and rooks and crows crept in under thorn-trees at the distant sound.

But that autumn was to bring the single biggest change in our lives, and it was not due to the war.

ii

On November the tenth 1915, my Father died. He had been ill for many months; how ill I, with a boy's carelessness, did not notice. He had spent some weeks in the summer in a nursing home at Limerick, and then, I imagine, realizing how hopeless his condition was, returned to die at Paradise, in the room overlooking the Italian garden. I should have been forewarned; for on the morning of my return to school for the September term, he called me to his room, with the dog-cart waiting at the door, made me kneel down and blessed me. No doubt it was a ritual handed on to him. I can remember little of what he said except: 'You are coming into the world. I am going out.' Yet it made a double impression, for in the middle my Mother burst into the room, impatient at the delay, saying that I would surely miss the train at the station, twelve miles off. Angrily he told her to go and leave us alone. We caught the train, and I went to school as usual.

On the morning of the tenth I woke up with excitement, anticipating letters and parcels for my birthday. These would be handed out in the eleven o'clock break. At about nine the headmaster sent for me and took me to walk round the paths of the big square walled garden. No doubt he was kind in breaking the news; but he kept on repeating (that is all I can remember of the interview) that though I was going home that day, I must be sure to return as soon as possible and make up the time I had lost, since I was sitting for a scholarship at the end of term.

The train left some hours later. It was bitterly cold with intermittent snow. I was sent to the matron's room to wait, and played idly with something, perhaps a jigsaw puzzle. It came with a curious shock, for I seemed wholly numb when after a long silence the matron looked at me and said: 'Oh, Henn, I *am* sorry for you.' I got on the train, which crawled wearily through the starved November countryside. At a desolate junction, I remember looking longingly at some dish or other in a glass-case in the waiting-room – sardines on toast – which I could not buy, for I had been given only my train-fare and nothing over. Finally, in the late evening I arrived at Ennis, the country town, where I was met by friends and put up for the night. The next morning I was driven out to Paradise. In the hall the impression was of an intense quiet blackness: my Mother and my sisters in the heavy veiled mourning of the time, all speaking with hushed voices, and faces that seemed unnaturally white. Two events stand out. My Mother asked me if I wished to see my Father before he was put into his coffin. I hesitated, and finally said that I did not. In after years this seemed something of a betrayal. I rationalized it by trying to convince myself that I wished to remember him as he had been that summer, in the low room looking out on the small Italian garden and the woods: I used to sit by his bedside after my return from the River, and go over with him the day's events, pool by pool and cast by cast.

The funeral was not for two days; my Mother decided wisely that there was little point in my hanging about the desolate hushed house, and suggested that I should take my gun and go out. I had never before seen the woods in autumn; they were lying leaf-meal, wet and cold, and I wandered round them with one of the boys. I cannot remember that I shot anything, and I think the people on the estate were rather scandalized.

The day of the funeral there was a high gale with sleet and snow; the great woods that screened the house from the south-west were in trouble, and a number of trees were blown down. It was a custom with us that the womenfolk should not go to the grave-side; my Father had thought it too great an emotional strain. The first part of the service was held in the hall, with its big glass door looking out over the Shannon: a faint light coming through the Victorian Gothic stained-glass windows at the sides, that carried various family coats-of-arms. There was an immense polished chest, holding tennis-gear and the like. On the walls hung curved cavalry swords in their leather-and-brass scabbards. I remember that I was taught to kiss weapon-steel if I ever had occasion to unsheathe it. (These swords were later taken by the IRA on one of their many raids.) The coffin stood on two stools, whose supports were negro boys carved in ebony. After the preliminary service it was carried on the shoulders of men, a great body of the tenantry following, half a mile across the fields, to the tiny burial-ground on the hill. The scene was impressed vividly on me, for this was the first funeral I had seen: the hill-top looking out over the estuary, with its screen of small storm-bent larches and firs, and clumps of rhododendrons below; the mass of brown-red shale and earth by the grave-side; the white surplice of the Canon; the driven sleety snow. The coffin was lowered slowly and clumsily on ropes, into some inches of snow and water; the three handfuls of earth sounded muffled upon its lid, even as Browne set them out in the fifth chapter of *Urne Buriall*:

Now since these dead bones . . .

Many years afterwards the emotion returned in verse:

Why should the dead go down into water, and the snowflakes
Melt on the coffin lid?
O but the empty house, and the rusting gun
And all that wisdom gone when I needed it so.

I went back to school, to return again for the Christmas holidays. It was then that the first numbness of loss, that is like the blow of a bullet, came back painfully into life. Part of the house was shut up; my Mother and I lived mainly in the library, which was small and relatively draught-proof. We still had two maids, but the whole establishment had contracted and changed. There occurred one of those small ridiculous incidents that loom so large and so bitterly in life. In the smoking-room which looked on to the inner courtyard and served as a study, gun-room and office, where the country-people came with their disputes and troubles, my Father had a large black desk. Many associations were clustered about it; it had been one of my earliest memories of Sligo. In it my Father had kept on one side his fishing-tackle, reels, fly-tying material; on the other, his diaries and miscellaneous papers. My Mother had taken the desk, tumbled the contents into a vast heap, and put them in a disused room. I was resentful and very angry, not quite knowing why. Some *mana* had passed, and the gulf widened between my Mother and myself. Only lately I read of a very similar incident – but with the parental situation reversed – in Richard Church's *Over the Bridge*.

There were other causes of friction. My Father had taken the keenest interest in my doings, both at school and at home; my Mother neither understood nor cared for school life, and, Martha-like, was obsessed only with my health and safety. I suppose that I looked – stupidly – to her to give me what my Father had given; their temperaments and sensibilities were utterly different. It cannot have been easy for her. I grew sullen and withdrawn in that wet storm-tossed winter, and went back thankfully to school of which I had become captain.

iii

I think that the teaching at the preparatory school was arbitrarily efficient, in a rather blind way. I remember doing constant sums about stocks and shares – neat mathematical formulae for present worth and such things – without any idea of what a stock or a share might be. We learnt a good deal of Latin grammar and Latin idioms, by memorizing each evening from a small red-bound book: I think this, and the stocks and shares booklets, had been produced by the headmaster himself.

But the real focus of life in the upper school was the examination for entrance scholarships at the public schools. Since we were in a remote part of the world, the papers were worked at the school, in the headmaster's own study, and with a system of special privileges for the two or three days that the examination was on. But one did not sit alone: if 'X' were the real candidate for, say, Clifton, 'Y' and 'Z', his competitors in the top form, would be told to take the same examination, at the same time, 'for practice'. We were invariably told to leave blank the nameplace at the top right-hand corner; I do not think that any of us tumbled to the significance of this until long afterwards.

A year or two after I had left, a major scandal came to light. A boy had won a valuable mathematical scholarship to a famous school. During his first term there his mathematical master had set his form a certain problem, which the boy was unable to answer.

'But you did that very question in our scholarship examination last May. I know, because I marked your papers.'

'No, sir.'
'Why, I can show you that you did!'

And the master went to a cupboard, and produced the six-month-old scripts.

'There, there's your own working of the problem.'
'This isn't my writing, sir!'

An investigation followed. The boy was right; the script was not in his handwriting, though the name at the top of the paper was his. The headmaster of the preparatory school, taxed with the scandal, resigned, and the school passed into other hands. It seemed reasonable to suppose, though there was no question of a judicial investigation, that he had in fact forged the name of the genuine candidate on the best of the worked answers. To this day I do not know whether I won my own scholarship fairly, or whether I was responsible for the successes of others. A year or two ago, driving from Fishguard to Clare with my wife, I found the school with difficulty, on top of a windy hill on the outskirts of Fermoy; it had become a slum tenement.[1]

That Easter holiday the Revolution broke out; the next six years were to be lived in a state of curious tension, erratic communications, rumours of every kind. In the autumn I crossed to England. My first sight of that country was the grimy platforms of Euston, in the very early morning, all under the general depression of two years of war, and the slaughter of the Battle of Ypres. School was cold, strange, but far from unkind to me, for my brother had been there six years before, and was still remembered. My second sister, then a VAD at a small hospital in London, visited me sometimes at the school. The eldest had long since married, and was much occupied with her family at Sligo; I hardly saw her for the next twenty years.

iv

The situation in Ireland changed the course of my education. My Mother was now virtually penniless, for no rents had been paid on the estate since 1916, and my Father's pension died with him; there was no money even to prove my Father's will, and to attempt to procure or borrow the small sum which he had left to

[1] The incident of the examinations is confirmed in Lionel Fleming's book.

me to provide for my first years at the Bar would have embarrassed the family finances still further. The will was not in fact proved until 1934, nineteen years after my Father's death; a legal delay which would perhaps have been possible only in Ireland. It was never clear from term to term how the fairly modest school-fees were to be met; my Mother, generous and spendthrift, knew that only her presence saved the house from being burnt and the demesne split up, and, like Lady Gregory[1] in the northern extremity of the county, was determined to keep it intact so long as might be. There was of necessity a slow process of erosion; the stock of cattle realized piecemeal, and not replaced; felling of timber, and finally the sale of silver and pictures, for a fraction of their worth, to antique dealers' agents who prowled the country. Out of her generosity she would send me, 'from the sale of a beast', odd small sums.

I had always intended to read Law, and go to the Irish Bar, where my name would perhaps have had some value in the early stages of practice; and in 1919 I had been accepted at Trinity College, Dublin. But it became increasingly clear that there would be no money to put me through the university, and that even if I did succeed in borrowing the money and getting called there was unlikely to be any Bar work for a Protestant in five or six years' time. (In this my judgement was wholly wrong.) But 'The Troubles' had revealed a substratum of religious hatred which was quite outside my imagining, though it seemed to have grown more moderate on both sides; veiled, paradoxical in its incidence, until the Ulster troubles of the late 60s and 70s. On the other hand, if the Bar were out of reach, the traditional alternative of the Diplomatic Service was likely to be more so, even under the assumption that the promised reorganization after the war might make a private income less essential.

I had started life at Aldenham as a mathematical scholar on the foundation; but though I find that I won the sixth-form prize for mathematics in 1918, I had little real aptitude. I had not taken Greek seriously, though my Latin was up to scholarship standard: German, in which I had been fairly fluent at the age of nine because of the Prussian nursery governess, I had only revived again at the age of sixteen; my French was good, but I had never, because of the war and lack of money, been

[1] See her admirable *Journals* vol. 1. edited by Daniel Murphy, Colin Smythe (Gerrards Cross) and Oxford University Press (New York) 1978.

Preparatory School 71

abroad. On the other hand, I was captain of the school, a quadruple colour, and most of my friends were going to Cambridge or Oxford; so with no very clear ideas in my head I sat for a mathematical award in December 1919. I did not get anything except an offer of admission, and decided that scholarship mathematics were beyond me; so I returned to Dublin, to lodgings which my Mother had found for Christmas 1919. There we were sometimes visited by a magnificently handsome old man with snowy hair, who had been a noted Nationalist. His name was Swift McNeill. He had been one of my Mother's many admirers forty years before. Paradise had been temporarily shut down, and it was said that I myself would be none too safe in the West since I had served in my school OTC, and because of my brother's implication with the Munsters in 'the Kaiser's War'.

Dublin was still suffering from intermittent shooting, the curfew, and outbreaks of IRA guerrilla warfare. Above and behind there seemed to be 'dilated consciousness',[1] a relic of the days of shelling and the burning city. One evening my Mother and I went by tram to see a performance of *John Bull's Other Island* at the Abbey; a good play, which then assumed a strong unintended irony from contemporary events. As the tram passed Trinity College, there was a loud explosion from the area of Harcourt Street. This, I learnt afterwards, was an incident in a private vendetta and had no political significance. A number of thugs had broken the windows of a large piano-shop, and set a quantity of gelignite among the pianos, with a time-fuse; ivory keys and pieces of wire littered the streets the next morning. It must have been about that time that Oliver St John Gogarty made his celebrated escape from the IRA who had kidnapped him and were holding him in a house on the banks of the Liffey; he escaped from the house, and jumped into the river, and afterwards in gratitude presented a pair of swans to the river.[2] A Dublin ballad celebrated his agility and courage with a pleasant ironical humour, and (I gather from a contemporary) with much poetic licence.

But Dublin that winter was cold, wet and rather dull; and though it was said that the West was too dangerous to visit, I longed for the mountains and the snipe. My Mother knew no

[1] The words are AE's.
[2] See his book of verse, *An Offering of Swans*.

young people of my generation; I worked in the mornings in the library of Trinity College, but it was a dreary Christmas.

Towards the end of 1918 I had my first experience of London, which had hitherto meant no more than early-morning arrivals on the Irish Mail at Euston; crowded trains that sometimes started or stopped in air-raids or the school train from St Pancras to Radlett.

During the whole of my schooldays my stammer had troubled me. I do not know the cause. It may have been inherited in some slight degree, or developed through my being made – so my sisters have told me – to use my right hand when I was left-handed. Probably the extreme loneliness of life at Paradise, the strain of the continually-awaited raids by the IRA, the uncertainty as to whether there would be enough money to keep me at school, all contributed.

Anyway, my second sister, who had been a VAD in a hospital in Kensington during the war, found an 'establishment' that advertised itself as curing stammering. It was in Bloomsbury not far from the British Museum; I went there for the Easter holidays in a mood of despondency at missing the River and Paradise in spring-time. The school was, in fact, a large flat with four or five bedrooms, at the top of a tall block of buildings. The proprietor or director was a large, suave and good-looking Jew of Germanic origin, who was patient and efficient. There was a little grey-haired housekeeper who was kind to me: I think that from time to time one or two pupils lived in, but I remember nothing of them. Most of the class of a dozen or so came daily, in various stages of inhibition. The exercises were simple; control of breathing, singing words rather than attempting to speak them, reading aloud. Outside the 'classes' there was little to do, and I knew no one in London. There were the usual things for a boy to explore; the museum, Covent Garden in the early morning, the Tower, but I was too despondent to have my heart in it, or to read systematically as I might have done, or even to unpack my emotions in verse. Always there was the longing for the open country and the sound of falling waters. One game I discovered early. My bedroom window looked out on a mass of untidy mean walls and roofs with many London sparrows, and these were busy nesting. Tiny pieces of cotton wool, teazed out, could be floated down into the chasm of buildings, and the birds would

Preparatory School

pick them up gracefully, or quarrel over them as they fell. The nests in the area must have been very luxurious that year. They brawled all day long, like Yeats's sparrows in the eaves. One day the old housekeeper told me that I was going to have a treat; 'one of the most beautiful women she had ever seen' was coming to stay. Foolishly I enquired if she was the principal's wife or daughter. A tall and well-groomed blonde appeared, who proved to be his mistress, and the pace of our work slowed appreciably for some days. I remember being priggishly shocked; I hadn't run across that sort of thing before at such close quarters.

Then there was Aldenham again for the Lent term. There was only one further chance to go the way of my friends; most of the Cambridge Colleges had finished their scholarship examinations, but St Catharine's held theirs at the end of March. There seemed little likelihood of going to Cambridge anyway, but there might be a chance of getting one's name on the honours boards. I had been writing a good deal of schoolboy verse, and translating much from the French, especially from Ronsard and Villon; the authorities thought that I might try for a modern languages award. I sat and was given a senior scholarship; more, I suspect, on my English than anything else. The headmaster, that great man A. H. Cooke, greeted it with: 'And even poor old Henn's got something.' It was not a traditional college from the school's point of view; most of us went to St John's, Caius, and Pembroke; nor were there family connections, since two uncles had been Fellows of Trinity Hall, two cousins had been Fellows of Trinity, and my brother was an Exhibitioner of Magdalene.

That Easter holiday I spent in lodgings in Bloomsbury, going out to Aldenham each day to train for the public schools' boxing championships. Though I was fighting light-heavy only, there was no one in the school of my strength or weight, and in the previous term they had set me to fight three rounds against a middle-weight London professional, 'in order to get knocked about'. He was of course infinitely faster than I was, and hit me more or less at will, but I stayed on my feet, with some discomfort but with renewed self-confidence. The training, on the other hand, was sheer joy; a journey from London, and gym work, a rub-down with olive oil, and six miles back running and walking. I have never known such harmony of physical fitness. In the competition I met the ultimate winner, who was a stone and a half heavier, and was beaten on points. Only twice afterwards did I use my knowledge, and then with a fierce atavistic sense of exaltation.

Meanwhile the scholarship had been offered; the School was prepared to offer a leaving exhibition, making in all £100 annually for the three years. It was said that £250 was necessary; this was an underestimate for one who had to travel to Ireland, and the Irish estates seemed unlikely ever to pay any of the theoretical arrears that had piled up. At this point an uncle, who was Bishop of Burnley and who had become an authority on dry-rot in churches and on ecclesiastical law, intervened. He had obviously a poor opinion of the college that had elected me, but Cambridge was Cambridge, and when he and G. G. Coulton had sat for the same classical scholarship at Trinity Hall in the 'eighties, he had won it, and Coulton had gone to St Catharine's. (Coulton was immensely kind to me when I came up.) Therefore, he would allow me £130 a year for three years only, provided I or my Mother could make up the rest. The future was in doubt, anyway; I accepted, and finished out my last term with a good deal of cricket, an OTC camp, and the coming of a new headmaster. The Irish situation was at its worst. I had to come back to school from camp at Strensall to change into civilian clothes before crossing, for I might well have been shot if I had gone in corps uniform, and I arrived to find my home practically in a state of siege. The cardinal error of turning loose the Black-and-Tans with, it was said, orders 'to knock hell out of the natives', led to reprisal and counter-reprisal:

> Now days are dragon-ridden, the nightmare
> Rides upon sleep; a drunken soldiery
> Can leave the mother, murdered at her door,
> To crawl in her own blood, and go scot-free . . .

That is based on an incident at Kiltartan in Co. Galway, when a lorry of Black-and-Tans drove down the village street firing promiscuously. It gave rise to another poem, the fourth of those on Major Robert Gregory, the 'Irish Airman' who was killed fighting for the British:

> – Yet rise from your Italian tomb;
>   Flit to Kiltartan Cross and stay
>   Till certain second thoughts have come

> Upon the cause that you and we
> Imagined such a fine affair:
> Half-drunk or whole-mad soldiery
> Are murdering your tenants there . . .

I have a letter from Yeats to Sir Herbert Grierson describing another reprisal: how the Auxiliaries took two young men from a village, tied them by the heels to the tail of a lorry, and dragged them on the metalled roads till their heads came off. And Yeats described how an old man said to him: 'There was nothing left for the mother but the head.' But Yeats did not use that episode to make such a similitude as he loved: with Hector, Tamer of Horses, dragged round the Walls of Troy.

V

'THE TROUBLES'

i

'The Troubles' or 'the Bad Times', as the old country-people call them, have never, so far as I know, received adequate or balanced treatment in history. The picture that comes nearest to my own experience was given in some numbers of *Blackwood's Magazine* between the two wars. In the last resort, there is blame on all sides, and I have no wish to revive the stories of threats, burnings and murder. 'The Troubles' did, in fact, lend colour to most of my school and undergraduate days. The Easter Rebellion of 1916 came during the holidays; of which, as usual, I spent all the time I could on the River. 'The Rising' was marked for us by the complete and sudden cutting of every communication; the usual crop of rumours of a German landing in support of it, and the complete impossibility of taking any constructive action:

> We are closed in, and the key is turned
> On our uncertainty; somewhere
> A man is killed, or a house burned,
> Yet no clear fact to be discerned . . .[1]

At that stage there was no real question of our being burnt or murdered. The battle in Dublin, 'that crazy fight', was quickly over. Not for many years later (though the celebrated *Easter 1916* was written that same year) did it assume as in Yeats's eyes, the status of a complete heroic action: it seemed then rather a sordid and militarily hopeless adventure pursuing the age-old maxim that England's need was Ireland's opportunity. A letter from my brother, with the Munster Fusiliers, described the anger of those troops and their desire to return to Ireland to deal with the 'traitors' who, they felt, had stabbed them in the back.

---

[1] Yeats: 'The Stare's Nest by My Window'. I have written of some aspects of this in the Warton Lecture on Poetry before the British Academy (1965).

In a week or two all seemed normal, and I returned to my preparatory school for the last term, leaving my Mother alone. The chief conversation among the country-folk was the possibility of the British introducing conscription as a result of the Rising;[1] and since many Irishmen had left England in 1914-15 expressly to avoid this, it became an important issue on which I was questioned constantly on my fishing expeditions in the mountains. An aeroplane appeared, the first that had ever been seen in that part of the world. Its noise was described to me by an old man: 'Your Honour, I heard a noise below at the crossroads, as it might be two motther cars, and them all drunk; and I threw myself into the ditch and I started to pray to the Vargin.' One school of thought held that aeroplanes would come over trailing long ropes with grapnels at the end of each, to carry off to 'the con-*scrip*-tion'. I remember vividly one incident of that time; I was far from a main road or village, fishing, in a wild district with the picturesque name of Furróor. I went into a cottage beside the little river to ask for a drink of water, knowing that I would be given, Biblically, milk. In the chimney-corner sat a very old man, wearing the knee-breeches and swallow-tailed coat of a past generation. He had little English, but we talked for a while. He was obviously curious to know who I was, but was too well-bred to ask; finally it came out. He got up with great difficulty, knelt down on the clay floor and kissed my hands; it was a shattering and very humbling experience for a schoolboy of fifteen.

Something of this kind, courtesy and friendliness, was common on such wanderings. At the time one took it for granted. The family had never, I think, been absentees. The great Famine, the incompetence of government and the horrors of starvation, must have been well within the memories of the older people; yet I never heard it mentioned by them. (My Father was born in 1848, at the height of the Famine.) Nor did there seem, in our immediate part of the world, any agrarian discontents. On the demesne itself there were five cottages for the men working on the place, and one farm under tenants. I never saw the rent-roll, but there were the usual small farms scattered over a wide area

[1] Many thought that if it had been imposed then and there all future trouble would have been avoided. But all that tragedy is loaded with 'ifs': *if* the Home Rule Bill had been cleared in 1919. So Yeats again:
    'For England may keep faith
    For all that is done and said . . .'

on the mountain, and I did not hear that there were evictions.¹ The wages on a place during the first war now seem derisory: a pound a week, a free cottage, firing, milk, potatoes, land for a garden and grass for a cow; yet they managed to rear healthy families, and my friends among them tell me that they were 'well off' then. They had long memories, and talked much of past families, in the winter evenings over the turf fires. On the roads one met tramps who talked in such a way:

> And there is an old beggar, wandering in his pride –
> His fathers served their fathers before Christ was crucified.
> *O what of that, O what of that,*
> *What is there left to say?*²

Indeed the war scarcely touched those remote villages, except by way of rising prices, and money coming regularly as separation allowances from those who were fighting with the Irish regiments.

My first term at my Public School followed in September 1916, and from then I was to lead a curiously double life. Aldenham was near enough to London to see though not to suffer some of the bombing raids; there was no question of shelters, and I saw one or two daylight raids in the near distance, as well as the blazing Zeppelin that came down at Potter's Bar. The contrast between school and life in the West of Ireland was unbelievable. Rationing was in force, and for the next two years we were all perpetually hungry; to return to Ireland was to find abundance of meat, butter, eggs. But the pressure of the war on a school was by 1916 beginning to be intensified in more important ways. The officer shortage was becoming acute, and the age at which boys could be accepted into officer cadet battalions was falling steadily. I was due to go to the Irish Guards four months after my seventeenth birthday, which was the day before the war ended. In consequence the turnover of boys leaving school was extremely rapid, and promotion to the ranks of the praepostors unduly so; the abler boys waited just long enough to sit for their university entrance scholarships, and left without taking them up.

As one consequence the OTC loomed very large in our lives;

---

¹ It was interesting to see, in 1963, a picture-map of Clare, perhaps designed for American visitors, showing that some 600 evictions, of women and children, took place in our village in 1898. This, when checked, proved wholly false.

² Yeats, 'The Curse of Cromwell'.

by 1918, as a senior NCO, I was doing some twenty hours a week in parades and lectures. Most of that training seemed singularly unintelligent; there was little attempt to tell us the reason for anything we did, though many of us would be subalterns within a few months. It was more important to spend hours seeing that one's puttees – and how we loathed those inefficient relics of Indian soldiering – should finish in the right place than that we should know the real purpose of the endless arms-drill. It was not till I temporarily became a sniping officer in the second war that I realized the true function of that drill: you cannot shoot, quickly and instinctively, as a boy throws a stone, until you have achieved complete unity with your weapon. We did much bayonet-fighting in all its brutality; I remember that the German saw-toothed bayonet of those days, plunged into the stomach with the twist-and-withdraw, grew for a time into a nightmare. I suspect that the emphasis had shifted from games to war, to swing back again in 1919; in any event travelling for matches with other schools was difficult. And there were long spells, on half-holidays, at various kinds of 'war-work'; cutting wood, hoeing turnips and such like for neighbouring farmers. A generation later my son did just this work at his school in New England, driving a tractor, ploughing, husbandry. Our wages were given (rather to our disgust, for it was back-breaking work) to war charities. All the masters, including those who were the corps officers, were in some way unfit, and as time went on the staff acquired 'temporaries', some of them very much 'dugouts', and once, for a short period, a mistress to teach the smaller boys.

By 1919 the situation in Ireland had become steadily worse, as the Irish Republican Army reorganized themselves after their defeat and started their systematic and highly intelligent guerrilla warfare, which served as a model nearly forty years later for the 'campaign' in Cyprus.[1] This took various forms. The first was the burning of the barracks of the RIC, and the sporadic shooting of policemen from ambush. I returned for the holidays to find the barracks in the local village a black ruin, much to the indignation of the villagers. One policeman was said to have been shot a mile or two from the house, and his body buried in a bog-hole, from which it was irrecoverable; though it may be found, centuries later, preserved perfectly in the brown half-liquid peat.

[1] The best account I know is in *The Secret Army*, by J. Bowyer Bell (Blond, 1970).

Then guerrilla warfare increased its incidence upon us. Bridges were blown up, or knocked down, leaving a narrow way for foot-passengers, so that it became common for the Model-T Fords to carry long planks strapped to the running-boards, and skate precariously over the gaps. Over many rivers horse-and-foot-traffic quickly discovered passages or fords, often involving long detours. The return to school became something of an adventure. Telegraph wires were cut and remained so. Sometimes, where the road went through a wood, or over a hump-backed bridge, strands of wire were fastened across at throat-height so as to catch military dispatch-riders on their motor-cycles. A favourite form of ambush was to dig out the road, preferably at the bottom of a steep hill, into a pit some four feet deep and the width of the road. This was covered over, first with stretched wire-netting, and then with mud and the broken metal used for making up the road. The IRA would take up their positions on the hillside above, and open fire when the lorry or Crossley tender crashed into it. To fall into one on a bicycle was an unpleasant experience; I know, for I did this in a south-west gale and rain.

Paradise was raided repeatedly on the pretext of obtaining weapons for the IRA; field-glasses, fishing-tackle, even the old swords were taken, with other loot of all kinds. The shotguns had been handed in to the military authorities, from whom some were reclaimed, hopelessly ruined through neglect, from Woolwich after the Treaty. I kept hidden among the rafters my own battered and pitted Belgian sixteen: a Purdey muzzle-loader that had been built for my Grandfather; and, young and foolish as I was, a Spanish 9 mm automatic pistol that lay cocked under my pillow at night. For there was always the chance of a 'serious' raid, of being made to dig your own grave on the lawn before being shot, and a dramatic vanity made me think that I might be able to do something about it. Of course, this was very stupid. One of my acquaintances did try to protect himself. He had been forewarned of a coming raid; the normal process was to terrorize the servants into leaving a back-door unlocked. At the end of the long passage that so often connects the front of Irish country houses with the back he built a barricade of furniture, and waited all night with a deer-stalking rifle to which he had lashed an electric torch. He was a good shot, and took the first seven men through the head; but a few weeks later he was himself ambushed and killed.

'The Troubles' 81

After one of the raids I went in to see the OC troops at Ennis, explained our standing as loyalists, and asked for protection. The colonel was charming and apologetic; he said that he did not dare to move a platoon even five miles. Meanwhile British troops were selling to the IRA, in the public-houses of Ennis, the ammunition which would be used to shoot them. The price was reputed to be one shilling per round of .303, or a pint of porter.

During most of the raids my Mother was alone in the house, except for two faithful maids; and the house was surrounded by woods, far from the main road and more than a mile from the nearest village. She was then in her late sixties. Yet it became a legend in the countryside how, during one of the 'looting' raids, they had put her in the smoking-room with two men with cocked pistols standing guard over her: and how within minutes she had them singing songs and dancing to entertain her. A party of Free State troops raided us early one summer's morning, and wished to shoot me when they found what they thought was a bomb, but was in fact the detachable sound-box of an old-fashioned gramophone. We convinced them of this by playing the gramophone, and then gave the firing-party breakfast; afterwards they posed for a photograph (which I still have) in the inner courtyard.

As in most Irish affairs, the 'Troubles' had their comic side; or rather, the perpetual ambivalence that seems to permeate all things Irish from the time of Swift onwards. Late one night in the Christmas holidays there was an authoritative knock at the front door. The house was in any event quite indefensible, with its enormous windows and many entrances, and because of the laurels and rhododendrons that pressed close upon three sides. One of us opened the hall door. A masked figure strode in dramatically, flung down on the floor a heavy package that might have been a bomb, and went out without a word. The package, gingerly opened, contained some boxes of sixteen-bore cartridges, then unobtainable. A label, in disguised handwriting, had these words: 'Wouldn't it be a pity for Master Tom not to have his bit of shooting, and he home for the holidays?'

As it happened I was only shot at twice, and then ineffectively and perhaps unintentionally; once by a lorry-load of 'Black and Tans', the British Irregulars, who went charging through the countryside in their wired-in tenders, shooting up villages in futile attempts to create a reign of terror. I was ferreting on the top of a wooded hill, below which ran the main road; a lorry passed below me, travelling fast, and let off half a drum of Lewis-gun ammunition at me. On the second occasion I was sailing alone, half-way between Foynes and the Clare shore: a rifle-bullet passed some distance away. It was only a ranging shot, probably fired by some enthusiast who wanted to see how – and if – his rifle worked. Much the same thing happened to me passing through a wood near Versailles, after the liberation of Paris; when a small boy of the Resistance fired his Sten gun at me, also to see how it worked. That is a fatal temptation if one possesses a weapon of any kind.

There were times, from 1919 to 1921, winter and summer, when I forced myself to walk the round of the woods along the northern and eastern boundaries: sometimes because there was a rumour of a raid that might develop that night; more often, I think, to fight my own cowardice. It was a circuit of perhaps a mile. Forty years later (but long before the final burning) those walks gave rise to a poem, which I called 'Dark Journey'.[1]

Clare was one of the worst counties, for no very obvious reason, though it had long had an unenviable reputation in matters of violence: even at the turn of the century it was said that one could get a man murdered for a five-pound note, with the cost of the cartridges as an extra. At any rate, 'The Troubles' ended with most of the big houses burnt. Atrocities seemed about equally divided between the Black and Tans and the IRA. Armed guards were posted when officers went to play tennis; the roads were nearly deserted at night. Again we must go to Yeats's *Nineteen Hundred and Nineteen*:

> ... The night can sweat with terror as before
> We pieced our thoughts into philosophy,
> And planned to bring the world into a rule,
> Who are but weasels fighting in a hole.

The last image is a living one: I remember on a summer's evening lying on the quay at Paradise, watching the sea-wall with its unmortared blocks of limestone facing where the weasels[2] lived; and seeing in the stillness two packs, perhaps families, come out and quarrel, with their short high chittering and sinuous delighted movements. Then they vanished into the

[1] See p. 267.
[2] So called throughout the country; but in fact stoats. We used the terms interchangeably, as with heron and 'crane'.

brambles along the wall, and presently I heard the shriek of a rabbit, as one of them fastened its deadly hold, just above the eye.

ii

So the last days at school merged through Ireland into the first October at Cambridge. School had been good, in spite of the tensions of the two wars, the uncertainties at home. In many ways I had been supremely fortunate. Aldenham had had a very great headmaster, A. H. Cooke; broken by the death in battle of his favourite son, he retired to an Eton living at the end of my last term. A great classical teacher, a leading conchologist, and once, it was said, wicket-keeper of the Eton XI, he did the administration of the school himself without clerical help, taught the Classical Sixth, and divinity at intervals throughout the school. He used a feigned or real deafness and short-sight to select what he should hear and see publicly, leaving much to his praepostors; privately he seemed to know everything that went on. He believed in an old-fashioned ceremonial, to which the school responded; at morning chapel he stood robed outside the gate, while a member of each form came before him and, raising the straw-hat which we still wore or carried, told him the names of those absent or ill. There was also an age-old tradition that the school could not have its hair-cut – a full day's job – unless the captain of the school had first presented to the headmaster a copy of Latin verses, sprinkled with contemporary allusion or scandal, invoking the presence of the barber. Since I was quite incompetent in Latin verses, I got the senior classic to compose them, and copied them out in my own hand; it then became a courteous fiction between the headmaster and myself that I had written them, and he would question me about quantities and metrics.

The four years at Aldenham had passed quickly and with a fair measure of happiness, except for that continuous anxiety over Ireland and my Mother's affairs. At first everything, in form or on parade, was hampered by the bad stammer of which I have spoken. The school, like so many others, had been an Elizabethan grammar school, and flamed into prominence when John Kennedy, son of the great Latin scholar, came from his tutorship at Pembroke to take over the headmastership in the '80s. Thereafter, until North London and the motor-car encroached upon its characteristic tradition, it drew largely on the sons of professional men – doctors, ICS, and an unusually large proportion of Cambridge Dons: Grays, Searles, McNairs, Sykeses. Its tradition was almost wholly classical: its size deliberately kept down to some 250 or so, its endowments, then as now, liberally augmented by the Brewers' Company.

As I look back, I realize that there were many interesting things about the school. Many of the masters were bachelors with private means; which meant freedom from domestic cares and a certain liberality in spending. My friend, R. C. Clift, an athlete, soldier and poet, went back there deliberately after the First World War, and gave most generously to the school: to die, wastefully, playing squash in London. The three 'out' housemasters, Paull, Beevor, Gilbert, were far from typical schoolmasters; the first two more like country gentlemen, sometimes appearing at morning school in plus-fours with a spaniel at heel. I think their scholarship was probably adequate but hardly more; their methods of teaching were certainly individual and exciting. My own most fruitful hours were with Cooke for Latin prose, and translation with the Upper Sixth (I still had little Greek), when some glimmerings came to me of the excitement he felt in the accuracy of the precise word, the process of making ancient life a living experience transposed into modern terms. But most important of all was G. C. F. Mead, sometime of Pembroke, a brilliant classic who also took us for English; without any perceptible plan, he read aloud to us exciting things and made us write essays on every imaginable subject. Out of this writing, and much reading of French and German, and French poetry classes with F. H. English, there grew, I suppose, a crude schoolboy's feeling for a comparison of literatures. All my teachers were outspoken in their comments, and intolerant of nonsense. I remember reading with Fred English some passage of Victor Hugo – the sixth-form linguists were a small group, and we had something like university tutorials – in which that flamboyant poet writes of 'le valse lascive'. There was a hush, a disgusted wrinkling of his very characteristic nose:

'Tom. This man has the sentiments of a third-rate methodist baker.'

War and its casualties brought me up the school probably more quickly than was good for me. It ended in the middle of the terrible epidemic of 'Spanish Flu' in November 1918. The school dispersed; several boys staggered into their homes to die there. I and a few others, Irish or Scots, whose homes were too remote, remained on at school, flu casualties in a single dormitory. One night from the window I saw the black dog cross the playing-field; legend said that it appeared whenever a boy was about to die. It seemed, and no doubt was, a very ordinary black retriever. Years later, I met someone who had studied the appearances of the Black Dog in Devon and Cornwall, who told me that these places, joined on the map, corresponded to prehistoric folk-tracks.

VI

CAMBRIDGE

i

Cambridge in October 1920 was a strange contrast to the life of semi-siege in County Clare, then at the height of 'The Troubles'. I had visited it two or three times already for scholarship and other examinations; and I remember being shocked at the state of my future college, without baths, lit by oil-lamps, and with many men sharing in pairs the shabby eighteenth-century rooms. It was an exciting time; two-thirds of the undergraduates were ex-servicemen, of every rank up to full colonel and of every experience in war; I was to meet their like again, and sometimes to teach their sons, as senior tutor of the college, in 1946. The remaining third were, like myself, fresh from the public schools, and, with a few exceptions, from the smaller ones. Between them and the ex-servicemen there was at first something of a social cleavage; caused as much by adult habits and money, and by a sense of optimism as to the future, as by their own seniority and experience. Most of them had money to burn; partly because of saving while on service, partly because of the system of gratuities for officers, which left many with a capital sum, that must have seemed substantial, to be spent on their Cambridge career. And after four or even five years of war, and the devastating casualty rates among their friends, a sort of desperate light-heartedness was in the air. This was concentrated, in a sense, in the body of Naval officers in Caius; from whom emerged much of the gaiety, and most of the superbly organized 'rags'. Of them Kipling wrote:

> Hallowed River, most gracious trees,
> Chapel beyond compare,
> Here be gentlemen tired of the seas,
> Take them into your care . . .

This world was brave and new and a little confused. At first I found myself sharing a large room with a schoolfellow of whom I had seen little, as he had been superannuated from school a year earlier while in the lower fifth. He was a superb natural athlete and quickly won his soccer and hurdles blues. But we had different sets of friends, who were always clashing at meals and evening coffee. After a term I was moved to a tiny room in the attics of the same staircase, remote and secure and with a magnificent view over the court; in summer one could sit out on the leads above Queens' Lane.

I had a large circle of friends from Aldenham, mostly at Pembroke, Caius and Queens'. Among them was Rupert Clift, a good poet and witty parodist, a fine soccer player, who had had a couple of years in the army. It was through his urging and example that I took the first unusual step: I asked the college to allow me to read for the English Tripos, though I was senior modern language scholar, promising that I would return to languages in my third year. The college did not care much one way or the other. After some experience of the university and of men I am convinced that, apart from the technological subjects, it doesn't matter in the least what one reads; provided only that one can be fired with interest for it, and have the chance – and it is a chance – of reading it under the direction of someone of stature and the gift of giving fire. Years later, W. H. S. Jones referred me to the quotation from *The Taming of the Shrew*, which governed his own classical teaching:

> No profit grows where is no pleasure ta'en;
> In brief, Sir, study what you most affect.

The English Tripos and its growth have since been celebrated in E. M. W. Tillyard's *The Muse Unchained*, and it was to him that I went for supervision.

ii

Cambridge in 1920 was full of exciting personalities, particularly in the English school. The English Tripos dated back only to 1919; it had been established by 'Q', H. F. Stewart, Chadwick, against implacable opposition. For a long time it was not considered a 'serious discipline' (this is a heavy stone invariably thrown at any new academic subject by the extreme conservatives); even today, forty years later, some colleges refuse to admit men for English.[1] But whatever its respectability, it had then the supreme advantage of complete freshness and vividness as a subject. Practically all the dons who taught us were ex-classics, and so brought to English a characteristic sanity and judgement. Further, they gave the impression – which was correct – of working things out for themselves as they went along. One was an ex-philosopher; another perhaps the most widely-read linguist in the university. Thus we had light turned upon our subject from every conceivable angle. There was no 'professionalism', and I think that something of Walter Pater's opinions about criticism was still valid. 'Eng.Lit.' was not to become a term of abuse till a quarter of a century later. No one thought of the Ph.D. as a vital step on the academic ladder; we knew of it, vaguely, as something that had been introduced to meet the American market. It is interesting now to think of the literary gods of the early twenties, and upon their place in the whirligig of taste. I had read while at school the normal volumes of Georgian Poetry, Masefield, Kipling, Owen, Sassoon, most of Shakespeare, and a good deal of French and German, mainly the romantics; but the library at school was then very poor, and that of Paradise belonged mainly to the eighteenth and nineteenth centuries.

Rupert Brooke was close in time and famous, but even then receding a little in spite of, or because of, his legend while at King's; it was not yet fashionable to sneer at *The Soldier*. Flecker of Caius we read; *Hassan* was running in London, and was being skilfully parodied by the Co-optimists, and *To a Poet a Thousand Years Hence* did not seem sentimental. Masefield was in full cry, though getting, we thought, a little passé: Rupert Clift had done for the *Granta* a superb parody called *Leonard the Cox,* taking off all his mannerisms and literary tricks. I had read all Shaw and Synge, but was suspicious of Yeats as at best a spiritual protagonist of the IRA in 'The Troubles'. Eliot we were just beginning to hear of; Grierson's great edition of Donne was beginning to take effect, though, following 'Q', we admired the Sermons rather than the verse. In general the Romantics were still 'in', and I read much of the Victorian poets; a strong Blake

---

[1] I do not think this is true any longer. It is perhaps ironical that what was contemptuously known as 'The Novel-reading Tripos' should now have a paper in Part II on the English Novel.

revival was in progress, led by Mansfield Forbes of Clare. I. A. Richards was giving the 'Practical Criticism' lectures with the first protocols; the nonsense that one had written three weeks before he would read out, gravely and quietly. Morning lectures were apt to be strenuous: most of them were given in college halls or in special lecture-rooms within the colleges, so that we dashed on bicycles from place to place. My own work centred on Tillyard's supervisions in his little house in New Square, with Godfrey Webb-Peploe, later to die as a missionary in India, and Alfred Stephenson, afterwards to become a headmaster. I do not think we were overworked, and I remember that I got a third in the Mays; partly, perhaps, because I was fighting for a place in the first boat.

Some of this breadth of interest we owed to 'Q', still lecturing memorably, wisely, and with what I can only call 'nobility'; a generous breadth of knowledge that was in the great tradition of the Scottish universities – A. A. Jack, Macneile Dixon, Grierson, Bickersteth; and, earlier, of Gilbert Murray, Raleigh, Verrall. His public lectures, at twelve on Wednesdays, were always crowded; we queued for half an hour to get in. Then 'Q' would arrive, immaculately and rather loudly dressed, looking like a prosperous bookmaker from the Gold Ring at Ascot; wearing an enormously high Gladstonian collar, and a large flower in his buttonhole. The very mixed audience was always addressed as 'Gentlemen', for he would not admit to the presence of women in an academic exercise. His hands shook over his notes; I believe that these lectures were for him an exciting but intensely severe ordeal. I am told that when his manuscripts came to the press to be set up each sentence was found to be 'pointed' for rhythm, stress and tone.

On Wednesday evenings, in the rooms allotted to the King Edward VII Professor in – rather improbably – the Divinity School, he held informal classes in Aristotle's *Poetics*. These were, very properly, useless as regards reading for the Tripos, but were magnificently stimulating. We sat on the floor round the long low room; 'Q' would come in from Jesus, probably a quarter of an hour late, having, we believed, dined well. The game then was to keep him from talking about Aristotle; any other subject might be turned up by means of a leading question, and then he would talk superbly, wittily, with an immense sweep of reference and quotation. Two or three earnest Indians did not approve of these excursions and were obviously puzzled. On one occasion 'Q' was talking, high and wide, on the theory of the origins of Greek Drama in the Thraco-Phrygian phallic dances. An Indian in a dark corner shot up a hand and said in a loud shrill voice: 'Pleese, Sirr, whatt ees "phallic"?' There was silence; perhaps 'Q' was meditating on the implications of the question from a Hindu. Then he grunted, and looked over his spectacles: 'Huh; look it up in the dictionary. Under P.'

He became to us a legend, though a dwindling one; his absences at Fowey became longer and longer, till, in the late thirties, he might appear only for the last fortnight of term. The charming old Senior Clerk of Jesus, when asked when the professor was expected in residence, shook his head sadly and said: 'Ah, Sir Quiller tarries!' He still examined for the Tripos, and there is a story of an Indian who believed that he had been unjustly treated in that examination, by being given a Second instead of a First; he therefore committed a sacrificial act of 'revenge', lying rigid across the threshold of 'Q's' rooms for several days, so that 'Q' had to step over the body as he went in and out. I remember him with gratitude, and I have hated steadily those who have sneered, and taught others to sneer, at everything he wrote.

Then there was G. G. Coulton, certainly the most eminent mediaevalist in Europe; once of my own college, which had not perceived his stature before he was snapped up by St John's. His story has been told in his own *Four Score Years,* and, naughtily, by his daughter in *Father.* I went to his lectures on *Piers Plowman* and Chaucer; lectures packed with information, a little tedious, occasionally enlivened with flashes of wit delivered in what would now be called a 'dead-pan' manner. He was a great and merciless controversialist against the Roman Catholics and Jesuits; challenging them (and Belloc and Chesterton in particular) to debates in the Town Hall with stenographers present, and publishing the results in pamphlets. Anything more unlike Hilaire Belloc's

> Remote and ineffectual don
> Who dared attack my Chesterton . . .

it would be difficult to imagine. His learning he hid under great courtesy and charm of manner. As I went down the towpath with the boats I would often see his tall, spare figure, aquiline and ascetic face, walking by the river; head bowed, talking earnestly with his great friend and disciple, Stanley Bennett, on whom the mantle of mediaeval scholarship descended after 'G. G.' retired, but who was also a distinguished Shakespearean scholar. Bennett had lost a leg in the First War and while in hospital at Cambridge had met his wife Joan, who soon became a Fellow of Girton and an eminent writer on the seventeenth century. I saw much of him on all sorts of occasions; when as a newly-elected Fellow I persuaded my college to hold an entrance scholarship examination in English, I was lucky enough to get him to examine with me, and to *viva* the candidates. It was mainly because of him that we had such a large proportion of firsts in the thirties, and when I went to the war I handed over the St Catharine's men to him and to his wife. One of my ablest pupils, Colin Eccleshare, married one of his daughters.

At King's there was F. L. Lucas, perhaps the wittiest, most epigrammatic of our lecturers. He had been through the First World War, and wrote of it memorably and briefly; almost alone among us he foresaw the Second World War,[1] and immediately prepared for his move into important secret work. Of all the Cambridge figures he had the widest range; his classics were always alive, seen constantly in allusions, illustrations, parallels. He knew French and Italian well; he had been to Iceland to see for himself the background of the Sagas. All that he said or wrote was pointed, clear, intolerant of pretence or folly; and the sheer range of his intelligence left one breathless. He reviewed much for the old *Statesman and Nation,* and, alone among the dons of the time, he was acutely conscious of the folly and stupidity of the contemporary political scene. He was shy and difficult to approach; but once approached, infinitely generous and gracious with his learning and criticism.

The most striking eccentric of the time, perhaps our only genuine one, was Mansfield Forbes of Clare. He was a bachelor, living in large and lovely rooms that looked out over the River, where he entertained with erratic munificence. On Sunday mornings there were breakfast parties of a dozen people; they started at nine a.m. and were apt to go on indefinitely. It was said – I was not there on that occasion – that he had scoured the country

---

[1] His *Journal under the Terror* is worth reviving.

to collect seven red-haired curates as a sort of centrepiece to one of his breakfasts, and on another occasion a large number of guests all of whose names ended in —bottom or —botham, and left them to mutual introductions. He lectured, rather sporadically, for his health and energies were uncertain, on Blake, and I think the Pre-Raphaelites. A slight elfin figure, with a hint of a lisp; his spectacles always mended with sealing-wax or plaster and padded on the side-pieces with pipe-cleaners. His mind was erratic, brilliant, metaphysical in its habit of producing the most astounding and improbable illustrations to literature or architecture. Manny had a theory that Blake's poems were written to be sung, and he would chant them in his lectures. But his originality extended far beyond literature. He was an expert on Scottish Baronial Architecture, and had an immense collection of slides: I remember that one night he came to lecture on that subject to the literary society of my college. We started at 8.30. At 11.50 he was still in full flight, and announced his intention of coming back to finish next day.

He later bought an ugly Victorian house, 'Finella', on the Backs opposite Clare; and with the most brilliant of the 'advanced' young architects of the time[1] proceeded to modernize and decorate it with the newest materials and fantastic architectural jests. One of these was reputedly a perspective drawing of a soldier, full length, on the interior of the maids' bath. He succeeded in obtaining the loan of Epstein's *Genesis* which he exhibited in the drawing-room; one condition was that it must never be left, day or night, and some of my young men had to sleep in the room with it.

Forbes' mind was fertile, always breaking out in some new direction; he was a 'Man of the Trees', a begetter of wildish theories about the Tuatha-da-Danaan and Shakespeare, an admirer of Wyndham Lewis, to whom he introduced me; restless, eager, erratic. I suspect his college found him, at times, a trial. Sometimes he would refuse to see his pupils for supervision for a whole term, and then, in the last few days, take them each for eight consecutive hours. He was a keen supporter of the Festival Theatre, then making its name under Terence Gray.

His epigrams, delivered with the slight and charming lisp that his friends will recall, were characteristic: 'One visualiseth Keats

---

[1] Raymond McGrath.

across a sea of chestnuth-coloured women with corkscrew neckth and working Adam's appleth, who MOB-ilize their neckth, and DE-mobilize their sexth, at one gulp.' All his behaviour was original; he would arrive late for our lunch parties and borrow the fare for the taxi. He was certain that only by living in a double cube[1] had his spirit a suitable space to expand.

In his library he had a number of books, some of considerable value, of the kind classified by the University Library as *Arcana*. There was, I think, some contemporary row in progress over pornography, which was perhaps related to a journalist's attack, ending with: 'Damn Cambridge! Damn the Dons! Damn the Dirt!' This was taken up in the famous Festival *Review*, mainly the work of Clinton-Baddeley:

> What's the matter with Cambridge?
> Why does Douglas damn?
> For we must say we think it's a little bit curt
> To damn all the dons and to damn all the dirt. . . .

Manny in a sudden access of fear or righteousness decided to throw all these books over Clare Bridge into the Cam. Next day he was smitten with remorse, and suborned one of his favourite pupils in another college, who was an unusually good swimmer, to come in the small hours of the morning and dive for them: I do not know how many were recovered. It was said, too, that he arrived to stay with his cousin in his Scottish baronial castle with all his belongings, including his dress-shirts, stowed in a single golf-bag.

At Clare, too, was A. D. Nock, just brought from Trinity: he was reputed to have three thousand classical books in his rooms, all of which he had read, and it was said that by the end of his first year no don in Trinity could teach him anything. Nock alone of all those I knew seemed to have been born a don, and soon became Professor of the History of Religions at Harvard. One of Manny Forbes' projects was to erect a sort of Cherry Kearton 'hide' in a corner of the Clare Combination Room, to take a 'nature film' of Nock handing round the port. He died at Harvard in 1963.

---

[1] That is, composed of two rooms in one, each being a cube of equal height, length and breadth. *Vide* the famous room at Wilton House, near Salisbury. See p. 134 *infra*.

But his great friend was I. A. Richards, and Forbes' death in 1934 was the loss of an important stimulus to Richards's thought. I went first to his lectures in 1920; I must have been, too, among those that appeared, who set down their naïve views for *Practical Criticism*. Like Forbes, he was a slight, eager figure, lecturing to crowded audiences who found it difficult to follow his complicated symbols and diagrams on the blackboard; a first-rate mountaineer; living a hermit-like existence in his rooms on King's Parade, where, so rumour said, he sat on the floor in a space cleared among the piles of books, feeding erratically on biscuits. I did not get to know him well at that time; nor, indeed, till after the Second World War, when he and his wife Dorothea used to visit us yearly on the way from Harvard to the Alps. Of his lectures I remember his exquisite reading voice, in especially from *The Brook Kerith*; his supreme ability to communicate pleasure and excitement; the complete absence of dogmatism in his explorations. Perhaps he had too many interests; psychology, basic English, Chinese, aesthetics, methods of visual training. He did not reveal himself as a poet and dramatist till well after his sixtieth year. In the early twenties it had seemed that, partly as a result of the vastly increased knowledge of the brain through war surgery, a theory of value related to physio-psychology might become valid. That hope was to die, but was set out with clarity and startling emphasis in his small book *Science and Poetry*. Magdalene lost him to Harvard, who were wise enough to give him a loose rein, but not until he had taught William Empson and Sweeney, among many others. I remember Richards saying to me with a rueful smile that Empson had 'driven a coach and horses' through his own *Mencius on the Mind*. Our friendship became steadily closer.

At Pembroke there was Aubrey Attwater; also an ex-classic, our best Shakespeare scholar; badly wounded while with the Royal Welsh Fusiliers, and 'Brains' of Robert Graves' *Goodbye to All That*. One of his best stories concerned the very Welsh Chaplain at the depot exhorting a draft about to leave for France: 'And I pray that God Almighty will go with you in all your wayss; and I myself will go with you to the sta-shon.' He hobbled on a stick, and lectured sitting down in the noble Old Library of Pembroke. Always in pain – he died of his war-wound in the middle thirties – he could not sleep at night, and read or entertained undergraduates in his rooms far into the dawn; for his men knew how ill he was and took it in turns to visit him each night. About him there were many legends; it was said that he and half a dozen officers of his mess had gone out with sticks and cleared the City of Limerick of some thousands of rioters. At that time he had met some of my family, and since most of my friends at Aldenham were at Pembroke, I got to know him well. His gifts of wit and gaiety, and his ability as a raconteur and mimic, were only paralleled by those of S. C. Roberts[1] and of Edward Wynne.[2] The Pembroke High Table was probably the liveliest and most charming in the university.

S. C. Roberts, then Secretary of the University Press, used to lecture in the evenings on Johnson; he later became acknowledged as the greatest authority on a strangely-assorted pair, Johnson and Sherlock Holmes. His range was wide; though he lectured seldom; everything he wrote had the precision, grace and wit of his friend Max Beerbohm, on whom I heard him give a lecture, shortly after Max's death, at the Royal Society of Literature. Indeed 'S. C.' had written a sequel to *Zuleika Dobson*, on the basis of her next manifestation in Cambridge.

The most important of my friendships was that with E. M. W. Tillyard, who had been my Director of Studies and Supervisor for my first two years. He had been a Fellow of Jesus before the First World War, a First-Class Classic and a leading authority on Greek Vases. He had ended the war in Salonika as Liaison Officer between the Greek and British Armies; there he had met his future wife, Miss Mudie-Cooke, who was driving an ambulance. When I first met him he was living in a tiny house in New Square, with a young family; later he moved to an old and charming house at Sawston. His college did not immediately re-elect him to a Fellowship, though he was destined afterwards to become Senior Tutor and then Master. He was a brilliant teacher, co-operating with his pupils rather than attempting to impose his personality upon them; infinitely wise and mature, with a love of all great literature which he invariably managed to communicate. To all his students he gave unfailing courtesy and encouragement, tempered with a certain humility, even deference. He was one of a group of us who met in each other's rooms in the early thirties to read poetry together. Among them

[1] Master 1948-57.
[2] Afterwards Bishop of Ely.

were Paul Sinker, Ivor Richards, and Leonard Potts. As his interests developed, he became one of the best-known Milton scholars of the day, and did much Shakespearean work as well. Of all the dons of the time he and Lucas had perhaps the most Catholic range of interests. I saw much of him during his last illness in 1961-2.[1]

iii

Among the great Cambridge figures was Steve Fairbairn, greatest of all rowing coaches, a massive, quiet personality whom one saw every afternoon on the towpath; the centre of fierce, almost religiously fierce controversy, through which he took his quiet way unperturbed, bringing his Jesus boats to the head of the river year after year. It was largely his influence that abolished the torture of the fixed seats on which I first rowed, for orthodoxy thought them essential to the development of the ability to swing. Fairbairn's ideas were more liberal, and centred on the moving of the boat by the natural thrust of the thighs, the draw of the muscles in back and shoulder. At least his crews enjoyed their rowing; and one of the sights of the Cam was a one-legged ex-serviceman, G. C. Adami of Jesus, who drove his crews relentlessly and with success.

I had been concerned with boats from early childhood, and, without any great skill in school games except cricket, fives, boxing and shooting, it seemed natural that I should row. My father had rowed at Radley, and two uncles, both afterwards Fellows, for Trinity Hall. In my second term, when I had strained some muscles, I played fives with my school partner, Philip Whalley of Caius, for what I suppose was the equivalent of the university side (there were no blues then); and I also played a little light-hearted cricket in the Long Vacation. But the river seemed to me then infinitely worth while. In the twenties the pre-war tradition, that the good name of a college largely rested on the performance of its boat club, still persisted in some measure; the rhythm of our year was fixed by the various races, eights, fours, pairs and sculls, culminating in the exciting vast crowds of the Mays.

[1] There is an admirable account of his life by another of his friends, a former pupil, Basil Willey: *Proceedings of the British Academy*, Vol. **XLIX**.

But of rowing itself, the very essence, the 'inscape' of it that has never been caught in poetry or prose, is this quality of rhythm: at its subtlest in the light sculling boats, steered by imperceptible pressure from the drive on the stretcher, and communicating through the fragile skin of the boat the living intimacy of water, solid under the blades, thrust away by the drawing muscles of shoulder and arm, then seeming to fling the body forward on the long smooth run of the slide as one gathers to strike again and again. I have sometimes thought that this rhythm, perhaps akin to that of the heart-beat, is a basic one; like those of the Atlantic groundswell on a calm day, flowing and gathering and ebbing in the inlets and lagoons. That rhythm of the sculler, because one was solitary, because one's power was all one's own, gave a sensation comparable in quality to that of sailing a dinghy single-handed in rough weather; though in this the danger, and the wholesome sense of 'scale' in the conflict, the double power of wind and sea produces an exaltation all its own.

Noël Annan in his *Leslie Stephen* has a long passage on rowing, which, he thinks, 'remains such a popular pastime at the universities because it gives the otherwise inept what they want but cannot get from games. The happiest hours of rowing are when it is over; the sensation of having overcome the weariness and desperation which afflict an oarsman in rowing a course produces after the event an extraordinary pleasure.' This is, I believe, a little less true of rowing than of other branches of athletics; the joys of rhythm, timing, and delicacy of coordinated movement are common to many other games. In the boat in which I rowed for the best part of three years, there were two outstanding rugger players, and one who, in off moments, ran the mile and three miles for the college. But the greatest joy of rowing, which Annan does not stress (for his real object here is to depict Leslie Stephen as a great coach) is the gradual apprehension of the meaning of rhythm, and the intermittent experiencing of it in its delighted perfection; intermittent only, because the power, as it were something external, which takes hold of a crew and welds them into a unity that seems so that they move mysteriously and without effort, the crew at one with boat and river, is not often achieved. This fact or experience of rhythm seems to me of supreme importance; it comes almost by accident, a mystical experience of momentary unity with one's body and environment. I have known it once when riding, on a prize-winning heavy-weight hunter on Exmoor; and at intervals playing fives, when hand and eye become co-ordinated to produce shots that were seemingly impossible. I gather from my mountaineering friends that it is the delicacy of harmonious muscular rhythm, harnessed to overcome immense difficulties of the rock, that produces their calm satisfaction. Cannot all supreme pleasure, aesthetic as well as physical, be related to this rhythm?

iv

At the end of an undergraduate's time at Cambridge, perhaps during the greater part of the last year, there is always a reckoning to be made of many kinds. That concerning one's career is not always the heaviest. But in 1922 and 1923 my friends were often going down to whatever jobs they could get. The ex-servicemen who had lived lavishly and counted on the promises of the politicians found themselves disillusioned. Here, I think, was the germ of the bitter mood that I found on my return three years later. Commercial travellers in soap, small farms that were doomed to failure from lack of capital, little newsagents' and tobacconists' shops in the mean streets – any kind of job might have to be accepted, since many of these men were married. Some of my friends, like Colin Hunter of Pembroke, who was afterwards best man at my wedding, and Rupert Clift the poet, went into schoolmastering. The luckier ones had careers in the professions or in business mapped out for them; and many came from established families and paid their own fees without scholarship or subsidy.

My own future was particularly confused. Money was shorter than ever, and though I had avoided debt and the long tempting credit of those days, I had not been able to get abroad to consolidate my rather academic brand of languages. I went up for a preliminary interview for what was then the Diplomatic Service, in which my cousin, Tom Spring Rice, was then serving, and was put on a short-list of fifteen or twenty out of some eighty candidates. But then we were told that the Commissioners advised us to go away and coach at Scoone's for a year, for an examination which might offer four or five vacancies; I suspect because many ex-servicemen with diplomatic or para-military experience had (very properly) been chosen. Most of those on the short-list already held college fellowships; there was no chance of one of these in an impecunious college which was then running on five Fellows only. In any event they had already in residence an ex-serviceman, a double first in English and a brilliant musician, who seemed certain to be retained. The prospect of a career at Cambridge never crossed my mind.

So I came up in Michaelmas 1923 for one extra term, partly to play for time, since the prospect of the Diplomatic Service was negligible, partly to work for a university scholarship and a prize essay. The first had meant reading and re-reading the whole of Shakespeare, and much of the related scholarly writing on him. The previous year I had been *proxime accessit,* and Aubrey Attwater and Tillyard had encouraged me to try again. This year George Rylands, fresh from his triumphs in *The Duchess of Malfi,* and subsequently creator of the Marlowe Society tradition in Shakespearean production, was *proxime* to me. I made a little money by coaching, and right at the end of term spent a peculiarly happy fortnight as a substitute modern language master at The Leys School. There I played a great deal of Eton Fives with the original of 'Mr Chips', Balgarnie, who was so greatly loved by all Leysians. I was semi-engaged to Enid Roberts, whom I had first seen in a lecture. She was reading languages at Newnham. But I was clumsy, shy and awkward; for many years I had scarcely spoken to a girl, for the good reason that Co. Clare was denuded, by threats and burning, of all young society.

At the time the great oil companies were starting to recruit university graduates, with a strange but wholly justifiable preference for those who had read classics. I still think of Matthew Arnold's: 'I know not how it is, but their commerce with the ancients appears to me to produce, in those who constantly practice it, a steadying and composing effect upon their judgement, not of literary works only, but of men and events in general.' Among the amateur soldiers in the Second World War the most brilliant minds seemed often to be classics or lawyers; the former included J. L. Austin the philosopher, Enoch Powell and Bill Williams who also became brigadiers; among the latter my one-time pupil R. T. H. Redpath.[1] Two of my friends were

---

[1] Afterwards Fellow and Tutor of Trinity.

just starting in what were to be financially successful jobs with Shell in China. I was offered a similar job, but in a different country. The information about it was scanty, and, as events proved, inaccurate. I was told that my life would be, in the main, remote from civilization and in the open air.

At the back of my mind were various confused issues, romantic and stupid. I would break into commerce, away from the three-hundred-year-old family tradition of the three professions, make money and buy Paradise from my brother. I might realize during leaves my ambition of being called to the Bar; and perhaps become involved in the international-legal side of the oil business. Once, towards the end of the eighteenth century, Paradise had passed out of the family, who had held it since 1673; it had been bought back after a few years, rebuilt, replanted. This might be done again.

A series of interviews confirmed the appointment. I was to sail early in January. I had a last visit to Clare for ten days' shooting, bringing with me Ivan Barling who had rowed with me as bow of the first boat.

v

That last visit was dominated by a mood of nostalgia blended with a certain self-dramatization. 'The Troubles' were over and the Free State Government was beginning to feel its feet. There were still odd shootings of a semi-private nature. But life between the Rebellion and the end of the Civil War had taken its toll of my Mother's health and mind; she was then over seventy, yet was to live for twelve years more. Her courage and humour had kept the house unburnt, and herself unharmed in spite of the many raids; but she refused to leave for the security of Dublin and the terrifying lonely comfort of an old ladies' home. At night I used to find her, wandering in her night-clothes, candle in hand, through the long corridors, looking for the fires that treachery might have begun in some remote corner. The gate-lodge, indeed, had been set on fire, though ineffectively, and her mind could not rid itself of the image of all the burnings round.

I shot a good deal, rode about a little on a stout pony to say goodbye to relatives some distance off. The woods and the uncut laurel coverts dripped dismally, and the house and its surroundings were beginning to decay.

VII

INDIAN INTERLUDE

For three days out from Rangoon the tide ran muddy from the great river, and baths on the s.s. *Lancashire* were strictly rationed. I saw the East – I had read Conrad's *Youth* – for the first time as we laboured up the channel between the low banks, with their groups of huts and bright green foliage washed in a strong light. We berthed in the middle of Rangoon, and I was taken with my kit to one of the company's 'chummeries' where the bachelor assistants lived. After a brief interview in the office it was clear that there was no place for me in the organization there – there had been some confusion of staff-work – and thus one's dream of being up-country in Burma was shattered. I was to be sent as soon as possible to the Calcutta office; meanwhile I was introduced to the staff, and sent to look over the refinery. I can recall little of that visit except the extreme brightness of the Burmese dress, the neat vivid women, the leisure of their lives; and at night, sitting on the balcony of the chummery, the hordes of flying foxes flighting home to roost, so that I remembered the pigeons in the Shore Wood. On the third day I was packed off on a BI boat for the four-day trip to Calcutta; monotonous except for the passage of the Hooghli, and the incredibly skilled navigation of the Bengal pilots. I had read enough of the intricacies of the River to pick up some of the landmarks; the treacherous shoals and quicksands; and on either side the mysterious Sunderbunds, with the little mud villages all under the implacable light. Some of the landmarks were in Kipling:

> Last night, when through the mooring chains,
> The wide-eyed corpse rolled free

> To blunder down by Garden Reach
> And rot at Kedgeree,
> The tale the Hooghli told the shoal
> The lean shoal told to me.

Here they were, and the oil-tank installation at Budge-Budge which I was to get to know well.

The boat docked; a junior member of the company was waiting to meet me and took me in his car to the office, an enormous flat in a building looking out on Hong Kong Square. There I was given a desk, facing one Beresford who was curtly told to 'put me in the picture' (though I doubt if that phrase had come into its own yet). At lunch we adjourned to the office canteen and ate an enormous meal of curry and apple dumpling, wholly unsuited to the climate, and, at best, calling for the siesta that would have been normal further East, say in Singapore. But here strict English office hours were kept, and the afternoon was a long struggle with sleepiness. Finally I was driven back some four miles to the Chummery in Ballygunge, a big square house with cement floors, a tennis court and a host of servants. One had been allotted to me; presumably because he spoke English of a sort, and I began to experience the first indignity (but an essential one) of the East; that of being perpetually watched by servants, with every detail of one's life wrenched from any possible privacy. I changed and started to make the room habitable. I had brought out from England a case of books, not foreseeing how they would suffer in the rainy season; a guncase and the usual kit, much of it useless, that I had bought in London. Then I took stock of my 'chums'.

They were all a good deal older than I. There was Beresford, whom I was to relieve; Matthewson, a silent highly-paid accountant with a slight stammer; Banks, short, stocky and vigorous, who kept a horse and rode in the Maidân every morning before breakfast; Valentine who acted as Mess President, and four or five more. Of these I took instantly to a small reserved Scotsman called Fleming of Glasgow University. Again not foreseeing that a quarter of a century later I was to admit his son to my college and teach him.

We sat on the verandah drinking whiskey: it was explained to me that each member of the chummery kept his own bottle, with one over for the common hospitality. The more suspicious marked their bottle-levels in pencil each night. Various other matters were made clear; there was a surprisingly high monthly messing charge, which included the wages of the native staff. I was expected to provide myself with some kind of mechanical transport, a car or a motor-bicycle; and as the newest-joined member I was detailed to decode the sheaf of cables that arrived each Sunday morning. This became the most loathsome of tasks, since none of these could not have waited till Monday. I was expected to learn Urdu as quickly as possible, and the bonus that the company gave for passing the intermediate examination would help to pay for a motor-bike; and much other information. Gradually it became clear that the majority of my fellows had grievances, which they aired as the whiskey warmed. In the early years of the war the staff of the company had been divided over the matter of volunteering for service, since they were not liable to conscription; about a third had gone to the war, two-thirds had remained where they were, even at the price of no home leave. So in four years these latter had been promoted with great rapidity, and were now holding important posts; the others had had their billets kept open for them, but returned to find themselves infinitely poorer, and well behind in the race; which was, proverbially, to make 'the last ten lakhs' (a lakh is 10,000 rupees) and retire at the age of fifty. Two of them who did just this found themselves badly caught by inflation after 1946; what had in 1925 looked to be a substantial provident fund was producing a small income by 1950.

Dinner in Calcutta is served at a very late hour, nine or after. But that first night we had all been bidden to dine at a neighbouring chummery – I forget the company – a few hundred yards away. The party went there, dined and drank; after a couple of hours the Mess President decided that we should all adjourn to 'The Road' – Khariya Road, the enormous brothel quarter of Calcutta, of the same status as Grant Road in Bombay. The President made a ribald issue of contraceptives; we packed into various cars, and drove to 'The Road'.

It was a curious sight, and suggested immediately one reason why the British were losing India. From behind lightly-curtained doorways came the incessant blaring of automatic pianos and gramophones; red-plush couches, and heavily-painted women, the off-scourings of the brothels of Paris, Vienna, Marseilles; fat madames presiding and dispensing bad Japanese whiskey. From time to time a Buick taxi drew up; the magnificent bearded Sikh taxi-drivers standing at attention beside them, while the Heaven-born staggered in or out like drunken wasps out of beer-and-treacle. Two of us, David Fyfe and I, excused ourselves on the grounds that we were engaged, an excuse accepted tolerantly though not thought to be cogent, for several of the party were in that position, and we went for a walk together. We had known each other vaguely at Cambridge; he had recently arrived, like me. He was the son of an eminent architect, and was passionately interested in art. I remember that we walked round Calcutta till the dawn broke, talking of many things.

The pattern of living soon became established. Office hours were from nine to five-thirty; for the first few months I got a lift in one of the cars belonging to a more senior assistant. Once there, I sat at a desk in the vast open office. Mail appeared intermittently, carried by chokras, the native office-boys, and calls for them were continuous. It was soon clear that out of the long day – and lunch was invariably taken in the office – there was no more than an hour and a half's moderately serious work. The real business was carried out in cubicles where the senior assistants and the Burra Sahib, the general manager, lived. Day-to-day business and the whole of the sales side was run by our managing agents; high-level policy was decided at London, Glasgow, Amsterdam or Rangoon. Calcutta appeared to be a mere clearing-house, and in fact the whole set-up was reorganized some years after I had left. So each day resolved itself into a few trivial matters – asking for quotations from business houses for various domestic and engineer stores required by the agencies or by the oilfields up-country; comparing them and placing orders; carrying out interminable investigations as to the proportion of expensive tin to cheap lead that was to be used for soldering petrol-cans; experiments as to the kind and colour of paint which would best protect the tank-farms at the ports against evaporation; downgrading stocks of kerosene that had gone yellow; investigating complaints of leaking tins. I can only remember one serious piece of work: the planning, in accordance with the rules of the Chief Inspector of Explosives, of a bulk petrol depot at Bangalore. Even that was an affair of elementary mathematics; I cannot even remember that it was built. For the rest there were endless copies of in-and-out correspondence to be read and initialled daily; large numbers of technical journals,

Indian Interlude 105

mostly American in origin, on oil prospecting, drilling, refining. Bit by bit I acquired some knowledge of the vast oil empires of the East; the Indian market in kerosene (far more important than petrol) and the religious significance of the brands on the tins in which it was sold. 'Elephant' was then the popular one, but the empty tins were put to endless uses, including the walling of the huts in Indian slum quarters. I learnt of the tightness of the agreements of the world 'ring' that controlled prices, and shared world markets at high political levels. I learnt, too, that the price of petrol at the refinery at Rangoon, where it might have been sold for a few annas, was in fact governed by the price at which competing petrol could be shipped from the Gulf of Mexico, and this was somewhat higher than in England. Also the complex business of tanker charters, loadings, steaming-out of tanks for different types of oil.

'Big business' seemed on the surface peculiarly unattractive and not very efficient. The general manager was chronically overworked and overanxious, and indeed died young; the number two spent much of his time playing golf, for he was the Indian champion. Promotion went either by seniority, or by having the right connections at home, or very occasionally by outstanding merit. In this class was my friend Fleming, who in the Second World War, seventeen years later, made a name for himself in Assam when confronting the Japanese invasion. Certain lessons came home to me; the fatal ease with which a headquarters can become clogged with useless paperwork (I saw this later at Versailles with SHAEF); the importance of giving responsible people adequate work and trusting them to get on with it; and the need to ensure that a staff is permanently, but not too heavily, overworked. In terms of percentages this seems to be about 120, taking 100 as the 'comfortable' day's work. At 140 I think that people begin to crack.

In youth one adjusts fairly rapidly and, for a time at least, in a satisfactory manner. It was obvious that I must learn Urdu, not only because my English-speaking Christian bearer was stupid, dirty and dishonest, but because I must buy some form of transport. By sheer luck I chanced on an outstandingly good *munshi,* a teacher of native language, one Abdul Habib Khan; a handsome black-moustached Mohammedan with flashing teeth, who had been brought up in Turkey by an Englishwoman (I never got to the bottom of that story) and was reputed to speak fourteen languages. He came at seven each morning, for an hour: I learnt the hard way, with a handwritten vocabulary and declensions of nouns. Then it turned out that he was an enthusiastic and knowledgeable shikari, so that when I got free of the loathed Sunday coding duty, I often went out with him, either into the suburbs of Calcutta to shoot snipe, among a strange network of little muddy streams, swarming with fish, where lived an aboriginal people who caught them in traps of bamboo wickerwork; or, taking a night-train to one of the buried cities north of Chandernagore, returning in time for office on Monday morning. Abdul Khan was the best shot with a rifle that I have ever seen; though with a shotgun no more than moderate. Always on these expeditions he took with him a small boy, armed with a large and very sharp knife to cut the throat of any flapping bird before it died, thereby making it *halâl*, ritually clean for food. I suspect that this was more a gesture than a reality.

Two incidents of these expeditions stand out. Once we shot a large green and golden water-snake, of a beauty that Coleridge would have envied, at a ford across a small river. The villagers came down rejoicing and garlanded us, for the snake had killed several people. And once I was called away from our path to see something important in the jungle; my Urdu was not quite good enough to follow the first explanations. Presently we came to a clearing, and a grove of trees, as of Ashtaroth. In the middle of a large tree, that had been trained to grow round it, was a twelve-pounder brass gun; I judged it to be a company's piece of about 1760. The breech had a garland of flowers on it, and a Hindu caste mark; just inside the muzzle, a little horse in clay. The two nations were worshipping it as a double fertility symbol. Nearly twenty years later I thought of that episode when I was helping to site a pair of German 105 field-guns, captured by the Navy with a thousand rounds of ammunition at Narvik, in the heather above Weymouth:

> I think it good that men should worship the gun
> As I saw them worship it once in the jungle near
>   Chandernagore.
> The twelve-pounder buried in the living tree, for seed
>   and fruit:
> The clay horse at the muzzle, the garland round the
>   breech.

The gun makes each St Peter, holding the keys,
Bright and beautiful pressed home in the magazine,
Power and dominion over the Kings; and at the temple
Swifter than asp at breast when the bolt goes home,
Accident shackled at last.

It was clear that I had little satisfaction to get from life in the office or in the Chummery. We played some tennis in the evenings when the light allowed, and on Saturdays and Sundays, but it was dull enough, since inevitably we had the same players. For a time I tried squash, playing often with the native markers, who could give me or any other European, seven points a game and a beating, moving with incredible and lovely ease; but squash in the sunbaked open courts was too much. Then I discovered the Calcutta Rowing Club, just about the time that the Chummery was moved to Alipore, and therefore close to the canal. There were fours, a few sculling boats and thirty or forty rowing members. The course was a short one, four or five minutes at most, for the exertion of anything longer would have been too great. Three Cambridge College boat captains, and one from Oxford, made up our first crew; we went to Rangoon for a week-end to row against Burma, and were beaten. I remember the exhilaration of the outings in the very early mornings with the Shwê Dagon Pagoda as a glittering back-drop to the lake. I sculled a good deal, enjoying the solitude and the lonely power of the boat; I won the India Sculls. Once during practice I drove heavily on top of a charred body pushed out half-burnt from one of the Ghats along the canal, and upset on top of it. In one sense it was rowing at its most luxurious; there was a squad of boatmen to lift the craft in and out of the water, and a butler waiting with a tray of drinks at the raft. I remember that one of a scratch crew that I was stroking trained largely on whiskey, and collapsed after a couple of minutes of the race.

Calcutta is not a healthy spot even with plenty of exercise and not too much drink. I acquired on hire-purchase a small and not very satisfactory motor-cycle to take me to the office. One day I was knocked off it by an erratic water-buffalo, and grazed an elbow and both ankles. In that climate it is wise to report quickly to a doctor, which I did. He dressed the abrasions and I went on to the office. Late that night, the right arm went up above my head, and stayed there. I knew what that meant and took a taxi to the nearest European hospital. They operated immediately and removed a fragment of splintered bone from the elbow; for some days I knew the extremities of pain. Perhaps a horror of hospitals goes back to that time, from being tended by a Eurasian nurse who chewed garlic. By sheer good luck I was invited to convalesce in the Archbishop's Palace; Foss Westcott, who was revered everywhere, had known my father, and was kindness itself. Perhaps not many people have played sardines in a palace, or sat down to dinner as the only layman among fourteen bishops who had gathered for some conference.

By this time I was growing very tired of the Chummery and all its ways. My rowing and shooting were both disapproved of by authority; I grew weary of the invariable drunken week-ends and the subsequent visit to 'The Road'; some of my colleagues had venereal disease. I do not say this priggishly, for I was then engaged and found it all not immoral but very tedious. In this I do not suppose that we were better or worse than other chummeries. The young assistant coming out to a commercial life was not then permitted by his company to marry in less than four years, and discouraged from doing so in less than seven unless he had private means. Unlike the subaltern, he had long office hours and none of the subaltern's encouragements to exercise and sport. It was a standing jest that if one went to consult the company doctor he assumed that you had one malady and one only; though in such an event one was supposed to bear the cost of treatment. To do them justice, the companies realized the situation and did their best to keep some surveillance of their young men. My company, after some months, magnanimously produced a billiard-table as a counter-irritant to the attractions of 'The Road'. I do not think there was any intentional humour in their action.

It was about this time that I sought permission to leave the Chummery and share a flat with a friend whose father had been a friend of my fiancée's people in London. He was Torick Ameer Ali, then a rising barrister, afterwards to become a Judge of the High Court before his fortieth year. His father was Syed Amir Ali, himself a former Chief Justice of Calcutta, a Privy Councillor, and the author of a classic book, *The Spirit of Islam*. Torick, afterwards knighted, had been at Marlborough and the House; his mother was an Englishwoman. In a rather stirring interview, the head of the company refused to let me live out of the Chummery, and warned me that I was to have nothing to do with 'bloody niggers'. It so happened that about the same time a managing director came out from England, and interviewed each of the assistants. He asked me if I were happy in my work. I replied that I was not, and we agreed amicably that I should resign and return to England in three or four months' time as soon as a replacement could be found.

There were several reasons for this. Apart from continued and compulsory life in the Chummery, it was doubtful whether I should be allowed to marry even after a further two and a half years, at the beginning of my second contract. I was suffering intermittently from malaria and dengue fever, and had lost a couple of stone in weight. Whatever the fortune that I might make in India in the next twenty years, there seemed no prospect whatever of my being worked up to capacity; if I had to have an office job, better one in London where there was some prospect of personal freedom.

Finally there was now a slight encouragement to return to Cambridge. In the Suez Canal on the voyage out, I had received two signals from my friends telling me that I had won the last two university scholarships and prizes for which I had entered. These were followed up by a letter from the Senior Tutor of my college saying that it was a pity I had not stayed on. (I learnt afterwards that the man who had seemed certain of a Fellowship in my subject had gone down under a cloud.) Spens of Corpus, afterwards Sir Will and my son's godfather, wrote hinting that it might be possible to pick up a living . . . if one were on the spot. So in April 1925 I returned to Cambridge, some hundreds of pounds in debt for medical expenses, subject to periodic malaria and without a job. On the credit side I had learnt about big business, spoke fluent Urdu and had seen something of the tougher sides of life.

VIII

RETURN TO CAMBRIDGE

i

I came back from India in debt, engaged to be married, and with no immediate prospect of employment. My college was only able to give me a very few pupils, and in any event there was little teaching to be done in the Easter Term just before the Tripos. I moved into lodgings. That term I made a few pounds from teaching, and spent many times as much. I was lucky enough to get some examining in elementary French, but that brought in very little. In August I went over to Paradise, where my brother and his family were staying, on leave from Egypt where he had become Chief of the Alexandrian Police; later my fiancée joined me there for a few weeks. My health was improving, but the future seemed precarious.

Quite unknowingly, I had arrived at a crisis in the affairs of the university. Under the old arrangements lecturing in the Arts Faculties was done mainly in colleges on a sort of freelance system. It was understood that men from any other college could attend; members of Newnham and Girton, not being yet full members of the university, had to seek permission through their tutors. Attendance at the first lecture was free, at the second, slips of paper were circulated on which the audience signed their names and colleges. At the end of the term the lecturer sent in a bill for 15/- a head for those who had signed on.

It was not a satisfactory system. A lecturer who offered a popular course for the first or second year might have a substantial audience, and make a reasonable living of £200–300 a year. His colleagues, lecturing on a subject that was possibly far more important, but which seemed to the undergraduates to be

Return to Cambridge

peripheral, might have a dozen or less in attendance. Yet there was probably some stimulus to improve and maintain lecturing techniques; people just would not come to a bad lecturer. On the other hand there was no real co-ordination of teaching. In my case I went to the Professor and said in effect: ' "Q", I want to lecture next term.' He replied 'Certainly, my boy, what do you want to lecture about?', and gave me a glass of sherry. So one put up one's plate, as it were, and hoped for the best. I had never lectured before; the remains of a stammer reared its head when I was tired, and I awaited the October term with very mixed feelings.

The term began; I was clearly on probation both in the eyes of my college and of the university. I was rapidly overwhelmed with pupils for supervision, lecturing twice a week, spending most of each afternoon on the River coaching crews, and trying to bring my scholarship up to date. I was fortunate in many things, chiefly in my pupils. Among the first were A. P. Rossiter, to die in 1956 much like T. E. Lawrence on a fast motor-cycle, and an ex-natural scientist, with one of the keenest and most original minds I have known. There is an account of that year and of the 1926 General Strike, in a slightly scandalous novel called *Poor Scholars* written while he was an undergraduate. There was C. R. Allison, afterwards a distinguished headmaster; J. B. Chutter, who achieved fame in South Africa: first as Chaplain to the Fourth South African Division (he was captured at Tobruk), and wrote *Captivity Captive;* his career afterwards included a Chaplaincy at Clifton, a parish at Bristol, and much pastoral work in industry in Bristol. In 1971 I stayed with him when he was Rector of the Drakensburg, in Natal. I became Director of Studies, at various times till 1939, for a number of other colleges including Trinity, Trinity Hall, Clare, Magdalene, Sidney Sussex, and Peterhouse.

Slowly there gathered round my rooms in an attic in St Catharine's an exceptionally interesting group of men. I believed, and said so, that one fault of the lecture system was that one's audience, dashing unhappily about Cambridge on bicycles to get to the scattered lecture-rooms, never had a chance to contest or argue with or develop what had been said to them. I therefore announced that I would be 'at home' with coffee and tobacco every Monday evening (with some memory of Sainte-Beuve) to anyone who cared to come along. So it happened that each

The Central Arch, St Catharine's College

Return to Cambridge 113

evening there were a dozen or twenty men in my rooms, talking and arguing about anything that came up. Once or twice a term we had an 'Original Evening', on which they could bring up unsigned prose or verse they had written, which was then read aloud and criticized by the room in general. The group, though it tended to become fairly constant, was spread over a number of colleges. Among those of particular interest were T. H. White of Queens', then a poet, afterwards to achieve fame with *The Sword in the Stone* and *The Elephant and the Kangaroo* (I choose the two which I myself most enjoy); Hugh Herklots of the Hall, then Editor of *The Granta,* afterwards a Professor of Theology and a Canon of Toronto; Ian Parsons of Trinity, afterwards a partner in Chatto and Windus, and in Air Intelligence in the war. There was Austin Lee of Trinity, who made a habit of breaking into my college late at night, and once arrived in my rooms to find the Dean there at 1 a.m. He was a colourful character, destined for a somewhat erratic career in the Church; slight in figure, outspoken, and a practical joker. It was said that for a bet he had stolen A. E. Housman's deerstalker hat, and had papered his attic rooms with his lecture notes, so that for a period each day he walked round and round revising them. He had a rich and indulgent aunt in Yorkshire who presented him at intervals with Daimler cars, which he sold at corresponding intervals to pay his debts.

Later there was H. L. Elvin of the Hall, who achieved a running Blue and the Presidency of the Union in the same week, and then a First in English; and after much service with UNESCO, emerged as Professor of Education at London. Many more came and went, leaving me with the warmth of their friendship. At this time one's 'circle' of men one knew really well, grew at the rate of about twenty a year, and that figure doubled when I became a tutor. After a time the numbers at 'Monday Evenings' became too large, and the 'open' invitation had to be restricted to members of the colleges where I had some official position.

In 1926 the present system of faculties, each with its own establishment of university- as opposed to college-appointed lecturers was set up. The choice of the initial appointments was made largely from those on the spot, as Spens had foretold; I was lucky to be chosen in the general mass appointments, which included I. A. Richards, Forbes, Lucas, Attwater, Tillyard,

Downs, H. S. Bennett, Rylands, and Potts. At the same time my college said that they would elect me to a Fellowship at the end of the year, but warned me that the college was so poorly endowed that its stipend would be nominal, and that until there was a vacancy on the foundation I should have to make a large proportion of my income from 'outside' sources. That meant only one thing; schools examining work with one or other of the large examining bodies such as the Oxford and Cambridge Joint Board, or the Cambridge Local Examinations. This latter body, with its enormous prestige and clientèle throughout India, Africa and the Far East, provided work extending through most of the year. I have always loathed large-scale and anonymous marking in English, but from then to 1940 this work brought in perhaps £100 a year, and was of course superimposed on one's normal term and vacation work. Broadcasting and television, which now supplement academic incomes so generously, were still to come.

In September 1926 I married, and after a short honeymoon returned to unfurnished rooms in one of the little streets. We had just enough to live on; the rooms were pleasant though noisy, being opposite a school and a church. After a few months a child was on the way; and it became necessary to look for a more suitable home. It has always been difficult to find accommodation in Cambridge; the large Victorian houses had not yet been split up into flats, and many of the small post-war villas were mean and badly built; neither university nor college then gave help with loans or accommodation. We decided to build our own house, on a plot of land which we bought near the college playing fields. We had no initial capital; the heavy mortgage to a building society took fourteen years to discharge. Plans were drawn up for a small house with large rooms, which was to be capable of additions later on. We began building in February. My daughter was born in August, and we moved into the house at Michaelmas 1927. I went through the usual exciting frustrations of building, examining and rejecting materials, and so forth; a little appalled, I think, at the commitment I had undertaken. Life was full and exciting; the perpetual stimulus of young men and their friendships, the making of the house and garden, had to be fitted into the pattern of a Junior Fellow's life. That pattern, being born of a monastic society, was in perpetual conflict with the needs of family life.

Yet if this conflict does not exist, and if one allows one's rooms to become an 'office' (in the American idiom), the collegiate system is in a fair way to break down, and the colleges will become little more than bad hotels. Here there are various factors at work; the pressure on accommodation near the university, the car which breeds a race of commuters, the loneliness and overwork of dons' wives who can get no domestic help. Clearly, wife and family were sacrificed to the needs of a system that demands, for its best results and a vital contact between teacher and pupil, something approaching celibacy. Perhaps, for me the situation was more acute than for most: for in addition to my teaching I was much taken up with the college rowing, which seemed a special task. It was an exciting one and rewarding: but it meant some two hours or more on the river every week-day and in all weathers.

I do not think that I took any conscious stock of the situation and this career as it appeared to be developing. College elections and re-elections to fellowships are made at intervals, usually every five or seven years; there is no guarantee that re-election will be automatic, though a University appointment, once confirmed after a probationary period, is for life and dismissal is possible only for the graver crimes. In the course of ten years I had been deflected successively from the Irish Bar, the Foreign Service, and a career in business; the last being something of a fiasco, caused by my own ignorance, inaccurate information, and a romantic optimism. I had always wanted a life that took me, if not out of doors, at least abroad, and that would give some freedom from routine. Until the Second World War came to enlarge the possibilities of action a don's life seemed to equip one for little except being a don; it lies open to a variety of gibes, some of which I had, earlier, made in verse. Perhaps the best defence of it is contained in the postscript to C. P. Snow's *The Masters;* yet that book, for all its devastating accuracy in the picture of a College election, gives an impression of day-to-day life, intrigue, wine-drinking and ceremonial that is in many ways false. The younger married Fellow, without private means and with extensive family commitments, finds himself on a treadmill of teaching, administration and endless committees; he has to attempt to drive the three wild horses of his routine duties, his research, and his family life. One curious effect of the war was to show a number of us that in fact we could undertake a wide range of wholly different jobs with some measure of success, so that many whose roots were not too deeply set in Cambridge moved afterwards to industry, the Civil Service or similar work. In 1946 I was offered three directorships in business, but it seemed too late, and there was much to be done in post-war Cambridge and particularly in one's own college. There were, too, the opportunities and advantages that an ex-officer possessed in speaking the same sort of language as the returning undergraduates, and in dealing with the War Office and the various Ministries who were still implicated in their affairs.

ii

In recollection there were a number of interests in the period 1927–39 that stand out. Our children, Rosalind and Desmond, were born in 1927 and 1929. At first we took them to the seaside on the Norfolk coast; then as they grew older we cast about for something more exciting, that would give again some semblance of my boyhood holidays. It had to be by the seaside, and there must be boats and bathing. It must be a rocky coast, for there the possibilities of sea-fishing would be greater. For preference it was to be on a farm, so that the children could grow with animals. If possible there should be a chance of some rough shooting. Finally it had to be within motoring distance of Cambridge, in one of the ancient second-hand cars of which we had an excitingly erratic series, varying in cost from £20 upwards. Ireland was too far, the journey too costly, for us to visit Paradise.

With the help of friends we found a farmhouse far out on the Lleyn Peninsula in Caernarvonshire, then unspoilt and little known. It was reached by a narrow track remote from the road; the sea was on three sides of us, with magnificent cliff scenery round Wylva Head. There were several good bathing beaches, including Hell's Mouth, afterwards to become a bombing range, where our friends the Hallwards[1] had taken a house.

There we spent good summer holidays; the farmer's wife cooked for us, and we went to a tiny village shop or to Abersoch for provisions. The south-westerly gales howled round the house,

---

[1] He was then Senior Tutor of Peterhouse: afterwards Headmaster of Clifton, and Vice-Chancellor of Nottingham University.

and rain drove in under the sills of the tiny windows, but the weather was much as one expects it in the West. The children throve, and became interested in everything that concerned the farm; we played about in boats, and visited the islands in Abersoch Bay. Soon after we were married we took one holiday alone together in Argyllshire; this was memorable for our being caught in a small dinghy, with a Scots ghillie to row us, in a sudden blow on the Sound of Mull. We had been pollack-fishing in the evening, and a black wind came upon us suddenly, so that Donald Cameron and I had much trouble in keeping the boat alive in the heavy seas. Later there was a trip to Norway with Colin Hunter, then a master at Winchester. He had been Captain of the School and of all games during my first term; then, after winning a mathematical scholarship at Pembroke, went to the war as a gunner. In 1919 he was invalided out with a bad head-wound, and partially paralyzed during his period in hospital. The hole from the shrapnel was still visible in his skull, but he had a slight steel cap made to fit it, secured with elastic. In succession he captained Cambridge, and the Corinthians, at soccer, and played first-class cricket when he had leisure. Then came the crisis that any athlete must suffer when he knows that coordination and speed have slowed up for just that fraction that puts an end to first-class athletics. It seemed likely that his superb physique would still give him pleasure if he would learn to sail and fish and shoot; so I took him to the Broads and Blakeney, to Norway, and to Ireland in winter.

Norway was peaceful, prosperous, hospitable and even then Americanized to an unbelievable extent. Near Rosendal on the Hardanger we saw a tiny wooded island, on which was a hotel kept by a philosopher. There were boats for his guests, a playhouse for their children, and great space and calm. I decided that if ever a war broke out I would retire to such an island and find peace in building boats. Later I did an army course with a Norwegian captain of infantry from those parts, who knew the island. Still later I was to negotiate with the Government-in-exile of Norway over their demands for rehabilitation when the ceasefire should come; miles of twine and rope for net-making; small diesel-engines for the fishing-fleets they would have to build; and, always, unbelievable quantities of tobacco. Lovely and vivid memories remain. An ice-cold night in a workman's hut on the snow-line by the Valley of the Bears, where a gale the next morning took the waves of the two lakes off the surface as they rose, and I had difficulty in getting a line out from the bank; of catching big steel-grey trout till we could carry no more; of the lonely farms and the fat sturdy ponies, of bathing in ice-cold water, of fjord cliffs painted with whitewash so that running fish would think they were waterfalls, and gather beside them to be netted.

iii

At an early stage, events in college were disturbed by something I had come to dread and loathe; the election of a new Master. When I was an undergraduate the Master was Bishop Drury, sometime Bishop of Sodor and Man and afterwards of Ripon. The college was then limited to candidates in orders, since a portion of the inadequate stipend of the office was derived from a Canonry at Norwich Cathedral, where the Master had to reside for specified periods each year. Drury had succeeded Dr Johns, who, it was said, had killed himself by overwork in straightening up the tangled affairs of the resurgent college.

Drury formed my own early ideal of what a Master should be. He was venerable, dignified, with charming manners, caring passionately for the college and particularly for our chapel; with sufficient liberality and magnanimity to entertain graciously. He was a Christ's man, of a distinguished Cambridge family. At first his hostess was his daughter, Miss Drury, who died while I was in India; afterwards, his grand-daughter Margaret Tait, the daughter of his son-in-law who was then Principal of Ridley Hall. She afterwards married Bertrand Hallward of Peterhouse, who is mentioned elsewhere. Her sister married Hilary Macklin, whom I had got to know well in India, and who had been my contemporary as an undergraduate and Captain of the Lady Margaret Boat Club. (His son, David, was a Rowing Blue). Drury was not a great administrator or scholar; practical affairs he left to Rushmore and Chaytor, then Senior Tutor and Dean respectively. But he had the supreme gift of making everyone love him, for he was a man in whose presence no evil could exist. At the Bumping Races he made a point of coming down to push us off from the Railway Bridge: we called it 'the Bishop's blessing'. We saw him wandering through the court, eager to talk to us, getting our names mixed, but always giving out an aura of goodness. We took a pride in doing as he wished; attending chapel before his Sunday breakfast and after Bump Suppers, cheerful pagans that we were.

Drury died in 1926. For some years negotiations had been going on to dissociate the Mastership from the Canonry of Norwich: it was taken for granted that Rushmore would succeed Drury, and he did so, with only a formal election in the chapel. But Rushmore held office for eight years only. During much of the time he was in poor health, and for the last three years ill almost continuously. It was said that he too had killed himself with work. He was not a scholar, and was of a vigorous and often dogmatic temper, conservatively minded; he had presided over the college's fortunes while numbers rose from some 60 in 1914 to about 240 in 1919. In dealing with the all-important problems of admission he sought for and achieved some balance between scholarship, personality and athletics; a good many of the men of his time were qualified under two of these headings, occasionally under all three. During the First World War he commanded the Officer Cadet Battalion of the university, coached the First Boat during my first year, and served as Senior Proctor. His wife was the daughter of Beck, a former Master of Trinity Hall, who had known my family. Though she had been born, as it were, into Cambridge life, she found the gloomy Victorian Lodge, with its inadequate accommodation and stipend, an almost intolerable burden in conjunction with her husband's illness.

At his death, an election was again necessary. Colleges vary a good deal in their procedures. A very few fortunate ones have their masters presented to them by outside bodies such as the Crown. Our own Statutes enjoined election within thirty days of a vacancy. As on all subsequent occasions, the Fellows now split into two groups. There were two internal candidates whose merits appeared equally balanced. Neither side would give way. The thirty days expired; the right of nomination passed to the Lord Chancellor, who appointed H. J. Chaytor, whom Rushmore had brought to the college immediately after the war.

iv

There was a curious interlude in the spring of 1936. Just before

I left Calcutta I had an emergency operation for appendicitis. The job had been badly botched; the scar was far too long and ill-stitched, so that the cut started to weaken again: further, the surgeon had cut a nerve which had formed a fibroma. I went into St Thomas' in January (my father-in-law, a London doctor, was of that hospital) and Mitchiner, whom I was to meet again in the War as a Major-General, operated and tidied things up. I was given a term's sick-leave; the children were left in charge of an aunt, and my wife and I went down to the South of France to recuperate. We moved eastwards from Marseilles along the little *Michelin* railway till we came to a hotel at Cavalaire which was quiet and cheap. There I convalesced for a month, writing among the pine-trees on the beach a longish poem that seemed to foreshadow the Second World War, perhaps affected by the atmosphere of concern among the French peasantry. I did not know then that the Germans had been using the Spanish Civil War to test out the Stukas and the 88 mm. gun, which I was to be concerned with later. For the rest we bathed, slacked, and walked in the Montagnes de Maures. There I saw for the first time the framework of pastoral poetry; the children bringing the flocks and herds up from the village in the early morning to graze on the upland pastures and lie down at noon beside the waters in the valley.

There were a few English people in the hotel, who gathered in the evening round the smouldering fire of vine-roots. Two ladies had come from Portugal, both crippled with rheumatism. There was an elderly colonel of a Scots regiment, who had been at Aldenham and had presented a cup for rifle-shooting. He was a noble and eccentric character with a fascinating range of talk. In the first place he was a British Israelite, who told me gravely that I belonged to the tribe of Dan. His co-religionists caused some trouble during the war. When things were going badly in the desert they were wholly optimistic, but were certain that Cairo must fall, and the Germans and Italians would capture Jerusalem. Thereafter, an earthquake would open up a geological fault running between Haifa and the Red Sea, and passing beside Jerusalem! This national canal could make the Holy City pre-eminent, commercially and politically, in the Middle East. Some British Israelites in Cairo had to be locked up for spreading alarm and despondency, since wealthy Jews were beginning their own Exodus in anticipation of the fulfilment of the prophecy.

Colonel Rankin was an expert on water-divining, earth magnetism, and such things, and had come to France for some sort of international conference in that subject. Human electricity was, he said, measurable and of great importance; it flowed up the right leg and down the left. Later I met a very senior officer who, whenever it was possible, went and stood barefooted on the grass outside his tent for just this purpose. It was important, he said, for one's health to make use of the earth's electricity during sleep by having one's bed properly orientated. He proved his power of divination both on the local water system, and by locating a gold ring hidden under a carpet while he was out of the room. He did this by means of a piece of watch-spring bent in the form of an omega with one end 'earthed' on his gold watch-chain.

I do not know the most up-to-date theories about the physics or psychology of water-divining. It is certain that it works, and that most people after a little instruction can 'divine'; at any rate the War Office had an expert on the staff at the outbreak of war, who had been used – no doubt among many other things – to locate buried caves near Woolwich. I saw him at work on our cricket field. He claimed to be able to indicate not only the direction but the depth of subterranean water; this he did by stamping with his foot, and watching the tensed twig for a delayed tremor that seemed like a returning echo. There is no virtue whatever in the twig itself; there is no need for it to be of hazel, or to cut it at the full moon. Any twigs from a hedge, tied at the thick ends with string, will serve perfectly. What is important is the correct grip, with arms, wrists and the abdominal muscles tensed. When this is learnt the twig writhes in the hands with an uncanny effect, and over strong water may strike the face with dangerous violence.

Gradually I came to realize that the English visitors in our Mediterranean hotel had come to visit one person in the neighbourhood. I had never heard of Maître Nicolas Angelin, but he is mentioned in one of Lady Fortescue's books, *Perfume from Provence,* that has its setting in that part of the Riviera. He was a natural healer; and in the First World War he was used as such by the French Army in one of its hospitals. He would sometimes drop into the hotel bar of an evening, and I got to know him after a series of Pernods and much talk about fishing and *la chasse;* for he had a passion for fishing from the rocks with hermit crabs, for the little fish that teem in that sea that are a convenient foundation for the over-rated dish of *bouillabaisse*. He was small, round, cheerful pugnacious, with wrinkled face and blue eyes, a bachelor and a strong atheist; voluble, garlic scented, and a strong drinker. (I mention these things to diminish the idea of any sort of faith-cure.) Nor did he have a 'practice' as a healer; he charged no fees, and was devoted to his vines and his boar-hunting in the mountains.

After a time I asked him to look at my back which had become troublesome. The process was simple; he used nothing but a box of French chalk and his hands which he passed over the site of an injury. He said that he had discovered his power as a boy by holding a kitten with a wrenched leg in his hands; it emerged cured after he had stroked it for a little. He would only treat certain kinds of sprains and muscular trouble. His theory was that muscles and ligaments became *accrochés*, and that all the power, that resided in his hands, could do was to straighten up muscles and let nature heal them. People went on crutches up the stairs to his little bungalow and come down in a few minutes walking normally. When his hands came to any past break in a bone, they 'kicked' violently, like a water-diviner's rod, and the process of passing his hands over a lesion seemed to cause him intense pain. He told me that I had been roughly twisted while on the operating-table, rubbed me for a few moments, and told me to go for long walks in the mountains. Years later I discussed the case with a Regius Professor of Physic. He listened carefully, and said: 'Yes. From time to time men like this are born – one in so many hundred thousands. We know about them, and there is not the slightest doubt that they do cure in this way. But we know nothing about *how* it works.'

v

I have seen the film of the nineteen-thirties,[1] with an acid commentary by Malcolm Muggeridge. Of the decade, the first critical year seemed to be 1934. Yeats had thought that somewhere round 1929–35 there was the falling apart of one of the long-spun gyres of history. There was the Night of the Long Knives, when

---

[1] This was at Christmas, 1959.

Roehm and his men were shot, and the strangely unchallenged rise of Hitler. Ironically, there was a general feeling that fascism, at least of Mussolini's brand, was what Italy needed, since the trains were now running to time and official bribery was discouraged. In Ireland there was the phenomenon of O'Duffy and his Blue Shirts – backed for a time by Yeats, who wrote some not very good 'marching songs' for them. These, like Oswald Moseley's men, seemed no more than a foolish shadow of bravado. My Mother died in Ireland, Paradise was closed, the furniture and pictures auctioned, and the house and garden became semi-derelict. I had done seven years' work for the University and College, and had seen the unpleasantness of two Mastership elections. I became a tutor with a 'side' of undergraduates, of whom I taught personally about a score. Salaries were still nominal, and I had to mark in my spare time some two thousand examination scripts a year. That hated form of self-prostitution did not cease till the War.

I think that it was about this time that the Oxford Group movement reached Cambridge. Four or five dons, of assorted but perhaps slightly eccentric reputations, became its leaders. One was the Dean of a large college, another an eminent mathematician. Some of my pupils became enthusiasts and attempted to convert me. There were various embarrassing incidents, including a statement by one of my pupils that he had been guided by God not to write his weekly essay for me! The answer was plain. But clearly I had to see the thing and judge for myself. The headquarters was at a famous London hotel, but the centre of events was Oxford. My wife and I drove to Oxford for a long week-end; it was a house-party held in Norham Gardens.

At first sight the set-up was remarkable. Numbers of young and attractive people, obviously sincere and with vast enthusiasm to communicate, were mixing happily and on Christian-name terms with artisans, business men and a few industrial leaders. The services were simple and impressive, particularly a mass one in Christ Church. By the third day one was aware of a strange and disquieting fermentation of the emotions, so that I remembered William James.[1] The pressure to confess seemed to reach enormous magnitude. It seemed clear as one watched that this was not wholly an emotional catharsis, still less a religious

---

[1] *Varieties of Religious Experience.*

one. By 'confession' it was obviously possible to attain to important stature in the group, and, if the sins were lurid enough, some sympathy from the many attractive and earnest young women. Yet many of the confessions seemed trivial, but magnified in the telling to a frightening exhibitionism. It was an emotional short-circuiting, a simplification, of the normal religious experience, and the group made many problems appear deceptively simple. The outcome seemed, so far as I could judge, for there was a strong infection of unreality, a temporary psychological relief rather than a permanent sense of grace or peace, for there was hardly time for any genuine re-assessment or re-integration of personality. Maddening slogans seemed to glaze the surface of the psychic situation, such as Buchman's cry 'It's the banana that leaves the bunch that gets skinned.' It is difficult to imagine a more vulgar or illogical exhortation for the solidarity of a group. We left before the house-party ended, perplexed and unsatisfied. Later, two dons who had joined the group had nervous breakdowns. Later still, Leonard Browne told me that in his view if ever fascism came to England, it would be through the agency of the Group. I think that the movement persisted in Cambridge with diminished energy till the outbreak of the war; two of its leading members in the college, both friends and pupils, were killed at an early stage.

A lucky chance brought me to Leonard Browne, one of the great London psychiatrists of his time. Some years before he had treated for delayed shell-shock, a great friend, who had gone from the army into the Church. After several months' treatment with him I came to know him well, and with ever-increasing admiration. The process of therapy has been often described, but my own case was linked to the events in Ireland and is therefore in retrospect of some interest. Among the undesirable symptoms was a sense of strain, and an undue tendency to worry that probably made me difficult to live with and tried my wife's unusually gentle temper. Perhaps the shortage of money, and the temptation of a profession in which a good deal extra can be made – at a price – were factors.

There was the usual period of preliminary interviews, and then it became clear that an emotional ice-jam was forming up. I went through a period of almost suicidal depression. On my next visit Browne questioned me as to what I felt. The nearest image I could find was to say that it was as if a large three-cornered lump of metal were turning round slowly in the region of my heart. He asked me three questions, and on the third I burst out weeping, and continued for some hours. When I recovered I asked: 'What happened?' He replied, quite simply, 'Your heart is breaking.' 'Why?' 'Because you've been living with a ghost.' Piece by piece he made me construct the pattern. My Father's death when I was just fourteen had left me numb; I suppose the fact of the coffin descending into the grave filled with snow and water, and later the presence of a rat-hole under the great limestone slab, had eaten deep like a tumour. I still believe that Sir Thomas Browne's *Urne Buriall,* as well as I Corinthians 15, are of central importance in combating the emotional aspects of death. But my father's death was followed almost immediately by the Rebellion, the poverty at Paradise, the raids and shootings of the Troubles, in which I had tried, quite unsuccessfully, to assume my Father's place in relation to the estate and to my Mother. Some nine years of acute strain, uncertainty and exasperation had produced an emotional state in which the adolescent was competing unconsciously with a grown and mature man; with the inevitable result of a perpetual feeling of inadequacy, whatever relief there might have been in action.

Leonard Browne had impressed upon me that no analysis could be of the slightest value without full co-operation, and much relevant reading. So it came about that I read, then and later, most of the standard works in psychiatry and psychology. I was about to become a tutor, and it seemed important to try to become competent, in so far as a layman can, to deal with the questions of mental and spiritual difficulty that are inevitable when large numbers of intelligent and sensitive young men are flung together to

> Endure that toil of growing up
> The ignominy of boyhood; the distress
> Of boyhood changing into man.

Perhaps the four or five years before the war were of special difficulty. The Spanish War, the rise of Hitler, and the uncertain aftermath of the depression, were all reflected in a number of 'breakdowns' of one sort or another. In subsequent years we have seen the fear of the Bomb, of the war in Viet Nam, with all their emotional consequences. Each generation of undergraduates seems to have its own peculiar *angst*. That of my own was lack of money, and the fear of unemployment. The tensions and their varied psychic compensations are very clear in the poetry of the time. Such troubles, merely taking the form of mental illness before examinations, and sometimes suicide, seemed to have a strong infective aspect; in 1938 the number of breakdowns throughout the University reached an appallingly high total.

From Leonard Browne I had learnt something of my own magnetic variations. I sent to him one or two undergraduates who seemed to be heading for serious trouble. But there were obviously a number of men for whom extended and costly professional treatment was neither possible nor desirable. Browne told me that I might do some good, and could do no harm, with the many people who came with a wide variety of problems, if I kept rigidly to three maxims:

> Get, somehow, the reputation of being someone to whom anyone can come, at any time, and talk. Never be shocked, never react angrily. Never be 'moral'.

> Learn to occlude your own personality at will. (This is the most difficult discipline of all.) Let the man do the work by talking. Never interrupt, or make suggestions as to a pattern of behaviour, until the man has revealed it to himself.

> Go on saying, *Why*? Why do you *feel* this? To get the answers to this at each stage is the most difficult and time-consuming of all, since the ice-jams of resistance must be slowly melted; and the process needs time and patience.

After the war I was faced with this problem in a new form. The war-damage cases among the ex-servicemen were in a class of their own; events which had given rise to traumatic conditions could be learnt or reconstructed, and handled accordingly. More significant was the renewed crop of breakdowns when the race of ex-servicemen had finished. There were, and are, many causes which might occur in sequence or simultaneously. The transition from home life to Cambridge accentuated social differences, since the Butler Act (1944) had opened a university career to all boys of ability; yet there were often conflicts, in themselves highly ambivalent, between the boy and his family on his return for the vacations. The intense competition for entry, and still more the knowledge that grants might be dependent upon success in examinations, can produce all kinds of tensions. Many boys had not slept away from home for a single night before they came into residence; this arrival in a new world, for which their background and schooling had not prepared them, was liable to produce grave depressions. It is significant that the two 'danger periods' are the first month of a freshman's residence, and the three weeks or so before he takes his finals.

Since 1946 we had kept fairly full records of men interviewed and admitted, with regard to background and personality as well as academic achievement. On these the psychiatrists of the newly-formed Medical Health Service at Cambridge did some important work. In 1951 my friend Sir Lionel Whitby, then Master of Downing and Regius Professor of Physic, asked me to read a paper called *The Causes of Failure in Examinations,* at the World Conference on Medical Education. This provoked some controversy and much correspondence.

It was clear that the problems facing the undergraduates after the Second World War were largely different from those in the period 1920-39. It seems to me that the whole ethos of universities is changing steadily, sometimes violently,[1] and will probably continue to do so. A vast expenditure of public money and perpetually soaring costs can only be justified if there is a continuous scrutiny of standards of admission and achievement. The pressure on admissions and even the breakdown of the machinery to assess qualities, other than those measurable by examinations, has resulted in a reliance, which many of us think unjustified, on the results of examinations taken at school. Competitiveness has resulted in a university career being overvalued as the golden key to the future; and in hopes, fostered by schools, that mere selection was a guarantee of success. There are so many factors that cannot be predicted. There is no measure for assessing, for instance, a man's potentiality to develop, whether he may have been overworked and his bearings as it were, burnt out at school; whether the superbly efficient teaching

---

[1] This is being revised in 1966-70. It is particularly true of the newer universities, here and in America, which have suddenly increased their numbers. The result is often chaos among the students, whose traditions have been swamped by these numbers.

such as one finds at some of the great schools, public or grammar, has done no more than put a deceptive gloss on a second-rate mind. Then there are the accidents of circumstance while at the university; the surmounting of inevitable love-affairs, difficulties at home, the demands made by athletics, dramatic or journalistic work. The adjustments of all these claims to the demands of his reading, his lectures and laboratories, as well as the proper use of the vacations, is the most serious problem of the undergraduate.

The impact of the post-war *malaise* began to be apparent about 1956. As usual the causes were highly complex. One was the emotional fear of the Bomb, which could produce mass hysteria, and a *carpe diem* philosophy not unlike that of the doomed youth of 1917. Another was the prevalence of neo-Freudianism, which seemed to have transferred responsibility from the individual to society in the present or to parents in the past. A third was the interest shown in existentialism by the more intelligent men; believing that the only right remaining to the individual was his right of choice. But it was not clear as to the hierarchy of the choices that might be made; and the end-result might be a kind of intellectual anarchy.

Superimposed on this was a variety of aestheticism which recalled some of the manifestations of the 1890s. A search for pure sensation as an end itself, whether through sex or drugs; an effeminacy in dress and appearance; a pathetic desire to achieve status by appearing different or 'kinky'; all these were intermittent manifestations. There was also the suspicion that a time of over-employment made money too easy to earn and to spend; to the detriment of at least the art students, who curtailed, for various kinds of employment, the vacations in which the State paid them to read.

But to balance the picture, I doubt whether the average undergraduate has ever been better off than in the twenty years following the Second World War. There is an initiative in travel, expeditions of all kinds, voluntary service overseas, social work and boys' clubs, which seems to be extending steadily. I doubt whether the intellectual standard at the very top has risen appreciably; and the tendency to admission by marks rather than personality has resulted in diminishing the third class, and forcing the second class slightly higher up the scale. There is a mass of relative mediocrity in all universities, ancient or modern; and at the lowest the standard can be contemptible. It is of course a matter of definition and standards, but I have long doubted whether there is an inexhaustible fund of university material that is merely waiting for a better system, for 'more opportunities', before it emerges.

America had shown me the appalling price that was being paid in their waste of teaching power by the admission of candidates who were not really qualified to read for a degree; in one university the 'drop-out' was as high as forty-six percent of the total freshmen entry. But there the problem was less pressing, partly because of the presence of numbers of secondary colleges of decreasing reputation who were capable of absorbing and ultimately graduating a high proportion of the rejects, however low the original 'flunking' standard may have been.

As I look over these pages in 1971 I am aware that the whole system of students' grants has become and will continue to be a perpetual bone of contention. They are not high enough to ensure what the undergraduate considers a comfortable living, and they never will be. A 'means test' for the parents is politically anathema. So is the treatment of the grants as loans, which would be a sensible solution. But the public sees that the tax-payers' money is being spent by a lunatic fringe, in all sorts of questionable ways, and therefore grows restive; the popular image of the student (not the undergraduate) has sunk low. A similar waste of money is apparent in the latest figure of a sixteen percent failure rate in British universities: and the figure, for various reasons, is almost certainly on the low side. With more efficient and far-sighted selection the rate should be a quarter of that, even taking into account the many hazards that, as the medieval writers well knew, beset the academic year. They include illness, family affairs, love-melancholy: but the chief one today is the lack of what the Americans call motivation.

IX

'MERE ARITHMETICIAN'[1]

i

During the autumn and winter of 1938-9 I had amused myself by building, in the back garden, a small pram dinghy for the children. I had also discovered at Portmadoc an ancient venerable boat-builder; a slow and thorough craftsman, the winner of several Bardic Chairs for poetry. He agreed to build a larger sea-going boat to my designs; she had to be strong enough to take the sand where I proposed to keep her near Abersoch, able enough to live under oars in fairly heavy weather, and somewhat under-canvassed, for I wanted to use her for fishing and expeditions to the islands, so that the children could learn to handle her safely. To my great joy, both Rosalind and Desmond had shown the family obsession with boats. Her launching and trials at Abersoch were to be the highlight of that summer holiday.

Meanwhile, the war came up over the horizon. A Cambridge don of thirty-eight was in a peculiar condition; technically we were all in a reserved occupation, and we were given to understand that the war, if it came at all, would be brief and highly professional. That spring I enrolled as a special constable, and did some training; then, with a number of my friends, joined the staff of Civil Defence Regional HQ, thereafter to be known irreverently as Spens's Circus, after the eminent Master of Corpus and Commissioner of the Eastern Region. It seemed likely to provide useful employment in the mass destruction, bombing, gas, which, we were told, would mark the outbreak of war.

As usual, I drove the family in the ancient Rover to North Wales about mid-August, and settled down on the farm. I went

[1] *Othello* I, 1.19.

'Mere Arithmetician' 131

to Portmadoc to fetch my new boat, and sailed her across the bay to Abersoch with Bertrand Hallward and his brother-in-law, André Tait, a Naval commander, later to go down with his ship. A blissful ten days followed; the children had the dinghy to play with, and the new boat was all I had wished for. Then a telegram arrived from Cambridge, ordering me to report at once to Regional HQ. I drove the car back through perfect summer weather, sought quarters with a friend in Pembroke, for both the college and my house were shut, and settled down to play at Civil Defence games and exercises.

War began; long hours in a gas-proofed room at St Regis, watching the teleprinter, coping with unrealistic paper exercises. September passed: my wife remained in North Wales with the children and their nursery governess, the much-loved Maria Lendvai, who had a genius for teaching, and I took stock of the situation. Term was approaching, military service was not yet in full swing, and the university was obviously going on. As for my own college, the Senior Tutor, Portway, an engineer and keen Territorial officer,[1] had left immediately to take command of a field company in France. The next Senior Fellow, a geographer, had been caught in the West Indies; Chaytor, the Master was near the retiring age. It was clear that for the moment I must help with the college. I resigned from the idle War Room at St Regis as a paid officer on £3.10.0 a week, and rejoined it as a volunteer for two nights a week. Term began fairly normally except for the black-out; I came on as a Special Pro-proctor, and started to walk the streets, seeing Cambridge in a clear unlighted beauty which I had never dreamed of.

I gave my first lectures, quoting (with unnecessary melodrama) Housman's words:

> We for a certainty are not the first
>   Have sat in taverns while the tempest hurled
> Our fruitful plans to emptiness, and cursed
>   Whatever brute or blackguard made the world.
>
> The troubles of our proud and angry dust
>   Are from Eternity, and shall not fail.
> Bear them we can, and if we can, we must –
>   Shoulder the sky, my lad, and drink your ale.

[1] See D. P. Portway, *Militant Don*, and, later *Old Contemptible*.

As the term went on I grew steadily more restless. Some of my friends, wiser than I, had taken up work in intercept or cipher, training for it months before the war. Others whom I knew pulled all possible strings to ensure that they should not be called-up; and indeed the scandals from France, of troops making golf-courses and the like, seemed to indicate the futility of the 'phoney war'. But I did not feel that I could bear a university life which would certainly change its character as fundamentally as it had in the First World War, and I went to the Intelligence Personnel Branch at the War Office to ask for employment, on the strength of reasonable French, German and Urdu; for I had kept up this last language in odd moments. Though my name was taken, I was told that I was most unlikely to be wanted and was in any event far too old. I returned to Cambridge in dejection, and spent a week's leave at Christmas with the family in North Wales. Our house at Cambridge was let, but I still had my set of rooms in college.

Early in January I heard from Admiral Sir Herbert Richmond, then Master of Downing, that the Admiralty were taking the names of yachtsmen of the small-boat variety who knew the West Coast of Ireland, for certain possible contingencies in the Battle of the Western Approaches. I sent in my name, but was told that I could not be considered unless I had reached the stage of being able to take a Master's Certificate in navigation. I returned to plunge into spherical trigonometry and text-books of seamanship. Early in April before Dunkirk I again reported to the Admiralty, and after extensive medicals was told that I could not be accepted since one eye was ten per cent below standard. I pointed out that I had shot at Bisley without glasses off the left shoulder. For the third time I returned dispiritedly to Cambridge.

Then came Dunkirk; and towards the end of the time a telegram from the War Office telling me to report at once as a subaltern in the Intelligence Corps. The commission was on two counts: firstly because I had had the appropriate certificates at the end of the First World War (I had been due, as I have said, to join the Irish Guards in the spring of 1919), secondly because the university would not release me except in commissioned rank, in view of my age, reserved occupation, and their commitment to make up part of the difference between service pay and the university stipend.

ii

I was told to report to Swanage, where the Army had taken over a hotel to set up a series of streamlined courses for intelligence officers; there was as yet no 'I' Corps, and we wore General List badges, vulgarly known as 'Crosse and Blackwell'. There, in perfect summer weather, we met; perhaps a third of us were officers who had just got out of the Norwegian debâcle or the Dunkirk retreat. These were – by comparison – seasoned soldiers; one noted curiously how they shrank into a doorway when a German reconnaissance plane came over, or how as they crossed a field, they watched instinctively for any small hollow, even a furrow in the ground into which they might flatten themselves in case of need. Another third were the notables: explorers, mountaineers, racing motorists, men who had lived in various European countries, and were often bilingual. The rest were a strange mixture: a few dons, including John Masterman, afterwards to be Provost of Worcester and Vice-Chancellor of Oxford; a few schoolmasters, mostly linguists, and oddments from many professions.

The course itself combined the atmosphere of a school, a boy scout camp (exercises on the desolate moors to the north-west), with the moderate excitement of war, for we were under orders to march inland at short notice in the event of invasion. Occasionally a minesweeper, destroyer or submarine appeared in the bay.

The directing staff were charming, and reasonably tolerant of our unsoldierliness: they included a professor of Greek archaeology, a keen Territorial officer who was the head of a great firm of brewers,[1] and a few regulars. One of the latter I came to hate, mainly because of his habit of thinking that obscenity was wit, and writing it as such on my essay papers. That was probably good for me; though I could not foresee that I should have thrust on me four years later the possibility of a mean and petty revenge when this officer, still an acting lieutenant-colonel, came to ask me to find him a job.

Swanage was exquisitely beautiful; the hastily-built defences

---

[1] John Buxton, afterwards a Fellow-Governor at Aldenham.

touched only parts of the bay, and there were magnificent walks along the cliffs. One night a friend and I went some distance along them, and were challenged by two LDVs, the forerunners of the Home Guard: huge square slow-spoken fishermen, wearing blue jerseys and armbands, with obsolete Lee-Metford rifles and five rounds of ammunition apiece, guarding a tiny cove. We stopped to chat with them; not of war but of boats and lobster-pots and mackerel. I had done much with the sea; we exchanged methods of making and mounting gear, and parted on good terms. After we had gone some distance a rich deep Dorset voice came looming through the night: 'Now fancy yon gurt big ugly bugger knowing about things like that!'

iii

The course broke up at the end of June 1940 in the midst of the regrouping after Dunkirk. I had been told by the War Office that there was unlikely to be employment for me for many weeks, and that I had better return to Cambridge to await orders. I remember driving to Bournemouth a brother-officer's car with a seized-up clutch. Cambridge was normal but crowded, and much occupied with ARP, and the dispersal of its treasures, and the guests whom we had received from various London colleges. But within a few hours another signal came from the War Office; I was to report immediately to Salisbury.

There I found that HQ, Southern Command, was just in the process of moving to Wilton House; the officers' mess was in the pub opposite the entrance, and I was billeted in a villa in the town some distance off. I was now a second lieutenant in Intelligence with no clear duties, catapulted into a new and bewildering life. It seemed that there I was the only IO, perhaps the only officer in the HQ for the moment who could read and speak German. I was promptly ordered to make myself an expert on the German Army and everything that concerned it.

The surroundings were exquisite. The Double Cube in Wilton House, one of the most famous rooms in England, became the operations room with Intelligence in a small passage-room beside. The furniture and many of the pictures had been removed, the mouldings partially protected, but the great Van Dycks remained. On a low trestled table was a one-inch map of Southern England, covered with talc. In addition to the marked headquarters, units, airfields, the beaches were marked in red strips varying in width according to their vulnerability to invasion. Outside, beyond the still-mown lawns with their Greek temples and statuary, was the Palladian Bridge. All history was in the place, gracious even in the first turmoil of war. Security demanded that the endless hutted camps should be hidden in the woods, for German reconnaissance aircraft were constantly over us, and they were finally covered with a roof of green painted steel wool, piled on nets slung from the trees. Of defence there was none; a single light machine-gun was sited, hopelessly and ironically, by the Palladian Bridge. Once a casual raider returning from the Midlands dropped a string of bombs beside the room where I was on night duty, and killed some woodpigeons.

Immediately after my arrival my wife and I had to take a decision of appalling difficulty. Yale University had offered, with a generosity that to this day seems overwhelming, to take over all the children of Oxford and Cambridge dons, and to be responsible for them, including a university education, if the father were killed. We had cables from our friends urging us to accept. There were many arguments for and against. If the battle came to England there would be no opportunity for evacuation. My son had been sent early to his preparatory school to be near the sea, because of health, and the school was being moved away from the Sussex coast. At that stage both children needed good food. By then I knew a good deal of German military methods, and I had seen their films of the Polish campaign. I imagined, stupidly and dogmatically, that I would have my wife and children shot rather than see them under a German occupation; though I was not then, as I was later, 'listed' as one of those who should not be captured because of what I knew and had written. So far as I saw the situation in July 1940, the invasion would come in September or October: none of us then knew how greatly Hitler's advance had outrun the German logistical resources, or the mistrust of the Continent for the sea, or Hitler's obsession with the ultimate necessity for conquering Russia. The appreciation ran that, in the first battle of the beaches, the Germans might lose 10,000 men. If they had command of the air, the Navy would not be able to intervene decisively at once, being based far to the north. The successive battles for England – they could be no more than delaying actions – would be fought on the lines of the Thames, the Humber, and finally on Hadrian's Wall. Daily the reconnaissance photographs showed the build-up of barges in the French and Belgian ports.

Against the evacuation of the children there were great arguments: the separation of the family at a critical time for an indefinite period. When and if they returned they would be, in part, foreigners and strangers. The rhythm of their education would have been broken. Worst of all, subtle psychological factors might be dangerous in the extreme, not least if we eventually came through the battle. Against that was what seemed then the supreme risk of gas; we had not foreseen the mass bombings. For a week or so the scales seemed equally balanced. Then we decided that they should go; but I made the condition that my wife, for the first years at least, should go with them. I got a day's leave to meet them in London: and my wife left with our boy and girl, a younger nephew and niece, and three children of Cambridge friends, their father having just died. I returned to Wilton and the prospects of the Battle of Britain.

Of that time, its excitement, emptiness, exhilaration and despair I have written a little in verse:

> Then in a moment flung
> To the high room where the Van Dycks watch the maps
> (Half a million rifles guarding King Charles' country)
> And the beaches marked blood-red. . . .

But there were only rifles, and no ammunition; I remember that there were reported to be 150 rounds for all the anti-tank rifles – in any event a futile weapon against German armour – in the whole area of Southern Command. Anything that would fire, however ancient, suddenly became valuable, and I saw a naval four-pounder of pre-1900 date taken from a museum and sited on an esplanade. The Home Guard were arming, variously and not without danger to themselves. In the local contingent at Wilton, A. G. Street was prominent. With his massive cheerfulness, his country skills, and his exquisite farm, he seemed to stand for all that was most typical of England. I remember that the headquarters raised an eight to challenge the Home Guard at small-bore shooting matches, and that we ate pickled onions and drank beer afterwards.

I am aware of many moods at this time. One was an enormous

exhilaration; of being alone, without continental embroilments, in a repetition of the classic situation. Never before, and certainly never since, was the unity of the country so fiercely light-hearted. We played endless war-games, anti-invasion exercises: the chief (at first Auchinleck, then Alexander) sitting on a dais that overlooked the maps: very quiet, a word now and then to the waiting staff-officers at his side, a telephone call to a corps commander. So Yeats' poem came to life:

> That civilization may not sink,
> Its great battle lost,
> Quiet the dog, tether the pony
> To a distant post.
> Our master Caesar is in the tent
> Where the maps are spread,
> His eyes fixed upon nothing,
> His hand under his head.
> *Like a long-legged fly upon the stream*
> *His mind moves upon silence.*

We pretended to repulse attacks on the headquarters; on the lawn where *As You Like It* was acted in Shakespeare's day, the house where Sidney's *Arcadia* was written; exercising with the Home Guard, using hand-grenades made of mud and bran, and wooden rattles for machine-gun fire. It was all deliciously unreal, but we might have been enacting the prelude to a saga:

> But the Palladian Bridge guards the River
>   and the gun-pit guards the Bridge
>   and the trout hang poised in the shallows above
>   the weir
>   and the moon lights up the River to guide the
>   enemy home.

The raiders homing from the Midlands picked up the tributaries of the Avon, which led them down to the sea.

> Whom do I sup with tonight? (The Pleiades
>   are gone.)
> Yeats and Donne and Landor – three races and
>   three men –

Guard me from the terror by night, and my own
   thoughts worst of all
In the blankness of the night.

Yet imagination was mainly submerged in exaltation, of loneliness, of having much to do and more to learn about everything that concerned my new trade. One of my civilian hobbies had been guns and gunnery and light automatics. I became obsessed with the idea that our men and the Home Guard should be able to use captured enemy weapons (it was later said that when our troops captured Italian 81 mm. mortars in Libya, they left their own behind) and should also know something about the characteristics of the enemy that they would face. From various sources I collected a sort of museum of German and Italian weapons, documents, uniforms, and I was frequently sent round to give lectures to officers' schools, and in the evenings to Home Guard battalions: Bulford, Swindon, Alton, Oxford and Reading. At Reading a couple of bombs landed outside the hall at the most impassioned moment of my denunciation of German war crimes, to great applause from the audience.

In Bristol I was caught in their biggest raid, and, having cancelled my lecture at the fort, for I had learned earlier that the city was 'on the beam', went to work at Civil Defence headquarters, one side of which was blown out in the raid. It was a memorable night, and several incidents stand out: a very ancient Civil Defence watchman, in a genuine bowler-hat, on the roof of a building where he had been stationed with one bucket of water and a stirrup-pump to put out incendiary bombs; a solitary AA gun firing hopelessly through the mist and smoke; the noise of the approaching engines, as each aircraft made its methodical run-in, knowing that there was no opposition; the clangour as of armour when the sentry outside flung himself to the ground, equipment and all, when he heard the whistle of a bomb. My FANY driver and I were staying with Bertrand Hallward, then headmaster of Clifton. When I learnt that the city was 'on the beam' I sent my driver back to Clifton with orders not to stir until I sent for her. That night the school was hit. The next morning I measured a great crater, thirty feet across, from a bomb that landed plumb between two brick shelters each packed with boys. No one was injured, but Hallward decided to move the school to Bude in Cornwall.

'Mere Arithmetician'

During the raid I worked in the Civil Defence headquarters. In the early morning the bombing ceased, but it was possible to read outside by the light of the fires. All night, by teleprinter and phone, the estimates for coffins kept coming in. The hit upon us caused no casualties, but spoilt my uniform. Thus far in my life I had been near death a few times: sailing, fishing on Irish lakes, but then with a certain security from the old prophecy; I had been machine-gunned by a casual raider in Dorset and bombed elsewhere.

iv

'The other night I stumbled at a skull.' Thus Nathaniel Wanley, that curious figure in the literary history of the seventeenth century. He has something of the poetic stock-in-trade of the later metaphysical poet, flourishing as he did about 1660. He can be in turn amorous, religious, morbid, and yet with a kind of gaiety in the Donne tradition; he achieves sometimes a vivid compression of phrase, yet the bulk of his poetry is of no great interest. But there is a single poem so typical of his century, and so vital in its rhythm, that it is worth consideration. There was, I think, a certain casualness in sixteenth- and seventeenth-century interments and exhumations which nourished the idea of the macabre both in literature and in painting. The system of limited tenancy for the body was in force in all the burial grounds of the city; necessarily so, until the purge of the Great Fire, and the subsequent expansion of London. The length of the tenancy depended, of course, on the nature of the soil, and on the quality of the body; hence the point of the jest about the tanner in the grave-diggers' scene in 'Hamlet'. That scene, indeed, must have been common enough to the passer-by: the diggers striking down into the old coffin, the bones flung up, to be collected or not as might be, and placed in the charnel-house, whose traditional horrors were all assembled in Juliet's dream. Or the bones might lie about the churchyard (as I had seen them in Ireland, and as Synge describes a burial on Aran); they might serve to play at loggats. That last indignity, or others like it, 'were tragicall abominations escaped in burning burials'. The scattered bones, too, lent point to Donne's and Herbert's great phrases concerning the dust of the churchyard, whose meaning we can hardly grasp now:

And when the Man sweeps out the dust of the Church into the Churchyard, and the wind blows the dust of the Churchyard into the Church, who will undertake to sift again those dusts and to pronounce, 'This is the patrician, this is the noble flowre, and this the yeomanly, this the plebian bran'.

So, too, the whole range of the churchyard imagery. It was not always morbid or unhealthy, in the modern sense. From one point of view it was the logical outcome of medieval theology. 'There is no life this side of the grave. Therefore look well into the grave. Keep its lessons ever before your mind: for thus you will be assured that there must be immortal life beyond.' So, in Lucas de Heere's portrait of the Betrothal in the Dulwich Gallery, the bride and bridegroom place their hands on a skull: below them, under the altar, there is a body in its winding sheet and you may see a wax effigy of a decaying body, behind a glass panel, under the high altar of a certain church in Quebec. Yet there is no morbidity, strictly speaking, in this. *Romeo and Juliet* might be overcharged with adolescent imagination playing on the worms and reeking chaps: but there is a steadier undercurrent of grave-philosophy which might be, in turn, the 'saeva indignatio' of Webster, or the gentle and inquiring humility of Browne, the quiet pulverescence of Herbert, the moral imagination of Young in his *Night Thoughts*; which, later, I read aloud in my rooms with C. S. Lewis.

In Wanley's poem, after that amazing opening, the monologue develops:

> 'And what?' said I 'is then death's belly full
> Or now the glutton has devoured the rest
> Is this the only fragment of the feast?'

The old image – 'What feast is toward in thine eternal cell?' abstract as in Ronsard's 'Ce qu'a rongé le temps injurieux' and more terribly concrete in the ballad: 'The channerin' worm doth chide'. Bed – lodging – the inn – the bridegroom – the train of association is familiar:

> 'Are beds of death so throng'd or growne so deare
> That a poore skull can get no quarter there.
> The grave that used not to dispute the stuff
> But took down all Doth it not cry, enough?'

The beds of death – even St Innocent's churchyard had grown too full: the horrible conceit was true enough. But Wanley goes on to speculate:

> 'Or have I lost my count? And is this day
> Good Friday, and this AEGYPT? For they say
> That yearly near Gran Cairo there is known
> To be a parcel resurrection.'

A 'parcel resurrection' – the bodies spewed up by the grave, yet lacking the spirit to cohere them.

But he turns back to the skull:

> 'Come thou with me
> Thou poor remainder of mortality . . . .
> For if we
> Rightly define the true philosophy
> To be a meditation of the grave
> Then while I hugg thee I am sure I have
> The best philosopher.'

The secret's out. The true philosophy *is* a meditation of the grave. The search for a balance between the emotional and intellectual contemplation of it is a notable achievement of seventeenth and eighteenth-century religious thought. The medieval world had drawn from the contemplation of it the certainty of corruption; had underscored the lessons in the church monuments of medieval France; had jested with it, danced with it, and flaunted Holbein's Pageant on the church walls; had woven it into the fabric of the Moralities. Across that dark tide, when the churchyards 'swelled with the waves and billows of the dead', the healthy sensuality of the Renaissance had flowed: sharpening the sense of loss, and fusing in the imagination a thousand images to link the grave with the lover's bed, or with God.

How much was intellectual, how much basically a morbid emotionalism arising out of meditation on the Cross, it is difficult to be certain. The church monuments of fourteenth-century France had a terrible verisimilitude, even to the shreds of rotting flesh hanging on the skeleton. England, with a greater sense of both humour and of tragedy, does not seem to have lingered too greatly in the grave, except when Elizabethan drama overstepped the boundary line between Rowe's 'Horror' and 'Terror'. Webster's world is much possessed by death, as is Tourneur's and at times Chapman's: again, I think, finding its proper food in the sensuality of the opening churchyard. A literal resurrection meant that the phenomenon must be closely handled. Wanley goes back to his philosopher:

> 'For if thy cheeks should have on either side
> A piece of flesh more than half putrified
> If in the open casements of each eye
> A pale worm should be wriggling seen to lye
> As if it voided rotten juice that flows
> And trickles down the channel of thy nose
> Though damps of open's vaults were in thy breath
> And on thy front the worms had traced death.
> Yet such philosophers I'd wish to have
> And think them fittest to discourse the grave.'

Perhaps Marvell alone, in that calm balance which constitutes his greatness, passed through the two stages of petrarchan wonder, and sadistic sensuality, and emerged triumphant: and with the civilization of the Royal Society and the Roman dignity of the eighteenth century, our contemplation shifts from the skeleton to the urn. There is decency and restraint again, but perhaps the sense of tragedy is lost. Was Ridgeway right in thinking that tragedy originated with ancestor-worship at the tomb, and feeds from the pot of honey there? Or perhaps it is that the full sense of loss and emptiness – and through this the larger pattern – can only be realized if the death-emotions are brought into play? The range is infinite:

'La reine Blanche comme ung lys
   Qui chantait à voix de sirène . . .'

'Imperious Caesar dead and turned to clay . . .'

'Do you think Alexander looked so in the earth?' . . .
'And smelt so? Pah!'

'Isn't it a strange thing when there is nothing left of a man that was a great fisher and rower but a bit of an old shirt and a plain stocking?'

'Mere Arithmetician'

John Synge was right, I believe, in thinking that all great poetry has its roots among the clay and the worms: not all, perhaps, but nearly all. In his parable I understand the clay to signify the common basis of men: the loneliness and strength and misery of people who have also the sense of wildness and mystery in life. By worms I understand that bitter sense of sorrow that sees all life brought down by the worm to its common level, so that the metaphysician can see, at one level at least, the final pattern that tragedy imposes on the world, and which is ultimately satisfying because it is final. Swift or Shakespeare, or a bone on the seashore –

> 'A man if I but held him so
> While my body was alive
> Found all the pleasure that life gave.'

– can make the particles cohere in that strange geometry:

> 'Unaccommodated man is but such a poor bare forked animal as thou art.'

That perhaps is why Nathaniel Wanley thought the skull to be his best philosopher: in part, no doubt, by reason of that strange shadowy melancholy that lay over his century; but more from a grim laughter – like Donne's railing at his mistress from the grave – and the certainty that the phantastic burial customs of the world must be quietly and scientifically explored: with voluminous learning, for knowledge was an attribute of God, and how else could he evoke the ghosts of the past? And so he rises to the majesty of the end of 'Urn Burial', and its crescendo from the fifth chapter on.

> ' 'Tis all one to lye in St Innocent's Churchyard and as content with six foot as the Moles of Adrianus.'

It was still light over the city of Bristol that December midnight. For nearly five hours the bombs had fallen: the guns had spoken through the low cloud, above which the invisible worm had passed to and fro on the run-up to the target. A dozen yards away, at midnight, one could read the number-plates of cars. Below ground it had been hot and stuffy, frightening, the white lights on the maps where the pin-heads moved from square to square as each message came in. The noise of the bombs died out, the first casualty-lists came in over the telephones as each district reported. The night air was a relief, though little patches of dust, mingled with very fine ashes, hung over the city. Many fires were still burning. As I moved northwards towards Clifton I passed a great church; inside, a hell of flame, still crackling fiercely among the pews. The east window with all its delicate shafting still stood, silhouetted against the flames, so that the light was shed outwards from where the glass had been, very stately in its momentary defiance of the flame:

> 'There lives one moment for a man
> When the door at his shoulder shakes
> When the taut rope parts under the pull
> And the barest hand is beautiful,
> One moment while it breaks.'

The firemen had just moved up, for there had been more urgent business elsewhere; hoses and pools of water lay on the road, and there was a wet ashen smell over everything. 'Been at another job,' a fireman said, 'cripples' hospital down there – direct hit. Can't do much for 'em.' I walked on; over rubble, and through pools of water, and over the hoses that throbbed to the pumps. There was nothing to say or do. A building seemed spread over the road, as a child's house of bricks is scattered on the nursery floor. And then my foot struck something that rolled a little, as an apple on its stem.

v

Before Bristol was the Battle of Britain: golden summer weather, with the German aircraft crashing all over the command, like wounded pheasants in the rear of the line of guns at a Norfolk shoot. One of my jobs was to go to investigate them and their equipment, riding a government motorcycle, a new and powerful Triumph, with some danger to myself and others. One particular bomber had come down on a long slant, crashed through the top storey of a house, and landed in the orchard beyond, where it had gone on fire. In the room through which it passed a child was asleep in an iron bedstead: the impact had folded this into a broad V-shape, but the child was taken out uninjured. In the orchard, roasted apples still hung on the trees; they reeked of the peculiar oil which the Germans used on their equipment and in their engines.

Once I went up to Basingstoke to see my brother's son, a fighter pilot who had been shot down in the Battle. After sorties that were almost continuous he had been called out early on a summer morning dressed only in pyjamas, and had been shot down in flames from a great height. As he descended, on fire, by parachute, his opponent sprayed him with machine-gun fire. In hospital there seemed little skin that had not been terribly burnt, and the nails were black lumps of carbon, yet he was flying again within six months. The torment of burning[1] exceeds all imagination. So we watched, we arithmeticians, the battle of the air. Each day the reports came – vastly exaggerated, as after events proved – of German aircraft shot down. We knew how low our fighter resources were falling; the invasion still seemed probable. The feeling was tense, and at the same time exhilarating. Something of that emotion, unfashionable but genuine, has been caught in Cecil Day-Lewis' *The Stand-To*:

> . . . and the wind blew fair
> From the east for men and barges massed on the other side –
> Men maddened by numbers or stolid by nature, they have their pride
> As we in work and children, but now a contracting will
> Crumples their meek petitions and holds them poised to kill.
> . . . .
> Since a cold wind from Europe blows back the words in my teeth,
> Since autumn shortens the days and the odds against our death,
> And the harvest moon is waxing and high tides threaten harm,
> Since last night may be the last night all thirty men go home. . . .

So September and October wore on. Though I was still a subaltern, I was allowed, perhaps because of my age, to take my

[1] Described in Richard Hillary's *The Last Enemy*.

turn as operations duty officer. I was acting on the night of the 15/16th September when wind and tide seemed right for the invasion. It was an unforgettable experience, at night in the Double Cube under the curved painted ceiling, taking the signals as they came in every five minutes or so. Many were ridiculous or trivial; a messenger-pigeon from the French bearing special wishes to the Royal Family, a German Cruiser reported heading straight for Plymouth, which she must have reached by then. But the most amusing episode that autumn was the Great Spider Scare.

It happened thus. As I walked across the lawn each morning to the mess, I saw large numbers of exquisite silvery spider-webs about six inches in diameter, lying on the grass and bushes. At that time British aircraft were said to be dropping on the German crops and forests incendiary wafers containing some phosphorous compound, so that when they dried they ignited whatever was near them. I do not think that they were of the slightest use. A signal came from GHQ to the effect that substances resembling spider-webs were being reported all over Southern England. It was suspected that they might be some form of German chemical retaliation. We were to warn all formations not to touch them.

I was frankly sceptical, refused to relay the signal, and collected some webs on a tray for a demonstration. I was reprimanded for disobeying orders, and one of my seniors sent out the signals. A day or two later a further message came from London, saying that a severe case of burns had been reported from the spider-webs; all formations were again to be warned. Again I refused to play. A week later came a further message. The reported case of burning had been traced. A lonely widower in the Marlborough area had pressed his trousers with an electric iron. As sometimes happens, he had burnt his hand with a delayed-action burn, which did not become apparent for a few hours after. Meantime he had handled, or thought he had handled, the suspected secret weapon. Spider-webs were off. But GHQ had not been idle. A genius in Intelligence there remembered Gilbert White of Selborne, and looked up that great and dispassionate naturalist's description of the mating habits of a certain kind of spider at that precise season, with the result that the silvery webs floated down everywhere, and Gilbert White's spaniels could not hunt because their muzzles and eyes were stifled as they worked the stubble-fields. Thereupon he wrote and

circulated, on a strictly demi-official basis, a Rabelaisian poem on the spiders and their webs, and their involvement in chemical warfare. But he did not mention Donne's *Twickenham Gardens,* and
> – the spider love, that transubstantiates all, –
> And can convert manna to gall.

There were other lighter sides to the life of the command. The chief issued an order that all chair-borne officers were to get out on visits as much as possible; and that in any event everyone was to have two hours off in the day, if work allowed, provided that he *did* something; that is, walked or rode or fished or shot. So it was that I caught up again certain threads that I thought had been dropped. The two rivers, the Nadder and the Wylye, ran through the park. Higher up the Wylye lived G. E. M. Skues, perhaps the most famous fisherman and writer of fishing books of his time. He was then old, bent and lonely, living in a little inn. Both his wrists had been broken in boyhood, yet he threw a perfect line, curving his casts to right or left at will. He could see fish, grey shadows in the weeds of the chalk-stream, where I could not. The few hours that I spent watching him taught me more than many books. Lord Pembroke let the officers fish the water on condition that we looked after it; it had been neglected and was overcrowded with grayling, large and small. A club was formed and the river was stocked: beats were allocated for two hours a day. It was long odds, of course, against being able to take one's beat at the time allotted, but there was always 'open' water where the grayling might be thinned out. I got some gear from Cambridge; that summer and the next I spent many happy hours on the water. Occasionally we went duck-flighting in the late evening at the little valleys west of Wilton; once I was given a day's partridge driving on the Downs in the company of some senior officers.

It was perhaps typical, in some comic fashion, that the ability to shoot and fish, to make gear or repair shotguns, did more than anything else to give me some sort of standing in the headquarters, and to break down something of the suspicion attached to a Cambridge don. I was, *ex hypothesi,* an eccentric, but even a knowledge of poetry could be condoned, and I was useful for clues for crossword puzzles. In the Double Cube was Jack Heaton-Armstrong, Chester Herald, and a distant cousin. He too was a keen fisherman, and, in addition to his duties in RAF Intelligence, had the task of preparing emblems and mottoes for the rapidly multiplying squadrons; a fascinating and difficult task, for each one had to be personally approved by the King. Problems of Latin or English were sometimes presented to me. But it was, I think, my ability to fish that gave me a start in my service career.

vi

Eighteen months passed at Wilton, with various intermissions for courses and attachments, during one of which I worked with a Scottish regiment. There, for the first time, I saw a full battalion on parade in the morning sunlight and thought of Sir Richard Vernon's description of the rebel army in *Henry IV*:

> All furnish'd, all in arms,
> All plumed like estridges that wing the wind,
> Bated like eagles having lately bathed.

There, too, I marched behind the bagpipes and understood something of their potency. For a month I went to Matlock to do a specialists' German course; we lived in a vast, gaunt hydro on the hill, while wrestling with the Gothic script I had learnt as a boy, and practising interrogation of prisoners. But the centre of my time at Wilton, because she gave me a welcome and houseroom, was Edith Olivier. A Swanage friend, Dick de Grey, had given me an introduction to her. She lived in a little grey stone house – The Daye House, once a dairy – on the eastern side of Wilton Park, near where the Nadder and Wylye join, very simply for she was poor. It was my fortune that about this time she decided to take an officer as 'billetee', and I became her second lodger; her experiences with me, and some of my successors, are told in *Night Thoughts of a Country Landlady*. She was then over seventy, Mayor of Wilton (which, she explained proudly, was the oldest borough in England), and the friend of countless young people who came to her. For she had, more than anyone I have ever met, the gift of spontaneous and warm friendship, a real concern for her friends and a profound absorption in their affairs. To these friendships she brought an immense gaiety, a lightning-quick but never malicious wit, a passion for the theatre (one of her books is called *Without Meeting Mr Walkley*) and an enormous knowledge of Wiltshire people and customs. Her Father had been rector of the ugly Italianate church in Wilton itself.

I may have been in some ways a model lodger for I was out all day, walking very early in the morning through the park to the mess at the Pembroke Arms, often loitering as I did so to watch the wild life of the place, and the trout and grayling in the streams and leats that crisscrossed the paths. But I seemed to grow into the little household, and took on certain duties; to do household repairs, to keep it in rabbits and pigeons, and, in season, trout and grayling; occasionally, on one of the rare days off, to act as a host at her little luncheon parties; once or twice, even, to read papers to her Poetry Society. She seemed to know everyone: at the house I met Rex Whistler, many of whose paintings hung in her rooms, and he designed the covers for her books; Sir Leonard Woolley the archaelogist; G. M. Young and Mona Wilson from Oare near Marlborough; Lord David Cecil, not yet appointed to the Chair at Oxford. Up the road, on the other side of Wilton, was A. G. Street, whom I used to meet when we shot against the Home Guard; Nancy Graves, the first wife of the poet, came over from time to time.

The house was within a few yards of the ornamental lake; on summer evenings when I got back from the headquarters, I often slipped on waders and went into the water, to rediscover its healing power, finding intense delight in the remembered rhythm of rod and line.

So the summer of 1941 passed and with it the fear of invasion, and the sense of excited strength in the country. Instead there came the news of the long series of defeats, the ebb and flow in the desert. My worm's-eye view was a little enlarged by having much access to secret material. I had a great many visits to make throughout the command, as well as lectures to cadet battalions and senior officer schools. There was a pleasant incident at Oxford; my immediate master, a regular major of the Rifle Brigade, was sent there for a day. He was to lecture on aerial photography at Brasenose in the early afternoon; I was to talk to the Home Guard, including many dons, in the evening. In the interval we had time free; my friend, who was an Etonian, had never seen Oxford, and I offered to show him round. We ended up in the gardens of Worcester, and then a thought struck me: 'Would you like to see a typical Oxford don?' He would; I rang up from the porter's lodge. C. H. Wilkinson was in and would be glad to see us. Worcester was our sister-college, and I had worked with Wilkinson in peacetime; I knew what to expect. But as the talk or monologue unfolded my companion's jaw dropped lower and lower. For Wilkinson was a colonel of guards – I think the Coldstream; he was running the University OTC; he was treasurer of the University Boxing Club; and he seemed to know all the War Cabinet by their Christian names. Somewhere in the background there was his grouse-moor in Scotland and his pheasant-shoot in Hampshire; on the shelves before us there was probably the finest collection of seventeenth-century first editions in the country. That afternoon he had just bought three Oxford Turners, and as we sat and drank quantities of sherry, a sumptuous and very expensive book on Persian carpets arrived from the University Press. So the amazing talk went on; until as a final gesture Wilkinson produced a book of atrocity photographs of the First World War, said to have been bound by the Oxford University Press in human skin. It looked rather like inferior parchment. This was the last straw, and as we tottered down the noble staircase from his rooms, my friend turned to me: 'I say – it's – it's rather an honour to be a Fellow of a college, isn't it?'

That autumn, authority decided that I had been long enough at Wilton, and that I should go on yet another course; this time, rather imprudently, to Cambridge. It was known colloquially as the Gauleiters' Course, officially as the Fourth Politico-Military, for the authorities had decided to train a number of elderly officers for post-treaty work in Europe on boundary-commissions and such like. So we assembled in St John's under Sir Ernest Barker, who lectured with characteristic vigour on constitutional problems and much else. I was allowed to live in my rooms at St Catharine's although I worked and ate in St John's, and inevitably became a sort of liaison officer between the course and Cambridge in general.

My own college had become wartime hosts to the London Medical Schools and to the Bartlett School of Architecture; the last included among its dons Corfiato, Abercrombie, and A. E. Richardson, after to become PRA. He was a striking, eccentric and most lovable character, fond of execrable puns (for which the High Table often fined him bottles of port) and of practical jokes of all kinds. One night I sat very late working in my rooms;

the door opened slowly and a figure glided in. The single reading-lamp showed it as dressed in a tricorne hat, a flowing black cloak, black silk knee-breeches and silver-buckled shoes. The rooms had long been haunted, but very beneficently; I had never seen, though others had told me of him, the old gentleman dressed in russet brown who used to come and lean over the back of my chair. I had brought some of the more startling manifestations in the early thirties to the notice of the Bishop, who had laughed, quoted 'Encompassed about as we are with so great a cloud of witnesses', and said in effect, 'If it's kind', which it surely was, 'why worry?'.

This time, however, my heart stood still. The figure was Richardson, who had bought the outfit that day from an antique dealer in Ely, and alleged that it had once belonged to Grumbold, the architect of Clare.

The course went on its way without incident; it included several MPs, Viscount Hinchingbrooke, Norwegians, Danes, Belgians, Dutch; and two charming 'free' Americans. This was my second meeting with the US Army: at Wilton I had had two colonels to show round in the autumn of 1940. They were polite, but expressed great contempt at the way we were 'running the war'. But this autumn it was different; I was in the Americans' room in St John's when the news of Pearl Harbour came through. They had taken the line that they would come into the war as and when it pleased them; now their consternation was beyond belief. Yet the whole course seemed unreal, its practical applications hopelessly remote in that time of defeat.

> Why have they brought us here to watch the pageant unfolding,
> Famine and fire across the fluttering maps?
> The slow oxen plod on, and the corn springs in the rain.
> Why must the great guns swing in their turrets, across the Straits,
> And the sunk ships guard the mole?
> (Because the cattle starved in a drought on the Steppes
> Because the lumps of amber must ring the neck of a queen
> Because a Nativity ikon burnt blue and gold at Kiev)
>   But to-night the air's a-whisper
> Hate and lust and intrigue, pity and lies and fear
> Brood on the Palace of Atreus.

We broke up in December; Ernest Barker called me in to help 'grade' my fellow-students (surely the first and last time this has ever been done on a course!); however, our records seemed, by the postings we were given, utterly disregarded. As events proved, mine must have been secreted for many months in some dusty archives of Whitehall. I took a week's leave at Wilton, and reported to Northern Command at York as a major in Intelligence.

The cavalry barracks, and the headquarters in a long street, was something of an anti-climax after Wilton. All tension over a possible German attack in the spring of 1942 had died away, and the command was almost entirely on a training basis. Even the happy eccentricity and enterprise among the Home Guard, which had been so refreshing on the south coast, was a little dulled here. I remember that I went to Leeds to open an intelligence course that we were running for them. At the door, checking the roll, was a somewhat shaggy-looking Home Guard captain; there was Bruce Dickins, then Professor of Anglo-Saxon at Leeds and afterwards at Cambridge, who had examined me in the Tripos twenty years before, but whom I had never met. He was then a widower living alone in the basement of his house: after the lecture he bore me off to eat kippers in his kitchen. I did not know then that one of the many subjects on which he was an expert was regimental histories of the British Army. There was a battle school at Barnard Castle, which I visited to teach German weapons and tactics, and once I had a day's shooting on one of the near-by big estates; but York, except for Milner White, Dean of the Cathedral, seemed cold and inhospitable.

The early spring of 1942 was probably the period in which morale generally was at its lowest. The two cruisers, *Scharnhorst* and *Gneisenau,* had survived countless bombings, to escape in daylight up the Channel; Singapore had fallen, and the desert war ebbed to and fro. America was in the war, but it looked as if the main objective of her ponderously-mobilizing strength would be directed at Japan. Russia was being driven back, and Rostock and the Caucasian oilfields might fall. The possibility of our invading Europe seemed infinitely remote:

A message falls on my desk.
A ship founders or a bomb falls or a cry goes out

To flutter the souls that crowd in the fetid shelters
(Coveys crouching in stubble, under the hawk's shadow)
To close the breech of the gun, or send the ammonal skywards,
Or twist the bridge-girders in torture.
                              The pendulum ticks on.
Bombs in the soft night on Pearl Harbour
Bombs on the cruisers at Brest, on the Baltic trawlers,
On the Shwê Dagon at Rangoon
                        on the steaming Perlis jungle.
And the limbs sprawl in the creepers for ant-folk and rat to whiten
Or the polyp to turn to coral, or crab to tear.
And in the beginning were words, and the soft-voiced diplomats talking
For the ant-folk must have room
              on the coral islands on the sands of Eritrea
Corn and wine and oil for their larger breeding
Copper and rubber and oil for their swifter killing
(And the desert thorn's aflame.)
                              Snow falls on the steppes.
Shells plunge and the diamond diapered patterns rise
To cover the creaking bodies. There's snow on the pinned maps
That weights them against rising in the winds of the world
                              The frontiers have gone.

One night as I walked back to the barracks with Charles Hirseli I had been in the depths of depression, and talked bitterly of these things. He stopped, and said, very quietly, 'Tom, I do not think it is the will of God that this great country should utterly perish.' I remembered that when I served Alexander again in Italy, and watched his immeasurable calm and certainty and humour in all crises. His personal chaplain always went with him. Perhaps a theologian would speak of his qualities as concerned with, arising from, Grace.

The spring came; a series of events brought me to London, to a job that did not really exist, and was clearly undesirable for me if it had. In the game of snakes-and-ladders I dropped again to captain and found myself, after some adventures and clashes with authority, on a tiny and highly secret staff called 'Plans and

Raids, GHQ'. This was a sort of offshoot of GHQ; we were attached for billets and messing to St Paul's School, later to become Monty's Planning Headquarters. The little party, some ten officers and a brigadier – Colin MacNab, who was later killed in North Africa – worked in a house in Queen Anne's Gate, and was in close touch with the underground fortress in Storey's Gate, where I was sometimes duty officer at night; and there met Martin Holmes of the London Museum, an authority on Elizabethan London, whose password of recognition was a quotation from Shakespeare while in the ablutions, one early morning.

Our brief was a peculiar one, and in less-than-military language ran something like this:

'Sooner or later we shall invade Europe. For the next two years, perhaps three, there isn't a hope. We shan't have shipping, men, guns or aircraft. Your job is a strictly paper exercise. Find out everything you can about the coast of Europe; how it's defended, the German strategy and tactics in holding it. Do some crystal-gazing and tell us what it might look like next year. Then say what forces you think you would want to do it. In the intervals, you will supply general and local intelligence for the people carrying out raids anywhere on the European coastline.'

The job and the personnel were an interesting piece of strictly British improvisation. Adequate information about France and its coast was hopelessly deficient; though no doubt there were admirable maps for the areas where the classic battles would be fought, as in the First World War, in the Low Countries. Charts as well as maps were hopelessly out of date. An organization called the Inter-Services Topographical Department was set up at Oxford, and sent out an appeal for any kind of postcard or photograph of the French coast and the seaside resorts. So Aunt Maria's postcard of the *plage* at Ostend, with her hotel-room marked X, might eventually have become incorporated in a beach report. We had to learn the lie of the buildings, how they might be adapted by the Germans for defence – even as we had built camouflaged sweetshops on the beaches in 1940 – and how groynes and piers might become obstacles. We knew nothing of the gradients of the beaches themselves, and these were finally plotted by low-level air-photography, the sorties being flown at different stages of the tide.

We provided some of the intelligence for the Dieppe Raid, and that curious adventure brought bitter practical lessons. Intel-

'Mere Arithmetician'

ligence work is, or rather was, starved in peacetime; there were no cadres for it in the Territorial Army, and to the regular officer it was traditionally a dead-end that seldom offered a prospect of high rank. With the outbreak of war, or just prior to it, numbers of amateurs and particularly linguists were hastily examined and put through various high-speed courses. With a few brilliant exceptions, they were unlikely to reach high rank. The information they produced was sometimes suspect. The arithmetician could only base his opinions on probabilities; Dieppe provided one example. The town was held by a medium-grade German division, and such a division included among its weapons thirty-six anti-tank guns of 37 mm. calibre. We were certain that there *were* those guns; but the planners of the raid pointed out that none of them were visible on air photographs, and therefore didn't exist. It was these very guns that did so much damage at the start of the raid (among other things they hit and blew up an ammunition barge) and we found out afterwards that some had been concealed in caves cut in the chalk, while others were run back each day into the recesses cut in walls and the sides of houses.

Standing Stones

X

INVASION AND AFTER

i

To an ex-civilian of middle age (I was then forty-two) the Staff College in January, 1943 was an exciting and, in prospect, somewhat alarming experience. For its function as I saw it was to train younger officers, mainly regulars, for staff appointments; it was therefore a waste of time and money to train anyone so elderly. For this reason I had refused, while at Wilton and at the War Office, three previous nominations; only yielding to a fourth after a row with a very senior officer. I argued that I was unlikely to be appointed except to a specialist staff, and that my general training would be of little value. I did not foresee the very real 'ring' of initiates represented by graduates of the Staff College, and the supreme value in any sort of staff relationships of speaking a common language with them. There were rumours of the ferocity and pace of the course – two years' peace-time training compressed into some four months – even of officers committing suicide during it. We were indeed ordered to surrender our pistols and ammunition on joining because, it was said, there had been three cases during the previous term. As a preliminary I had been ordered to do an attachment to a brigade or battalion; and since I was apt to be wanted for quick consultations in London, I stipulated that it should be somewhere in the Home Counties. Good fortune took me to the Fifty-third Division in Kent, and eventually to friendship with two remarkable men: Eric Dorman-Smith, my Brigadier, and Cyril Coleman, afterwards a Lieutenant-General, then commanding the Fourth Battalion of the Welsh Regiment. Dorman-Smith had served in the Burma campaign. He was bitter, cynical, and had a brilliant mind; intensely critical of the conduct of the war in the Middle East; full of violent and unorthodox ideas, and with an amazing fund of reading and knowledge. Coleman was quiet, carrying that air of well-bred leanness and tautness of mind that I was to notice later in several high officers in Italy, together with a gentle courtesy of movement and speech that I remember with gratitude. At first both Brigade H.Q. and the Battalion regarded an attached major as a nuisance, and showed some tinge of the usual suspicion of the staff. Later I was overwhelmed with kindness, and had the exhilaration of training officers in my favourite game, snap-shooting at moving targets. Those weeks remained in my memory as supremely happy ones. My attempt to rejoin the Regiment – which had most graciously taken me on their strength – for the invasion of Europe, was indignantly vetoed by my general, though Coleman had agreed to allow me to revert to the rank of subaltern, as a supernumerary sniping officer.

Early in January I joined the Staff College; my wife had returned to England a few days before, having enlisted in the WAAF in New York. This was the only way she could obtain a passage to get back to England. After some months in the ranks the authorities discovered that her German was good. She was borne off to secret work at Bletchley, and was finally in charge of intelligence concerning the German night fighters. The children remained in America with their hosts the Pages in New Haven, Conn. Contrary to my expectation I found Camberley enjoyable and immensely profitable. There was necessarily too much compression in the course, too little time to digest the reams of paper, précis, schemes, lectures, exercises, that appeared in one's pigeon-hole several times a day. It was an interesting experiment in returning to school again, and made me sympathetic three years later with the ex-soldiers who returned to Cambridge to take their Triposes and to rub off the rust of five or six years. The teaching was superb; far more logical, less stereotyped and with fewer dogmatic solutions of the many problems than I had been led to believe. Lectures were diverse and interesting; two stand out in my memory. One was by the defender of Malta, who, standing up before six hundred officers, ascribed his victory to the hand of God – and no one laughed! Another was on the writing of Military English, delivered by an officer who was said to have obtained a fourth in the schools at Oxford, at which I sat with a Fellow of All Souls on either side. I found myself sharing a room, and for part of the time in the same syndicate, with an RASC Major, who had been one of my pupils in 1939, and who was to distinguish himself later as commander of a beach group in Normandy. Of my fellow-students, about two-thirds were regular officers, in the 25–32 age-group: a third, amateurs like myself.

At the outset I realized that I knew far more about the German Army and its weapons than I did about the British. We went through the mill: staff duties, which seemed slightly ridiculous till one realized the compelling logic behind them, still more when we had to construct a common language, symbolism, and map-conventions with the Americans; the time-honoured exercises of the withdrawal, the attack, and the river crossing at night; a compass-march across country at night, in which one syndicate got itself beautifully enmeshed in the elaborate enclosures of a chicken farm, passing from pound to pound till it gave up in despair, like a salmon led into the innermost trap in a weir; many demonstrations of the latest weapons; tactical exercises without troops, which were problems of tactics worked out on huge cloth-models in the Rawlinson Hall.

There were no formal examinations. We wrote essays and military papers; we were told that we were, in fact, being 'examined' every week, and five or six students vanished quietly at intervals. We went for runs, and for ten days we were detailed to serve as umpires on one of the large-scale pre-invasion exercises, which involved a battle across the line of the Thames. We slept in outhouses and under hedges and saw much of the Chilterns and their surroundings.

The 'battle', as always on these occasions, seemed a little obscure. Various things impressed themselves on my mind. Strict wireless discipline was in force, and no messages were to be sent except in cipher; but a mobile column of armoured cars penetrated into the 'enemy' area south of the Thames, and sent back a message in clear giving the map reference of a large arms dump. Within a few hours the Germans had bombed it. Then there was the appalling toll taken of despatch-riders on these exercises, travelling fast with dimmed lights in unknown country; I think the casualties on this particular exercise were nearly a hundred. After each such exercise rumour told us of a long list of commanders, major-generals and above, who had been relieved of their commands for ineptitude of one kind or another. We became aware that the Thames could simulate, very fairly, the Loire or the Seine.

For ten days or so the Staff College course included what was obviously a psychological attempt to see which students would crack under strain; for we were loaded at quick intervals with a mass of paper exercises, running simultaneously – in each of them one played a different role as a staff officer – with much mathematical calculation, writing of orders and so on. The whole had to be done with very little sleep. I was familiar with this, but on a lesser time-scale, through the anti-invasion 'signal' exercises at Wilton. It seemed to make sense as a test, for it revealed the phenomenon of 'flap': a kind of psychological paralysis which sets in, with devastating results, when the clearing-house of the brain refuses to receive and order the messages coming into it, and to form them into a pattern of action. The centres become choked, as it were, through inability to sort the stimuli into an order of appetencies or priority of decisions. Such a mental state bears a close relationship to the matter of university students' breakdowns, and sometimes suicide, when confronting examinations.

For myself, I had determined that I would treat the course with a courteous levity, and that no one should commit suicide that term. Perhaps I am the only student who has sent in a poem from *Punch* (remembered from 1915, as it concerned Gallipoli and my brother) as 'Appendix C' to a military paper. I believe that the essay went up through the hierarchy of the college, with endorsements in different coloured inks on the way. The debates in the Rawlinson Hall, at which one might be called upon quite suddenly to speak *extempore* on a military subject, could be rather fun, though the regulars seemed for the most part to dread anything for which they could not prepare from 'the Book'. Towards the end of the course we got on to intelligence and information about the enemy, where I was on my own ground, and I induced the Staff to get a lecturer down from London to tell us about the all-important business of Combined Operations, a subject which was not yet on the official syllabus.

About a fortnight before the course ended a representative of the Military Secretary's Branch came to visit us, and had brief interviews with each. I did not then realize how carefully, and I think wisely, that organization plans and guides the concerns of officers over field rank. It is a peculiarly British, and in some ways quite irrational institution, in whose keeping there must be countless secrets and scandals; working very quietly, with a vast knowledge of human character. I never saw any of its dossiers; but for the German Army we had a secret document known as The Brown Book, in which were given brief sketches of all the characters, careers and personal lives, sometimes highly scandalous, of the more important German commanders. There are occasions when it is important to assess character in predicting how a general will act in a given situation; it may be even more important to know whether he has written on strategy or tactics. It was said that at the siege of Damascus the de Gaullist commanders knew exactly what the commandant of the city would do each day; it seemed that he was the supreme rigid, military arithmetician.

One by one the postings for my friends came through to every conceivable kind of job. There was nothing for me. I began to wonder whether I should find myself unemployed, one of the redundant majors. Finally a letter arrived marked Top Secret; within the second envelope were two lines, ordering me to report by a very devious security route to Norfolk House in St. James's Square.

ii

Norfolk House, which now carries a plaque commemorating its service as the Headquarters at which the invasion of Europe was planned, was a large block of offices. It was officially known as HQ, COSSAC – Chief of Staff to the Supreme Allied Commander, whenever he should be appointed. COSSAC ultimately turned most of itself into SHAEF (Supreme Headquarters Allied Expeditionary Force), probably because of the appointment of an American, and was reorganized on the American system as a fully operational HQ. It swelled to enormous proportions, and finally became wholly ineffective because of the mass of conflicting interests, the immense amount of paper which so easily flows from the modern duplicating machine,[1] and the difficulty of getting 'concurrences' (in American staff-idiom) to any matter that required immediate action. Because of the sheer size there

[1] Paper, floods of it, seems to me to be the curse of modern warfare and perhaps of modern business and University as well.

was always the possibility of what the Americans call, expressively, a 'foul-up' through lack of co-ordination. In that respect the complexities of the Pentagon and the State Department still have for me a nightmarish quality.

In May 1943, COSSAC itself was still small, perhaps forty or fifty officers, though even then it was swelling rapidly as US officers joined it. I found myself working in a small room with Colonel Alms, afterwards to be lost in a Dakota over Malaya, and Charles Wintour, a scholar of Peterhouse, a distinguished journalist, and afterwards Editor of the *Evening Standard*. There were several old friends; many of the small group that had been working at Queen Anne's Gate a year before had been reassembled.

The planning of Rankin 'A' – afterwards known as 'Overlord' – has been described many times in official histories; less often from a worm's-eye point of view. We began early in May; the plan was brought to Washington in July. During that period we worked all day and often through the night. The plan itself went through some twenty editions, each with many maps. Each copy had to be numbered and accounted for; every scrap of paper and blotting-paper had to be burned every night under the eye of an officer. The job of my own section was to set out under guidance the probable European strategy of the operation; I was therefore lucky enough to see the larger picture.

In essence planning an invasion is a vast mathematical problem, with a large number of 'unknowns'; these have to be estimated, or 'guess-timated', and agreed risks taken on them. Our job was to try to build a picture of the reactions of the German Army in Europe to the fact of the invasion of France. Before this could be done we had to have a complete picture of the whereabouts of every German division (there were many different kinds and grades), deployed for the defence of the 'Festung-Europa'. The German system of defence was broadly similar to what our own had been in 1940–41; that is, the coast was held by static infantry divisions and artillery, with mobile forces, armour and motorised infantry lying in reserve at various distances inland. The possible invasion area, from the German point of view, was split in two by the Seine; the most direct threat – because nearest in distance – was to the Belgian coast and the Pas de Calais area, as offering the shortest sea-crossing and the maximum air-cover. So long as the threat existed, their mobile forces had to be split, east and west of the Seine. Therefore the longer the German High Command was kept in doubt as to the real point of attack, the more difficult it would be for them to concentrate quickly the forces for the counter-attack.

The area selected for the invasion attempt must not, if possible, be one of those most strongly held by the enemy in anticipation of the attack; yet it must be well within range of effective fighter-cover from Southern England. The bitter lessons of Norway had been well learnt. It must offer possibilities of enemy airfields that might be captured, to provide further cover; or at least country in which airstrips might be rapidly made to provide operational bases for our fighters. The Invasion Exercises provided many rehearsals for this, often on the South Coast of Wales. It must be in such a position, geographically, as to give a prospect of the quick capture of deep-water ports which could be used for heavy-draught shipping, through which the American reinforcements and supplies must come; and these ports must be capable of being rehabilitated to receive a predicted tonnage within 'X' days, assuming 'Y' amount of damage to them by the retreating German forces. These conditions did in fact focus attention on the ports west of and including Cherbourg.

Once an outline took shape, a thousand details followed. Every bridge and water-way that might be blown up by the enemy had to be marked, measured, and a proportion of bridging provided. The daily expenditure of every kind of ammunition had to be provided for. Hospitals had to be planned and their capacities estimated. The RAF picture – of the German production switch from bombers to fighters (this they had planned too late), the effect of the next nine-month bombing programme on the German war effort, the delaying effect on reinforcement of the new rocket fighters – was central to the planning. Fighter support in the opening phases would be thin, because of the distance and endurance factor; therefore the new technique of quick construction of airstrips, using modern machinery, had to be developed, and troops practised in it. The slopes of the invasion beaches themselves had to be calculated. Indeed the beaches themselves were a perpetual source of anxiety: how would they stand up to the enormous weight of transport, especially tanks, even over steel roadways? Shortly before D-Day there occurred one of many scares in this connection. An academic geologist came forward with the information that one of the Orne beaches had a

Invasion and After 163

substructure of peat, under a thin covering of sand; this, if true, meant that any road-way would eventually disappear under the stress of heavy traffic from the unloading ships. It was necessary to lay on 'Operation Peat', which involved several geologist heroes landing at night, by submarine and collapsible boat, and boring deep holes with augers in the shore. Fortunately it proved a false alarm.

iii

The plans were sent to Washington in July 1943, with Morgan and Kenneth McLean to 'sell' them to the Combined Chiefs of Staff. Various subordinate, conditional, and ancillary plans took us through a hot and dusty August full of raids. Early in September an event occurred which was to change completely my own inglorious war.

The Joint Intelligence Committee in London issued a long paper, an appreciation of the strategical position in Europe. It was mainly concerned with the German war position: and it set out the opinion that – *but for one thing* – the German overall position was strikingly similar, from the point of view of manpower, manufacturing potential, and economic resources, to that which had obtained in September 1918. Thus, in the opinion of the committee, Germany was on the verge of collapse – might even collapse that winter or early next spring – *except* for the one unknown factor: the presence of the Gestapo and the SS Troops. It was impossible to evaluate their restraining influence, or the known internal dissentions in the High Command, or the personal loyalty of these bodies to the Hitlerian ideal, even in defeat, or to the possibility of a last suicidal stand, a Wagnerian Götterdämmerung. But – supposing Germany *were* to collapse early in 1944, without an invasion, and in the midst of the detailed planning . . . ? Nothing would be ready to cope with that vast house of cards, the infinity of resulting problems, the economic and transport chaos, the millions of displaced persons. Europe might have to face rehabilitation without the preliminaries of invasion and reconquest.

All copies of the paper were immediately recalled and destroyed. But the mischief had been done. Morgan sent for me and told me that I was to plan for the military government of North-West Europe; and to have everything ready by 1st January, 1944. By then I knew him well, admiring him above all measure; I told him bluntly that with the staff proposed – I was to be given a major and a GSO3 – the whole thing was unrealistic. He pointed out that I was the only member of his staff who had had any sort of training for politico-military work, and that I did at least know the invasion plans; therefore I should have to become the link between the operational staff and the military government organization. This meant the end of my hopes of going back to my regiment; worse still, it meant involvement in the political controversies and international jealousies that were even then apparent. Sir Roger Lumley, afterwards the Earl of Scarborough, became head of the new section. Six months later the staff of three was swollen to some two hundred and eighty, and moved from pillar to post round various commandeered houses, finally ending in rather grim quarters in Victoria Street. The political issues involved in the appointment of the Supreme Allied Commander still hung in the balance, and the detailed operational planning of the invasion began.

In all this work the expatriate Allied Governments were in close touch with us; they were in a position to estimate at least some of their most pressing needs. Their demands were fantastic in their range and diversity; hundreds of single-cylinder diesel engines to rebuild the Norwegian fishing fleets; miles of nets and twine for making them; enormous quantities of tobacco; massive pumping equipment for the Low Countries in anticipation of the damage to the dykes; equipment for posts and telegraphs; rolling stock, bridging equipment, and, above all, lorries and more lorries to replace the worn-out or commandeered civilian transport. All but a very small proportion of these things had to take a low priority over strictly military equipment; and no one could foretell, with a 'pipe-line' a year at least in length, when the demands would be met, or how they would ever be paid for. It was clear that by far the greater proportion would have to come from America; but how and when? In placing their demands, each country heavily over-bid its hand, and requisitions had to be scaled down and filtered to make some sort of sense.

In the spring of 1944 many American officers arrived to reinforce the staff, which now became SHAEF under Eisenhower. We saw in the headquarters the edges of two great controversies.

Who would have the supreme command, and who would command the British land armies? The former choice was clear, if only because the ultimate American component, including the build-up and the supplies, must so greatly outweigh the British. The military government component became the fifth of the Staff Sections, and was known as G–5. It was then that the Great Schism developed and its fires burned hotly until well after the invasion. The course it took was both amusing and terrifying in its implications. From the very beginning of the operational planning period we had been seeking direction as to how Germany was to be treated, administered, partitioned. I have little doubt that the 'unconditional surrender' formula was a temporary escape from the insoluble problem of a coherent inter-Allied policy, as well as an important factor in prolonging the war. Yet no directions about Germany were forthcoming from the only source competent to issue them – the Combined Chiefs at Washington. There were probably two reasons for this: the Combined Chiefs were too busy with the immediate operational problems, and it was impossible to get provisional agreement as to a hypothetical series of situations which could, at best, receive only provisional and theoretical solutions. So, lacking guidance from above, the Staffs had to follow what became known as the American system; that is, you wrote the orders which you thought might fittingly be sent down to you and which you could probably implement, and sent them upwards as drafts in the hope that they would be ultimately approved, at least in substance, and sent down to you again. Too often these draft directives seemed to get lost in the vast machine of the Pentagon; and, lacking any policy, the 'country handbooks' had to be printed as drafts. This hopeless and heart-breaking delay occurred again and again: notably when Eisenhower, having clamoured for months for directives from Washington, had to decide to go into Germany 'on a strictly military basis', and Alexander, nearly a year later, was forced to do the same thing at Trieste.

But when it came to writing the directives which we should have liked to have received, it became clear that there was a vast divergence of views between the British and American sides. The matter was still further complicated by the arrival of a number of US officers who had had experience of military government in Algiers and Sicily, and who wanted to administer France in the same way. To the British, the idea of administering the oldest civilization in Europe, down to low levels of the Civil Service, by American ex-business men who spoke no French, seemed ludicrous. But a certain American general, who became one of our few hated officers, collected a small private army of his own, and bore them off to Shrivenham to train them on these lines. The British worked on the assumption that once France was liberated, and certain preliminary but essential questions of finance were settled, the French would govern and rehabilitate themselves infinitely better and more rapidly than any US–British Staff. And the same was true of the Low Countries, Denmark and Norway.

Something of the same problem, but far more complex because of its emotional and economic connotations, arose over Germany. The American Presidential election depended largely on the Jewish and Italian votes in that country. Jewish opinion demanded, if not open revenge, at least the policy that Germany should be treated as a country from which all Hitlerite and SS elements must be immediately and mercilessly purged, replacing at once every petty official who had subscribed in any way to Nazism. Furthermore, and this is where the Jewish and big business interests converged, the great prize of the war was to be the Ruhr with its factories, patents, and trade secrets. As the armies lay in the invasion plan, the British forces on the left would be the first to reach the Ruhr; it was rumoured that business interests had attempted to have the plans changed, or, alternatively, to provide for the utterly fantastic operation of crossing the lines of communication of the two forces before the Ruhr was reached. (I have in my files a newspaper cutting from an American newspaper: 'Civil Affairs Lays Magic Carpet for American Business Men'.) When the Ruhr had yielded up its secrets it was to be turned into a pastoral area – the so-called Morgenthau Plan – so as to eliminate future manufacturing competition in Europe. That the Ruhr could never be pastoral, nor the European economy exist without its coal and steel, was irrelevant to this peculiarly inept dream of high finance. No doubt it was conceived in part by the fear of American overproduction, and of renewed German competition in the post-war period; but even Morgenthau could not have predicted that within fifteen years America would be begging Western Germany for financial support, that the Krupp empire would be more powerful than ever, that the German economic recovery would be the envy of Europe, and that Japan's industry would have outstripped all competitors.

A similar clash of views arose over the matter of collaborators in France and Italy, and Nazism in Germany. The American view was politically naïve, lacking the experience or the imagination to picture the conditions of a country in various states of occupation, terrorism, tyranny. We believed that in Vichy France many of the important figures – such as the factory owners – had been forced into collaboration of a sort, and that the 'Hun-happy' collaborators would in due time get what was coming to them. In Germany, myriads of small officials and factory-owners of every kind would have owed outward allegiance to the Nazis; it was the price of their livelihood if not of their lives. The so-called de-Nazification would be a slow, cautious and tricky process. There was one real priority after the occupation; to rebuild quickly so as to get the essential industries working again. The prime necessities for Europe would be steel and coal; a million tons of coal might save Northern Italy from Communism, given rolling-stock and lorries and fertilizers, Europe might have a chance to feed herself and avoid the horror of famine and the packed Displaced Persons Camps, within two years. Therefore, detailed de-Nazification must wait, and for the first phase we must work through Western German officials who were on the spot and could command some measure of co-operation from their fellows.

So the German Handbook was written, sent to Washington for approval, and returned to us with some violence of comment, saying that the policy which had been evolved for the treatment of Germany was insufficiently 'tough'. The Jewish tide was then flowing strongly, and a lieutenant of Morgenthau's, one Bernstein, was sent to watch our planning, disguised as a full colonel in the Finance Section. In the early summer during the invasion, Eisenhower's proclamation on entering Germany was drafted and redrafted countless times. Eventually it was approved, and handed over to the US side for translation.

The Proclamation came back to us translated. My own German was not good enough to spot its subtle bias, but the Foreign Office told us that it contained a number of *tourneurs de phrase* which would only have been used by a German Jew. We had it re-translated. While it was being printed, Bernstein had the presses stopped, and ordered the second clause to be cut out from the first sentence of the second paragraph, which ran: 'Wir kommen als siegreiches Heer, jedoch nicht als Unterdrücker.' (We come as a conquering army, but *not* as oppressors.) The omission was significant, and had been made on private initiative without the approval of the General Staff. I took it straight to Morgan. I was not in on the resultant row, but the agreed text was restored by Eisenhower's own order.

In the spring we moved to Bushey Park, to a hutted camp, which was steadily but inaccurately shot at by flying bombs. My own sense of futility and obstruction grew, though I remained as liaison officer between the operational section and military government; and the work on Europe's future acquired a certain unreality as the invasion date drew nearer. Meanwhile, men, armour and supplies rolled through England to the sea and the waiting ships; the magnificent spectacle undimmed by the knowledge that the dockers who helped with the loading would steal many batteries and tools from the vehicles to sell them on the black market.

My own depression increased. 'We fought at Arques, brave Crillon, and you were not there.' I moved restlessly between Advanced HQ near Portsmouth, and Rear at Bushey. The story of the terrible decision over the date of the invasion has already been told, and how near Eisenhower's gamble on the weather came to failure. Less well-known is the story of how the news of the invasion broke, twenty-four hours before it actually occurred. A journalist had bribed a clerk in the transmitting service of the only channel that was not then subject to strict censorship – the early morning service to Russia. He knew that the invasion was imminent, but did not know the exact date or hour. He therefore arranged that the news should be broadcast – and arranged with his paper to listen – *unless* he warned his accomplice by telephone that it was 'off'. The journalist went down to the West Country to see the airborne forces take off, mislaid his pass, got arrested, and was powerless to stop the message going out. There was nothing to be done; to the German High Command it may have seemed no more than another attempt at deception. We learnt afterwards that most of the German coastal troops had, in fact, gone up to breakfast after the morning stand-to, thinking that no landing would take place in that weather.

iv

In August 1944 I was sent on a mission to Italy; partly to find out something at first hand of what was happening in military government there, partly to liaise over arrangements for the Allied landing in Southern France in the Marseilles area, partly to find out the views of Allied Forces HQ as to what was likely to happen to military government when the armies entered Austria, since command responsibility for that country had not yet been assigned.

After extreme security precautions – the party was isolated for a day under guard in a country house in Hampshire – we took off late at night in a Halifax. It was said that we were to fly far out into the Atlantic, to avoid the German night-fighters who were still operating over the Bay of Biscay. We touched down for breakfast at Rabat, where I had my first glimpse of Africa; flew on in an ancient Dakota, that faithful packhorse in which I was to travel so much in the next twelve months; crossed the Moroccan mountains and the appalling desolation caused by the Arab and his goat; changed planes again at Algiers; thence over Pantellaria and the Straits of Messina which I had last seen twenty years before on my way to India. We came to Capodocchino, and I was taken to Caserta, the summer palace of the King of Naples some fifteen miles north of that city, and not far from the ancient town of Capua. I had no idea then that Caserta was to be my home for many months; that fantastic palace deserves some description.

It is a vast red-brick building of many courts, on the edge of a rather sordid modern town; built to compete in 'la gloire' with Versailles. It included a miniature theatre, of elaborate baroque decoration; endless passages that seemed to obey no rational plan, and often forced one to change levels to reach a given destination; huge rooms with ceilings and cornices decorated, rather uncertainly, with classical episodes in fading pigments; scanty and temperamental sanitation. The water-supply, precarious at the best of times, reached the Palace by an aqueduct some miles long, which followed the contours of the foot-hills to the north; its waters when they reached us reeked with chlorine, and the aqueduct itself was always liable to collapse unexpectedly.

To the north, a magnificent landscaped vista stretched up to the hills; ornamental waters and statuary of little merit flanking the great avenue that leads up step by step to a grotto and Actaeon's Fountain, a subject of ribald comment by the troops. West of the avenue was a mass of huts, tents and messes: higher up towards the hills, the villas where the generals lived. It was picturesque, unhealthy, and because of its straggling nature, a great waster of time in conferences and such-like.

AFHQ under F–M. Wilson had moved there from Algiers a few weeks before. The huge reception room at the head of the marble staircase still contained a number of bad and massive eighteenth-century pictures; it was said that one of them, *The Flight of the Children of Israel from Egypt*, was a fair representation of the HQ's move. The fighting troops under Alexander's Allied Armies in Italy were far up the peninsula: all we saw of the war was a few ineffectual raids, and one explosion of a nearby ammunition dump.

My business was quickly done; it involved a series of discussions with General Charles Spofford, later to become my opposite number in the integrated Anglo-American staff, and later still Chairman of the NATO Council of Deputies: in civil life head of a great firm of New York lawyers, a man of great charm, and with an immensely able brain. I met some of the Free French leaders, including de Lattre de Tassigny; the Marseilles plan was obviously unpopular, and landing-craft and stores were in short supply. As things turned out, this miniature and subordinate invasion was practically unopposed; it was of no strategic value in the over-all plan for the invasion of France, and did little except tie up vast quantities of shipping, landing-craft and stores which would have been far better employed elsewhere. The price of the slow laborious progress up Italy, where sea-power and landing craft could have outflanked the German defences at many points, reflected the perpetual inter-Allied conflict over allocations for the different theatres. The Resistance of South-East France, in which my friend and sometime pupil, Francis Cammaerts, had played a particularly gallant part for nearly four years, could probably have taken care of what German forces remained; for everything of fighting value had been withdrawn to the *Schwerpunkt* in the north.

I was then moved to Paris, to an office in the Petites Ecuries at Versailles, and a billet in the Rue de la Reine, a small house whose owner was believed to be in a German concentration camp and who seemed to have built up a specialized library of sixteenth-century French pornographic literature. Paris that autumn was cold and dispiriting, after the first honeymoon welcome. Relief at the liberation was balanced by much indignation at the needlessly inaccurate bombing, particularly in the suburbs through which ran the 'ring' lines round Paris. Many Frenchmen yearned openly for the days of the occupying Germans, who were, they said, 'très korrekt' in their behaviour. The domestic habits of the German officers were certainly strange; in a flat at St Cloud where I was billeted for a time my predecessors had apparently lit cooking-fires on the parquet flooring, and the bath was unusable because of the coating of carbonate of lime; they had pickled in it vast quantities of eggs. A little later I saw the torture-chambers at Gestapo HQ, including the 'wall of fire' and the apparatus for the 'Prefects' Beating', that refined piece of sadistic ingenuity. But for the average Frenchman life must have been tolerable, and there was much money to be made on the black market which had been developed with great and cynical elaboration. I got to know a family in the street of my billet where the meat rations would be delivered by the butcher early in the morning, and their black-market allocation, on a standing order, a little later in the day.

The battle was static. Eisenhower seemed effectively insulated from all contact with us. Planning for Germany seemed pointless, and SHAEF itself became, so far as I could see, buried under a flood of rather futile memoranda, papers, and such like. And my own work was quite insufficient to keep me busy.

In the midst of this period of despondency a signal arrived from Italy: could I be released to be DACOS[1] at AFHQ? My general agreed, and I flew down to Italy to be vetted by F-M. Wilson and the Chief Administrative Officer, General George Clark, before the appointment was confirmed. Again I went to Caserta; the interviews seemed satisfactory, but I learnt with some consternation that my two predecessors, both regulars, were being re-posted because they had 'failed to obtain the cooperation' of the thirty or forty US officers who constituted about half of the integrated staff of G–5. I was ordered to go

---

[1] Deputy Assistant Chief of Staff: that is, the British head of a staff section, the A.C.O.S. in this case being an American.

back to Versailles, and thence to London, to see what was happening to the Austrian planning and the setting-up of the Austrian Control Commission. The two flights were not without excitement; on the way down to Marseilles an American colonel and I had to go forward and tell the charming but very young pilot that the spot-heights of French hills were in metres, not in feet – this was after we had narrowly shaved two of them – and on the return the pilot failed to find the airfield at Orly, so that we circled the roofs of Paris for some forty minutes in the falling October dusk.

After a fortnight I flew back to Caserta, this time for good; within a week or two I was faced with a sequence of crises. For a start, the whole pattern of the headquarters changed almost overnight. Wilson went to Washington; Alexander moved back from Allied Armies in Italy, to become Supreme Allied Commander; and the move provoked the highly indiscreet signal which went through military circles like the proverbial dose of salts 'So the Poacher has now become the Gamekeeper.' Alexander brought with him as his Chief Administrative Officer Brian Robertson, with John Harding as his Chief of Staff. I had seen something of the system – a natural and efficient one – by which a change on this scale at the highest levels involved almost complete reposting at the lower levels. For the Services in wartime it does not matter greatly – save for personal disappointment and bitterness – since there is no real redundancy; I had vivid memories of what happened when Montgomery took over at St Paul's School in the autumn of 1943. But it seemed probable that I, as the nominee of those who had just been displaced, would be sacked also; and matters were complicated by Charles Spofford's recall to Washington; so that I was left for some months in sole charge of the Staff Section. It was clear that I was being watched with a view to dismissal; my masters knew, I think, that I knew this. It did not matter greatly; as a middle-aged ex-civilian – I was then forty-three – I could always return to Cambridge, and my 'war' had in any event cost me so far about half my annual stipend and earnings. For some weeks the situation provided excitement and amusement; then, I suppose, the decision was taken that I should not be sacked. Thereafter I had nothing but the utmost courtesy and help from Robertson and Harding, both among the very greatest of soldiers.

XI

ITALY, 1944-5

i

My American opposite number General Charles Spofford, left, as I have said, for Washington, and I found myself with a very large and miscellaneous staff section, which included seven full colonels, as well as the specialists in the different countries that we were concerned with, and a wide variety of personalities, British and American. We were responsible for the Military Government side in Italy, whose complicated and shifting status as a co-belligerent had exercised Macmillan's ingenuity – he was then Political Adviser to Alexander – in producing a paper called 'Muting the Middle C', when the Allied Control Commission in Rome became the Allied Commission. We were to assume a general responsibility for the rehabilitation of Greece. After endless argument it had been decided that Austria should be administered and fed from Italy, and planning for that was in progress. As and when the Germans left Jugoslavia that would have to be rehabilitated too.

The strategy of the slow and laborious advance up Italy was halted on the Gothic line, and south of Florence the country had to be rebuilt: the little white towns along the coastal road between Naples and Rome were still pulverized from explosives. Under the plaster or stucco surface the masonry was crude and loose. Only Gaeta, which I knew so well from a copy of Richard Wilson's painting in my room, was unscathed. Cassino seemed to have been driven into the very hillside by the massed artillery. There was an exquisite clear river running beside it, that looked as if it might have come from a Wiltshire valley, and surely held trout. And that springtime the splintered olives put out their new shoots and men began to plant corn in the valley.

At Caserta I shared a big hut with an RAMC Brigadier; the winter was cold and unpleasant. Every morning I was shown a long sick list of my staff, mainly from jaundice, which was taken very seriously just then. One does not often see oranges hanging on trees, with snow underfoot. Life was more strenuous than I had ever known it. After an early breakfast I went to my office to read cables: then held my own conference for the heads of sections: and then walked through the long corridor to the Chief Administrative Officer's Conference. Thereafter anything might happen; I kept check-lists, re-typed every night, with between one and two hundred items always heating up in their varying degrees, apt to be the subjects of midnight calls or urgent telephone summonses. I usually took a half-day off, once a month. On one occasion we collected some miscellaneous surrendered Italian shotguns and highly suspect ammunition, and went out, four of us, to shoot snipe in the Volturno Marshes where the battle had been. It was a bitterly cold day, with snow on the mountains; a gale was blowing on the Mediterranean, and the line of surf to the west looked as though it were towering high above the marshland. We picked up the Italian gamekeeper, and walked down a muddy lane to the marsh. Some miserable cottages fronted on the lane. In the vegetable patch in front of one there were three graves, a sapper, an infantryman and a signaller; the rough wooden crosses with the helmets still on top. I wanted to make a poem of that day, but it did not come. In the marshes I recall that I shot a mallard, already wounded, and bone-thin.

One was, I suppose, still an arithmetician, but at least there was the satisfaction of giving an order and seeing the results on the ground; as when we dropped supplies on a snow-bound village in the Appennines a few hours after getting the emergency call. Sometimes I flew to Athens for a day or two, and once to London to visit the Foreign Office on some matter which I forget. As the weather improved I took my monthly half-days on the Bay of Naples, sailing, alone, a lovely Star-Class boat; I climbed Vesuvius, which had recently erupted, and knew the exhilaration of striding down the ash-slide, twenty feet to a step. There was Cumae, and the Sybil's Cave, with the rusting

German machine-guns sited on the low shore where Aeneas landed; Avernus with a flock of seagulls on the lake, and an American rest-camp on the further shore, a loudspeaker playing jazz music, that echoed across the narrows where Caesar's fleet had lain. Once, on the way to Rome, I stopped with my driver to eat sandwiches on the shore of Lake Nemi, and saw the Sacred Grove across the water. A seedy-looking man came up to us wanting to talk, and we tried in various languages to establish contact. Finally we hit on dog-Latin; he was a Rumanian priest in some sort of disguise, who had escaped across the Adriatic to Bari, and walked across Italy. There was another occasion when I had to use Latin; the Archbishop of Bosnia and Herzegovina wished to visit His Holiness, and sought the permission of the Supreme Allied Commander. The letter was in Latin; staff sections were invited to comment from the political angle, and we achieved a Latin Minute. I think it began: 'Eructavit cor meum'.

Roosevelt died; and we had a terrific and badly-drilled parade of US troops. Psychiatrists talk about 'father figures' embodied in political leaders, and I had always mistrusted this; but there was no doubt as to the response to Roosevelt. My American friends seemed stunned, as if their world had fallen apart; Roosevelts' immense *mana*, his legendary power and control, his friendship with Churchill, all suggested that the new dispensation would see the gravest political changes. With my US officers I had no personal troubles; our views, policies, and behaviour were widely different, but it was essential to keep international friction to its minimum. So my first action was to invite each of the US colonels in turn to dine in my mess, and to drink and talk of their troubles in my hut afterwards. If there were difficulties with the US side I took them to my friend the Deputy Chief of Staff, Lyman C. Lemnitzer, whom I regard as one of the finest men I have met. It was he who, with Terence Airey, went to Berne to negotiate the surrender of the German forces in Italy, under the pretext of buying a dachshund in that city; which is the point of the verses quoted later.

My work took me often to Rome, where the Allied Commission lived in great luxury, presided over by Maurice Lush, with Tony Quayle as his Aide. I have never quite forgiven him for his (alleged) destruction of the whole of the edition of *Amgothic Rhymes,* written by various members of his staff, and reflecting wittily on Allied Military Government. Fortunately a couple of verses remain in my memory:

> 'We are Lord Rennell's Army,
> We never fire a shot –
> When danger's o'er we come ashore
> And set up as Amgot . . .
>
> Elect of Monty Norman
> Our heads are bankers all –
> The proud élite of Lombard Street,
> Cornhill and London Wall . . .

ii

I had two 'masters' in the hierarchy of the headquarters. I was directly responsible to Lt-Gen Sir Brian Robertson, then Chief Administrative Officer; I attended his morning conference daily, and went to see him, or was sent for, several times a day. The other I saw less of; he was the Chief of Staff, Sir John Harding. Both demanded that problems, or their proposed solutions, should be set out with the utmost economy of language. Robertson was rather silent, a little grim, appearing humourless; a finely-tempered brain, impatient of fools, and leaving one with a feeling that he was to be trusted absolutely.

In dealing with these men – and my luck in serving them never ceased to astonish me – I was continually puzzled by one thing. The very great men gave me, as their subordinate, the continual impression of being ahead of, or in control of, events, which in the last resort could be no more than a vast tissue of probabilities, themselves woven out of a very large number of variable factors. Or were they actually controlling, shaping events as they emerged out of time? This was obviously true when a battle was being fought, a campaign planned in all its chess-moves, and the counter-moves that might have to be rapidly extemporized but, in outline, foreseen; but this? By contrast the lesser men – I had served three, perhaps four of them – always gave the impression that they were running behind time, so that every mental movement was just that fraction slow; an oarsman's blade late into the water, the shot-column flung a foot behind the rising bird. And so a mental condition of anxiety, frustration, and perhaps – the outcome of both – of disloyalty, might build up.

Looking back, I do not think it could have been any kind of strategic clairvoyance or control of events. These men had been trained over the years to select what seemed to them the central issues, and to concentrate their powers upon them to the exclusion of anything that seemed to them of minor weight. The whole complex staff system existed to relieve them of all detail, while they retained the full responsibility for the operation. They had also been trained in the art of forming patterns, rapidly and surely, out of the multiple factors that the problems of war presented. Those patterns had to have, like Blake's pictures, the 'hard and wiry line' that made thought capable of being translated rapidly into efficient action. It is this speed of thought and action that makes the soldier turned politician or diplomat impatient of the slow maturing of political thinking, of the gradual manipulation of events in time. Behind each pattern there must have been thousands of factors, full of subtleties and ambivalences if one stopped to analyse, the stuff of politics but not of war, which they rejected ruthlessly, knowing that the problem was moving, and changing, even as it was being assessed, in the remorseless time-stream. By the very rapidity with which pattern was imposed the situation took as it were a consistent and comprehensive shape. But, while the solution in their minds seemed clear-cut, it had also to retain the potential for quick re-shaping. Perhaps the whole process was like that which I had watched in the mind of a great barrister; the mass of documents, instructions, evidence, that would finally be reduced to an opinion on a single sheet of foolscap.

I had to take stock of my American officers, and watch the tensions that inevitably develop in an integrated staff. Most of them were irregulars, university-trained; they included many lawyers. Several things struck me immediately. There was a fear of and respect for rank that seemed peculiar in a democratic country; even a half-step up made a difference, so that a major would not, unless driven to it, argue with a half-colonel. Perhaps that was because of the rigid, comprehensive and secret system of reporting on 'the man below'. There was also, I thought, a certain uneasiness in their relations with the enlisted men; long afterwards an American friend suggested the reason. There seemed to be no real system of selecting men of officer quality from the ranks, once they got overseas; so that a number of the officers seemed aware that their men might be more intelligent than themselves, and were afraid of giving themselves away.

In all this there was the inevitable and basic clash between the interests of different Staff Branches; and the conflicting claims were themselves susceptible of many shadings. We go into an occupied country with the commitment to rehabilitate the country only so far as is necessary to further the military effort, and to prevent 'disease and unrest' that might impede that effort. Clearly, transport – bridges, roads, railways – is a first priority. You must bring in food for the civilian population. How much? A theoretical 1,200 – 1,500 calories – the fashionable dieting figure, which is starvation for a manual worker. But how many extra calories will the average man or woman get from the country? In the country itself, quite a lot; in the towns probably very little. What about the fishing villages, with no agricultural hinterland, their nets rotted and their boats commandeered by the Germans or by ourselves? How will they live? What can you do about the black-market? Probably nothing. I had seen American troops auctioning their K-rations under the Arc de Triomphe, and knew that a million and a quarter five-gallon petrol cans had been abstracted from the great motor-convoy column that ran incessantly from Cherbourg and Brest to supply depots nearer the battle.

But in Italy the problem had all sorts of curious ramifications. Sicily, for instance, normally grows enough corn to feed herself, but the price on the Black Market was so high that the Sicilians were running it over the Straits of Messina in small vessels at night to sell to the mainland, and refused to release it to their own townspeople.[1] Therefore we had to take up valuable Liberty ships to run in some 5,000 tons of grain a month to Sicily. No doubt it would have been possible to have coerced the farmers, and stopped the smuggling; but all that meant troops, police, local riots and then more troops, who could not be spared. There was also an olive-oil problem; because of a fluctuating market, and no consumer goods to be bought in the shops, the peasants

[1] Much the same thing happened in the Irish famine of 1845-8, when quanties of wheat, barley and livestock were exported from a famine country, while maize was being imported from the U.S. But this was a failure of government.

held on to it, even sealed it up in walls. For what they did sell, the price they got was so high that they refused to undertake the labour of pressing it again and again; for out of these pressings came oils of successively lower quality, and finally residue used in soap-making. So there was no material for the soap factories, even if we could bring them caustic potash. Without soap they could not wash; lice appeared among the city populations; with lice came typhus. Anything that endangered the health of the troops – and there were many in and around Naples – could not be tolerated; therefore vast quantities of DDT powder had to be imported, and the inhabitants forcibly disinfected.

iii

'VE' Day came, the culmination of mysterious comings and goings, rumours and counter-rumours, which deprived the official announcement of any real exhilaration. That evening I took a truck and went up to the narrow valley that joins the walled city of Caserta Vecchia to the head of the valley in which the palace lies, and looked down on the plain and the modern rather sordid town. It was blazing with light, and even at a range of three miles was noisy and strident:

> The doors of the dovecotes opened one by one
> And the half-moulted birds blinked for a while at the light
> Looking for the withered olives we had made ready for them.
> Airey and Lemnitzer bought a dachshund in Berne.
> The delegates fawned in our tents, in the Palaces, and the scraps of paper were signed.
> And all the Americans shot off their pistols, and the RAF their flares.
> At the Headquarters they started to throw the files out of the windows,
> (So we had fought, four had died miles from the battle)
> – But that was wrong, for the Chief had to write his Despatches
> – So they threw out toilet paper instead.
> Sit back on the ridge above Actaeon's Fountain.
> Sit back and watch the lights come on in Europe.
> Lights in Turin, with thirty murders a night.

Lights in Klagenfurt, with the Jug patrols in the streets,
Lights in Macedonia, where the gold and the Stens are hidden.
Lights in the Val d'Aosta, where Allies chaffer for honour
(To gild Pétain's surrender, or raise the sunk ships at Oran?)
Lights in Damascus, from the bursting seventy-fives.

And a lady MP visited Buchenwald.

No one quite knew what might happen in the north. We had no idea where the Russians would stop, since the triple pillars seemed to have sold us to them at Yalta in an access of good-fellowship. Indeed, they claimed much; a Russian column even came down into North Italy and gate-crashed – literally – into one of our prisoner-of-war camps, taking many of them off in lorries to death and probably torture. A sealed train of refugees was returned to Yugoslavia to suffer the same fate.

Clearly there was no respite, only a horrible uncertainty:

So we moved the tanks to Udine, and the guns to Monfalcone,
And held our conferences, and printed more paper money,
And saw the weasels settle to wait on the river-lines,
Wondering what teeth should be sharpened   or drawn that peace might come.

I took a car and drove up through Rome to Florence, which looked sad and battered; thence over the mountains, and crossed the Po on a pontoon-bridge. Its bed was dry and sandy, and there was no time to look for amber there, as Euripides had written. Then on for a night to Udine, and afterwards a glimpse of the coast. All along it, from Venice to Trieste, every craft – down to rowing-boats and hulks – had a large red star painted on it, the sign that the Jugoslavs were claiming it as booty. They were in occupation of Trieste, and so were Freyburg's men, and the situation there was said to be hair-triggered. So up, over the Bolzano, where the great bridge was held at either end by British and Jugoslav patrols, fingering their machine-pistols uneasily and watching each other's every move. I remember that I stopped to watch a deep rocky pool that looked as if it must have held fish. Thence across the Pass and the spring flowers, into Villach and Klagenfurt, climbing the Pass with difficulty, for my Humber Snipe had served in the desert and was now growing very tired.

In Villach itself something of the complexity of the aftermath became apparent. Here Tito was running a private concentration camp, with some two thousand men, women and children in it; typhus had broken out, and no one was allowed into it, not even the Red Cross. It was quite possible that the Jugoslavs might try to hold Carinthia by force; they had already announced their intention of keeping Trieste permanently.

To the west of us reports said that the situation was almost as sensitive. The French were claiming the Val d'Aosta, which supplied Nice with water and electricity, as some compensation for their losses and humiliation; and the French Resistance of South-East France were for the moment out of hand. British and Free French forces were face to face there, with artillery laid on each other. In every town in North Italy the partisans, with the arms and ammunition we had dropped on them, were paying off old scores; each morning the lamp-posts had their crop of corpses, and bodies lay in the dark alleys.

Klagenfurt itself was in a state of some excitement; it too was occupied simultaneously by British and Jugoslavs. The town was beginning to fill with refugees trying to get away from the Russians, who seemed unlikely to stop for any political agreement; and the householders were imploring British officers to commandeer their houses to give them some measure of protection.

Next day I went out from Klagenfurt to see some of the local 'discoveries'; one was a series of caves full of pictures and art treasures, Nazi loot which had been concentrated in that area for the last stand in the mountain perimeter. All this would have to be sorted out some day. Another was the nucleus of what had been intended to be the Nazi National Library. The building was a huge monastery, with loggias and cloisters opening on the inner-courtyards. Every available space was piled solid with books, a librarian's nightmare: books of every language, binding and description, thrown together at random. I pulled out two or three; some from Polish and French universities, Czech private libraries, and – very strangely – a Victorian album of photographs presented to their English governess by some children whom she had been teaching at an Austrian schloss.

So back to Caserta, to make my report to Brian Robertson, and to try to meet the endless demands for men, resources, food and hospital equipment, and above all men to cope with the ever rising flood of displaced persons. There were some curious incidents: a party of VIP prisoners was found at a secret camp at Dobbiacco, and flown down to Naples, where I met them and talked with Niemoeller and a German professor of theology who had been scientifically beaten on repeated occasions. He bore little malice; the Nazis had done it, he said, not in any lust of sadism, but 'like a surgical operation'.

A Jewish commander of a certain unit took it upon himself to set up a private 'rescue line' for Jewish refugees, using service resources and sending them to the Adriatic for illegal shipment to Israel. Communism was rife in all the industrial cities, aggravated by unemployment and the presence of partisan weapons as well as by the lack of raw materials. In the great shipyards of Monfalcone there were many vessels half-completed on the stocks. It would take no great effort to finish them, and cut the unemployment there; but when we suggested this to Washington we were met with a flat refusal. There would be an immense surplus of Allied merchant shipping, and we must do nothing to enlarge it. The 'Liberty Ships', on which there were so many mixed opinions, would have to be used somehow, since they represented an enormous capital investment. In this there was again discernible a certain political naïveté; as there was in the proposal to send a mission to Greece – which had been the third largest maritime carrier in the world – to teach them to reorganize their mercantile fleet.

Strangest of all the crises that came my way, and one which made the signals from Washington and London 'hot' for some days, was the affair of what I shall call the 'X' Pit. Not far from Trieste, on a romantic-looking hillside, a British mining company had once sent a deep vertical shaft, in an unsuccessful quest for minerals; this was before the first war. The shaft had long been abandoned, but was still open, a circular hole perhaps a dozen feet across. On a fine June day a number of lorries, apparently filled with prisoners and a number of armed men, together with some horses, arrived at the pit. The only witnesses of what followed were a number of children, at play some distance down the slope of the big hill. They were unable to say – naturally enough – who the armed men were, and who the prisoners, but they thought there were some twenty lorry loads of the latter. Some, they said, were taken to the edge of the pit and shot in the back of the head; others were invited, at pistol-point, to leap across the opening. When all were disposed of, the horses were brought up, shot, and pushed into the opening. Then the lorries drove away.

No confirmation was possible. The evidence was the trampled mouth of the pit, a mass of empty cartridge cases, the children's story and a horrible smell. But there was a rumour in Trieste that two Allied soldiers were among those shot, and that didn't help the tension.

The physical difficulty of investigating proved insuperable. An officer was lowered into the pit, and taken out semi-asphyxiated. Then the Engineers rigged a gantry over it, and let down chains with grapnels; these came up covered with putrifying horse-flesh. There was only one possible action, to drive a tunnel at right-angles through the whole hill-side to intersect, if possible, the base of the shaft. That would have taken many months, and even if the base were found there would be no more than a mass of corruption. The pit was sealed and left.

iv

In the weeks that followed I have an impression of endless conferences, of the usual frustrations of trying to obtain directives for problems that had turned slowly from military to political and a good deal of travelling about the Mediterranean Theatre. I flew back to London to the Foreign Office; to Trieste with W. G. Morgan for a conference at Duino Castle with Tito's staff, and saw that loveliest of all views and the terraced gardens down to the Adriatic, and thought of Rilke. It was there that I collapsed one morning while waiting for a conference to begin. I remember that they put me in a caravan bunk, and summoned a very young Army doctor, who told me I had twenty-four hours to live. They took me to Udine to hospital. Four days later I flew back to Caserta, whence Brian Robertson indignantly sent me for a month's sick-leave to Positano. But then three of my colonels fell sick, and I returned after a week.

. . . What limb is set by honour?
In the hospital ward flies swarm on moist flesh
And Italian girls scrub the floors, and think of the evening's
  lover.

Ether drifts through the balconies.
   There's no reality here:
Or in the stone graveyard of the Acropolis, or among the
   gardens at Versailles.
No answer from Cumae, whence Virgil's lines are cut,
Deep in white marble, gold-lettered, smeared and defaced,
With pencil signatures of pilgrims.
   (*Si quid mea carmina possunt!*)
The Roman nobility sits in the night clubs, at cards,
Measuring out their lives and loves with Allied lire, with dice,
To raging saxophones, against the sea-blue night.

They did just that, the Italian aristocracy, and Positano was noisy with their beach-parties and dances. The future of the *latefundia,* their great estates, was in doubt. The currency was subject to a steady inflation and they were enjoying themselves while the money lasted. I spoke to some of them about the future; they shrugged their shoulders and answered that they would go to America and make their fortunes when the money was finished: meanwhile . . . Italy's bitterness, a selfish and absentee landowner class, recalled something of Ireland in the eighteenth century. I slept and bathed in the blue waters, and went back to the palace.

XII

CAMBRIDGE POST-WAR

i

I left Caserta at the end of August 1945 with no great regrets. Because I had joined up well over-age my release group was a high one. The work in Italy and Austria was approaching its next stage. A number of regular officers, who saw themselves getting involved in the snakes-and-ladders game of promotion (with the betting heavily on the snakes) were looking hungrily at my job. Worst of all, the highest-ranking officers, who, while the battle was on were content to let us work in our own way, were starting to take an embarrassing interest in our signals to Washington, London, Athens, Vienna, and to call for endless and needless explanations and statistics. Alexander had left for Canada to be Governor-General. Brian Robertson had been called north to impose order upon Germany, and to put into effect my friend G. D. H. Heyman's plan for Allied Military Government. On the morning he received the signal asking him to go, he sent for me, and questioned me about affairs in Allied Military Government in Germany. I answered as best I could: my friends had described them as chaotic. I had seen the Commission forming up at SHAEF, but I may have been exaggerating when I said that I knew of only two men who were able, and completely honest, in that formation at that stage. Robertson decided to go; perhaps I might have gone with him, but it would not have been right to have agreed to serve for less than two years. It now seems to me part of the tragedy of Europe that, at that particular stage, many of the amateur soldiers (and some of the professionals) who were called on to clean up Europe were of no great calibre or distinction. Often they had no jobs in civil life, and were very content to accept the immense tax-free salaries offered by UNRRA (whose personnel were tied to the US scales), or to enjoy for a short time more some official status and privileges (sometimes much abused) in the occupied countries.

A few days at the War Office and the Foreign Office, a sheaf of the last 'secret' letters to my Caserta friends; a solemn processing at Olympia and the issue of new clothing: and there was time to look round. A letter was waiting for me from one of my ex-pupils, a distinguished airman, poet, and afterwards a diplomat.[1] We had met at HQ, and after the battle was over, we used sometimes to take up a captured German aircraft from the little field near the palace, and fly her over the Sorrento Peninsula. Usually we took a Fieseler Storch, the equivalent of the old Lysander. My friend knew no German, so I had to interpret the controls. We always believed that a certain knob, if you pulled it, would blow up the plane. Here is the letter, which seems to me to express a dominant mood:

'I'm sitting outside my tent, three miles from the Northern mountains. There are no foothills between: these green, splendidly cultivated fields just end – Bump – *Finis,* like the writing on Puck's Wall. It's hard to trust the maps that there is anything beyond them. I've climbed and peered further, but there were only more rocks. My world has shrunk from Caserta's cocksure and dusty Olympia to a few fields. . . .

'Squadron life is utterly idle, and has been for three months. I came sleepwalking and yet was soon mistrusted as a dangerous, restless and dynamic person who wouldn't leave well alone. But for my drowsiness I too would have been shocked at the utter apathy and listlessness that hang down on all the veteran units here. There is no effort to face the fact that the fighting is over, for the moment, all over the world. The pretence is that ops. are suspended, call it leave or stand-down or what you will, and everyone joins in the conspiracy to exclude constructive thought, and to retain and recreate (so emptily) the devil-may-care atmosphere of the great days.'[2]

[1] R. A. Burrows: sometime Chancellor's English Medallist.
[2] I found this to be true: some of the ex-Service men turned undergraduate tried to regress into the security and good fellowship of some RAF messes near Cambridge, and, for a time, seemed unable to go forward.

The very name of this formation, Desert Air Force, is as outworn and as dustily nostalgic as the dying capers of the Two Types.[1]

'I think you will find this an outstanding problem, perhaps your most difficult, when the warriors begin to flow back to Cambridge. It will be penitentiary work, re-educating gangsters to take interest in intricacies that have no sharp solution, and beauties that are not sudden and fierce. On top of these will be the new, young lot who will tend to be corrupted into fashionable killing of memories they haven't got. Most dangerous of all will be the teachers who have not gone into the dirt (many of them will think they have) who may try to play down the past sufferings and deny shock to shocked minds. These may infuriate the older, experienced crowd and give false values to the new. If so, they will destroy much that might have been gained from the war years.

'That's where the few who have knowledge of both worlds can play so invaluable a part as peacemakers between fact and fancy and ideal. You alone can impress both the cynical experienced folk and the pseudo-cynical, inexperienced and eager newcomers. You can tactfully interpret to the veterans the well-meaning tactlessness of their masters who do not understand. You may even be able, very very slowly, to teach the lessons of experience to those who preach from theory alone. It'll be difficult, sometimes maddening. How will you keep from snarling when plump Dons are re-arranging Europe between liqueurs? They won't have seen the legions of DPs, nor the exhausted apathy of Italy, nor Tito's peasant, confident cunning. Their Russia will be that of the Left Book Club and the wartime press. But if you say: "I was there and I know . . ." you'll be described, first as an unenlightened simpleton who couldn't see beyond his nose, and eventually as a crashing military bore.'

---

[1] 'Jon's' cartoons were republished in 1960: they went well with the sugary sweetness of *Lili Marlene*, surely the most efficient of all war songs, and far from simple in its psychological implications.

ii

Cambridge was preparing itself for the first regular October Term for six years. Portway, the pre-war Senior Tutor, was still in India, where he was President of an Officer Selection Board, and seemed unlikely to return for some months. The acting Senior Tutor had clearly had enough of it. Six Fellows, two of them over-age for service, had been running the college, combining various offices and acting as hosts to the two bodies to whom we had offered hospitality.

It was necessary to take stock of the position and of the problems confronting us. First of all it was clear that there was a great cleavage between those who had gone to the war and those who had stayed (this I had seen twenty years before in Calcutta), and so it was to continue for a decade, perhaps more, and to influence many elections and appointments. Those who had stayed thought, quite naturally, that they had borne the burden of the day, while we had been 'swanning around' Europe. A newly-elected Fellow made this very clear to me. It was some years later that a famous doctor said bitterly: 'If you want to get on in this place, grow a beard and throw away your medals!' The majority of the dons seemed supremely uninterested in Europe and its problems; many of them voted left at the '45 General Election.

> ... 'A murmur comes from England, where the great men
> Sling mud against the moon, or claim their due
> Naked, for Corioli.'

I tried to assess my own position. As a result of the war I had lost six years of scholarship. Others had taken over most of the lecture courses which I had started, and I decided to settle down and write new ones. My rooms had been used as a guest-room during the war; one result was that a number of my books had been stolen. For those six years I had lost perhaps half my normal earnings. For some months the problems that I had played with in the Mediterranean Theatre kept circling in my mind and would not let me sleep; but that was nothing new, since I had not slept well since my boyhood in The Troubles. A rough landing in an Auster aircraft at Granville had left me with a damaged hip, though this was not to culminate in a major operation at a military hospital till ten years later. The college governing body was again facing the election of a new master within a year's time. Chaytor, who had come to the retiring age shortly before the war broke out, had been renewed annually till it was over; his experiences in the First World War, his silent imperturbability and wisdom, had been of long service to me and to the whole college.

I was asked to become acting Senior Tutor, at least until after the election; the problems of that post were complicated, and involved a great deal of work, though they bulked small beside the day and night pressures of my last year in Italy. Since 1939 the college had elected each March its scholars and exhibitioners. Some of these, the scientists and engineers, had finished their degrees; many others did a year only and were then called up. Numbers of the scientific bursaries had been given by the Government to men who had done two or three years' study. Many cadets, naval and military and air force, had done six-month courses, and felt that they had some right to return to the college that had taken them in. There were numbers of commoner acceptances; ex-servicemen who could now obtain further education and training grants; and continuous pressure from schoolboys who hoped, quite vainly, that if they could get admission to a college, national service might be over by the time they had finished. Men with a certain background, and their families, often had a particular horror of conscription. This problem was fully alive until 1958, so that some men would go to a civic university which would take them straight from school, rather than take up an award two years later at Cambridge. All the papers affecting these men were in a state of confusion, both because of a hopelessly antiquated filing system which went back to 1919, and because of the death of the tutor's clerk. My predecessor had left me an admirable secretary: I installed her in my rooms, and set to work.

The first thing was to set up a thoroughly modern office system and a card-index, which the college allowed me to do: the next, to plan what the composition of the college should be for the next ten years, for the job involved the control of admissions as well as the responsibility for what was, in army terms, roughly the 'G' side. Some hundreds of men had to be interviewed; the correspondence ran to between forty and sixty letters every day of the year. I drew up a working plan, and had it agreed by the college, building up to a total of about 360 undergraduates, or an intake of 120–30 a year. Before the First World War the total strength of the college had been about 60, for which number the college had been rebuilt in the seventeenth and eighteenth centuries. In 1919–20 it had risen to 240, and gradually crept up to about 320 before the war. The combined effect of post-war pressure, the further education grants and the Butler Act, produced this immense change. The college had built extensively, on a cramped and unpropitious site in 1928 and 1936; more building was now necessary. In addition to the tutorial work I found myself caught up in university administration, and served for five years on that central body, the General Board of the Faculties, and on several of its innumerable committees. Its Secretary-General, H. M. Taylor (afterwards to be Vice-Chancellor of Keele), had returned from Larkhill, where he had unostentatiously reformed the gunnery of the Army. All who knew him have reason to be grateful for his courtesy and charm, and his superbly keen brain. I took for granted a full teaching load, and the full-time university lectureship to which I had returned.

It was the post-war crop of undergraduates who provided the greatest excitement and interest. The roll of our dead was already large; many of them had been my own pupils. Those who came into residence then included the newcomers, ex-servicemen with no previous connection with the college. Among them a number of war casualties, physical and spiritual, men who seemed to me to have had unusually bad luck, but who might, perhaps, be set right in such a place as Cambridge. This would be in keeping with the monastic, or at least the religious, function of a college. We took these as choice or chance sent them: a polio case from a Jap camp at Singapore, who went to his law lectures in a wheelchair; the commander of a one-man submarine in the Adriatic, who had got claustrophobia (as well he might); a regular officer of the Dorsets who had been beaten-up for three years on the Burma Railway; a commander of a destroyer flotilla, with all the decorations, who wished to become a Borstal officer; and so on. They were superb people, wholly capable of administering themselves, prepared to work and to get the utmost out of Cambridge. For those years at any rate it was an advantage, in dealing with them, to have been in the service oneself. There were, of course, difficult moments. We had a few cases who were more or less neurotic, and had to be handled with care; I have seen a major of gunners, who had come through the desert with distinction, weeping in an armchair in my rooms because he dared not go into his examination next morning because he had already got one first, and feared he might not get the other. A captain of a tank regiment who had been trapped in the turret of a blazing vehicle tried to assault the Chairman of Examiners of his Tripos, late one night, when he found that he got a third instead of a second. But on the whole they came through it well, and their friendship was one of my greatest joys at this time and for long afterwards. Against all expectation, they mixed well with the schoolboys of whom we were taking the medically graded straight from school. There was none of the cleavage that I had seen in 1919–20, nor the cynical defiance of university authority that I remembered then. Indeed, if there was any complaint to be made, it was that the post-war undergraduate took life, and examinations, and perhaps the dons, too seriously; his horizon, because of lost time, tended to be limited by examinations.

Gradually the college took shape. The undergraduate is a great preserver of traditions, and after both wars there were enough 'links' to ensure that these were revived. As one might expect, with the arrears of scholars and exhibitioners coming back into residence, the Tripos lists made an excellent showing for the next three or four years. And when men had taken their degrees, there was no problem of the unemployment whose shadow had lain so heavily on the undergraduates of the 1920s.

For myself, I was fully occupied; a couple of hours' correspondence a day, normal supervisions and lecturing, and nearly every afternoon taken up with meetings of one kind or another, sometimes twice a day. Through these I was drawn into a mass of committees and sub-committees, and did my tours of duty as Chairman of the English Board, as well as a long spell of twelve years as Chairman of the Faculty Board of Architecture and Fine Arts. My knowledge of art and architecture was strictly amateur, but it sometimes happens that a smallish faculty will prefer to have an 'outsider' in the chair. In that time the school made its immensely important transition from a pass degree to an honours school, under the guidance of its first professor, Sir Leslie Martin.

iii

It was very clear that one had 'lost ground' during the war as regards scholarship. Before it I had published only one small and not very good book. Yeats had died in 1939. I was perhaps the only man in England who knew intimately his country, both in Sligo and Clare, who was, like him of Anglo–Irish stock, and who was thus qualified to have some knowledge at least of the background. With Tillyard's encouragement I started to write *The Lonely Tower,* in a mood of angry exasperation at the scandals and denigrations of Yeats that were then circulating in Dublin. In order to check some material, and to refresh my memory of the place (for I had not seen Sligo since 1913), I paid a hurried visit; greeted by Mrs Yeats in Dublin with that courtesy and unfailing helpfulness which she gave to so many scholars. Sligo was unchanged, in general, and people even recognized me in the streets; the house where I had been born was different. At the head of the stairs I was confronted with a three-quarter size plaster image of the Virgin Mary, complete with bleeding heart transfixed by a sword; executed with all the vulgarity of taste that belongs to religious iconography in Ireland.

'This land of saints – of plaster saints. . . .'[1]

In Clare I hired a small car, and drove round the known country, pausing to catch a trout or two in the River. It was heavily overgrown with ash and thorn, the hedges with briars more impenetrable than before; floods had shifted the gravel and bank, so that the remembered eddies were only in the pools where the rocks held them as before. I visited those who had been my Mother's servants in her last illness; many of the older people I had known had died. Strangest of all, and moving one to great humility, was that the countryside for a considerable area roundabout seemed to have been saying prayers and lighting candles for my safety in the war.

[1] Yeats: 'Beautiful Lofty Things'.

Thoor Ballylee

'Safety in the war.' And I knew well that it was for no quality of mine, but for the sake of the past. Memories here are long, and they talk of the adventures and manners of those in the big houses much as they do in the East, where I had been received with courtesy because of such tenuous links. Nostalgia rose up strongly, and is not to be repressed if it is firmly rooted in what is active and which can provide, in its concreteness, 'metaphors for poetry'. I found myself certain that I could never live that life of forty years ago; and it seemed to me right that three centuries of Irish aristocracy had served their turn in history. For a time I thought they had failed, having in the century neither given themselves to lead rebellion, or to crush it; we who had had

'. . . many pretty toys when young.'

All over the country the burnt houses stood blackened; the greater fields split up into little ones, going back everywhere to rushes, bracken, briar. Of our church at Kildysart nothing whatever remained, not even the scars of the foundations; the masonry and memorials had been removed (though in full agreement with our Roman Catholic friends) stone by stone, for new building.

In the north Lady Gregory's Coole Park had been taken down in this way, so that the caretaker had to dig away the turf over the threshold-stone to show tourists some vestige of the house, though vandalism had not yet touched the

> 'catalpa tree nor scented lime.'

Our own graveyard on the hill above the Shore Wood was clean as Martin Daly had always kept it; but that of Klondagad was choked with briar and ivy, except where new earth was spread over an old tenant. Later, at Yeats's Tower at Ballylee the 'storm-beaten cottages' were in ruin and filth; only in a dark corner a farmer had stored a cart and a plough, so that I thought of Blake's proverb.

> *'Drive your cart and your plough – '* said that fierce William Blake.
> (And there they are, the plough and the cart, in the great square lower room,
> Rusting, rotting in dung; the scratched initials above;
> The plaster chipped for souvenirs – *'over the bones of the dead.'*

So it should be; and I turn from their dark corner
To empty window, rain-starved river, weed-stalking moorhen,
Idly glance at his arrogant bad verses set in slate on the wall.[1]
Someone has smeared them with charcoal.

> 'Sure wasn't that fella Yeats
> A great imposther always?'

But they carted no stones of the Tower
To Galway housing estates. The Norman mortar too hard?
Coole's nothing, as he foretold; the walks for two ghosts ungravelled[2]
That gaping tourists can see how the house is killed.

---

[1] 'I, the poet William Yeats,
  With old mill boards and sea-green slates,
  And smithy work from the Gort forge,
  Restored this tower for my wife George.'
    'To be carved on a Stone at Thoor Ballylee'.

[2] ... 'Our shadows rove the garden gravel still,
    The living seem more shadowy than they.'
        'The New Faces'

Yeats drove nor plough nor horse: rode but mind's images
(Though envying always the riders, mounted men or women),
Voices of hounds and drumming of hoofs on Benbulben,
Horses of fire, of shadow, Blake or Homer or Spenser,
Tamer of horses from Troy – nightly over Drumcliff
Riven or ridden the tomb – under engine or plough?

Thick-sown the graveyards of Ireland lie to grey weather,
Nettle and briar and elder, that wrenches frost-cracked
   limestone.
Yet no man ploughs them to corn, or trenches for footings.
This is the Holy Ground; the dead imprison the living
Scatter Synge's skulls[1] and the coffin boarding to mark it
Only cram with more dead.

That is Blake's challenge: in symbols an ignorant farmer
Lent to the empty-eyed tower. Now let us take them from it.
The plough to break, the cart to carry; the graveyard walls to
   break.
Scour, sharpen, yoke, harness; rend the encircling briar
And honour the dead with truth above the stone.

iv

Paradise seemed empty, desolate, with that peculiarly 'blind' look of a house where the windows have long been shuttered and the frames are decayed. On my Mother's death it had passed to my brother, who could not live there: it was for sale at perhaps a tenth of the price it would have fetched in 1913, and for long there were no buyers. The outlying parts of the demesne had been eroded by the familiar process; squatters breaking down fences and moving in, cutting timber, breaking down walls. Even the magnificent view from the hall door had changed. A mile or so beyond the boundary the sea-wall had been breached. Local jealousies, the all-pervading inertia, and lack of capital had left its breach unmended, and now over a thousand acres of good meadowland the tides ebbed and flowed, depositing a layer of grey mud and killing the screens of trees. Across the fields where we had cut and carted hay the curlews and redshanks cried despondently. A mile or two south was the track

---

[1] *v.* the account of the funeral in Synge's *The Aran Islands.*

of the transatlantic aircraft bound for or leaving Shannon.

Everywhere I went (in 1948) I was met by the complaint of poverty, high prices, lack of capital, and the cry: 'God be with the old times!' The national budget showed an enormous annual deficit, to some extent offset, as I had seen in Greece and Southern Italy, by remittances from America and England. There was a steady flood of emigration; there were far fewer young people in the countryside than I had remembered; I was told that most of the girls went to England to be hospital nurses, the boys to work in factories or construction of one kind or another. Later I was to read the symposium of essays called *The Vanishing Irish*;[1] it seems to be the bare truth. By contrast the population of priests and nuns seemed to have increased fourfold since my boyhood; this was understandable in view of the shutting-down of so many missions, particularly in India and China. Any peasant family that was growing in wealth and standing had always looked to have one of the sons a priest, one daughter a nun; thereby confirming their social standing and perhaps their 'eschatalogical expectations'. I talked with some of the priests; they were nearly all Maynooth-trained, theologically narrow, highly disciplined, and authoritarian in outlook; of a very different stamp from the wise and kindly Father Clancy whom I had known in the old days at Klondagad. But he, like many of that generation, had studied on the Continent, was widely travelled, and had a European outlook.

I returned to Cambridge; *The Lonely Tower* was written, mainly in the small hours of the morning, which was the only time that I was free from routine and the endless callers that my job involved. Again the compensations were endless. My son and daughter had returned from America at the end of the war; the former to Rugby, the latter to Cheltenham. Both were now exhibitioners at King's and Newnham. I had picked up again my autumn shooting, on the odd days that I could get clear; and a black retriever with me. The River and the boats were unchanged; for ten years I became President of the Cambridgeshire Rowing Association, but there was now no free time to coach. Sometimes I was called on to give lectures on military subjects at staff colleges and the like, but the waters of the Services were closing quickly over those whom I had known.

---

[1] *The Vanishing Irish: The Enigma of the Modern World*, ed. J. A. O'Brien (W. H. Allen, 1954).

The beginning of the post-war period was embittered by another mastership election. I refused to be a candidate, and as the Senior Fellow remaining, took charge of the endless meetings and cabals that – see Snow's *The Masters* again – are the curse of all small communities which have to carry such a burden. It became clear that there was a complete deadlock, with a split corresponding closely to that between those who had gone to the war and those who had not. On the morning of the day that I had fixed to go to our visitor, the Lord Chancellor, one fellow suddenly announced that he had changed sides; he was to do exactly the same thing eleven years later, and with the same result; and the whole house of cards collapsed. But the scars remained for a long time. Indeed I did not know then that I was entering the fifth arch, and that the tide was on the ebb.

v

In retrospect the period 1957–69 seems to have had a watershed about 1963: someone has suggested that this was the year in which the Communist power had decided that the universities were suitable objectives, or nurseries, for subversion. The 'unrest' in Cambridge started to become perceptible by 1966, and culminated in the riots at the Garden House Hotel in the spring of 1970. They and the 'sit-ins' followed closely the American pattern, carefully planned in the 'urban guerrilla' schools, in Berkeley, Columbia, Kent; and those of the French student riots of 1967–8. It is perhaps worth examining their incidence on British universities.

It is clear that the lot of the 'student' today is in the main difficult and unhappy. From the historic point of view there is always liable to be trouble of various kinds when student numbers grow very large, when an inefficient selection process causes an inordinately large drop-out, where there is no strong tradition of university education as a platonic 'good', when social conditions raise doubts about the future employment of those who do become graduates, and where the subjects taught invite by their nature criticisms of a philosophical, religious and sociological nature. Of these last the disciplines of English, sociology and psychology invite a range of amateur critiques based on emotional immaturity, and the confusion is at once intensified by two major ideologies in conflict, Marxism *vs* The Western Tradition: with the various sub-ideologies based on contemporary hero-figures.[1]

Confusion is multiplied when those who teach those subjects are seen to be taking up conflicting viewpoints; either because of sincere belief or out of a desire to be 'with it'. Now this in turn may render suspect the nature of their examinations. One teacher may hold rightly that the university tradition allows a man to hold any opinion he pleases, so long as his facts are known and his conclusions reached by the laws of logic. If he suspects that his chances of doing well in a particular examination are increased by a study of the opinions of those likely to examine him, the result may be cynicism or despair. An extreme form of this, which I have seen in certain US universities, is known as 'playing ball with the prof.': that is, a meticulous deference to the views, notes, lectures, prescribed syllabus of the teacher. I have been told by an English professor that he never took seriously any essay written from a Christian standpoint, and a substantial body of critical behaviour has been determined by Marxist critics such as Lukacz.

There are several lessons. No university of which the staff is rent by internal divisions can present a philosophically-justified *Weltanschaung,* nor conduct its administration effectively, without involving a most serious political rift between right and left. Those disciplines which demand the mastery of a body of fact, and training in its manipulation according to certain established laws, do not experience this confusion and conflict. It is ironical to note that students whose mental balance is suspect often tend to opt for psychology, or one of its compounds, *without* the steadying effect of a supporting degree in medicine proper. The Scottish universities with their ancient and honourable traditions of learning as 'good' in itself, and of a social background that recognized them as providing an essential and civilized discipline (that had some foundations in philosophy, taught traditionally by its greatest men) seemed to stand aloof from these confusions: as in the main did all the schools of mathematics, the sciences, engineering whose students had much to occupy them, and little scope for intrusive ideology.

---

[1] Compare the cults of Che Guevera, Ho Chi-Minh, with those of Mazzini, Kossuth, Garibaldi in the last century.

At the same time the dons themselves – at all universities, and as far afield as Canada – seemed much to blame. In the rapid expansion of 1957–65 the supply of competent and experienced teachers was far behind the demand: men whose attainments would have been relatively insignificant in 1939 received rapid and sometimes ill-judged promotion. At Cambridge itself a number of colleges, self-perpetuating in their choices, moved leftwards for elections of younger men, and those in turn, following the familiar pattern, consolidated the 'cells'. This in turn changed the traditional pattern of the selection of undergraduates: more and more one became aware of political pressures (lest any instance of 'favouritism' should be brought to the attention of Parliament) to admit for sociological reasons. Here two strands, an ironic contrast, could be perceived. Good men from good schools were refusing places at Oxford and Cambridge because they had been taught that the colleges were 'homes of privilege', preferring a civic university. On the other side college selection committees openly stated that if a candidate with a clean record from a good school, whose parents were able to finance him, were in competition with one from a working-class background, the latter would be chosen. One sensed a marked decrease – this was to be expected – in college morale, loyalty and the cultivation of the elementary virtues. There was, incidentally, a decrease in the number of men who played games, particularly those which, like rowing, demanded a measure of physical discipline.

vi

When one is over sixty one must expect the loss of many friends of an older generation. Of the poets, the chief was Walter de la Mare, with whom I corresponded sporadically during the war. I think that he is the only poet since Coleridge to whom the supernatural world was wholly living. Children were attracted to him instinctively: he and they seemed to share some kind of secret. He always seemed under-rated as a poet. So, I think, was L. A. G. Strong with whom I worked a little: he died young. T. S. Eliot I knew only slightly, but I remember with pleasure hearing him read aloud the first draft of *Sweeney Agonistes* in my rooms.

Sean O'Casey came and recorded his experiences as my guest

in one of his autobiographies: James Stephens, an elfin-figure with an enormous head, which he seemed to withdraw, tortoise-like, as he spoke. Lord Dunsany came to stay and lecture, and produced one good poem, 'On a Surrealist Picture'. I have not seen it quoted, and I can only give it from memory:

> The kind of bucket that they use for tar:
> A pole: a button very poorly drawn:
> A cheese: and nothing in particular
> Lay in the light of an unnatural dawn
> In the Sahara Desert: drawn by one
> Who never went there. An old snail shell too
> Was in that group: and probably a bun,
> And one bright pin of an outstanding blue.
>
> And being asked what meaning might reside
> In such a picture, I replied it might
> Serve to present a rabbit's thoughts on first
> Riding a bicycle.   And I was right!

A frequent visitor was Roy Campbell who seemed to have done everything with an Elizabethan gusto: an African hunter, a soldier in two wars, boat-builder, bull-fighter, translator of St John of the Cross, and, I think, a neglected poet. His jovial ghost will laugh to learn that a PhD thesis is being written about him. F. L. Lucas wrote perceptively of *The Flaming Terrapin*:

> . . . 'it has no form worth the name; its philosophy is neither deep nor new: why then does it stand apart from the usual abortions of modern poetry? Partly because Mr Campbell has lungs, imagination and an ear; but much more because he has a personality – the charming, laughing, laughable earnestness of youth, that vigour which is still unwearied, that intensity unblunted by too much experience, that spontaneity which has not learnt to suspect. . . . Hence the blessed relief of a writer who has clearly written to please himself, and enjoyed it, because he loved shouting his thoughts in galloping rhythms that he liked none the less for being – like all the things that move us most deeply – old as the changeless hills to which men lift their hearts.'

Edwin Muir, most lovable of men, I got to know when he lived at Swaffham Prior, and lent him books: underneath a mask of great courtesy and charm there seemed a profound pain, perhaps from his childhood experiences. Later there were many other friends: I think that the best poet among them is Kathleen Raine, who has allowed me to use two of her verses as an epigraph to this book. She is one of the three best Blake scholars living, and as such supremely competent to interpret Yeats. More important, her views coincide at almost every point with my own, and are summarized in her book *Defending Ancient Springs*. At the centre is the question propounded by Malinowski, as well as by Plato, Plotinus and Paul:

Nothing really matters except the answer to the burning question, 'Am I going to live, or shall I vanish like a bubble?' 'What is the aim and issue of all this strife and suffering?'

I do not think it is possible to make the teaching of literature a living thing without attention to the transcendental values.

Ben Bulben

XIII

FALL OF THE HOUSE

i

When the tide turns in the great estuary, the water in the tributaries backs up quickly, driving the wading-birds from the mud-flats. There is a faint crackling sound as the seaweed comes to life again, little blow-holes fill and close, mussels, crabs and cockles begin to draw their food from the richness of the flood. Under the five arches the tide takes over, pool by pool, for perhaps a mile upstream; and if you time things right you may have ten minutes of profitable fishing at the head of each pool, where the fresh water lips into the salt, and the sea-trout come nosing up along the shallows. At the height of the flood there is a period of standing water, before the tide moves slowly down again. Perhaps this image is a better one than that of a turning wheel for this next phase; because the wheel, with all its complex meanings in eastern philosophy, seems too rigid in its determinism. So some new flood tide began, perhaps in 1959 or 1960. For a year I acted as master of my college, with much happiness. Choice or chance brought me back to Sligo, where I was born, and to work at the Yeats International School for more than a decade there.

After the end of the war there was a steadily increasing flow of pilgrim-visitors to Sligo and its surroundings. Yeats had died in 1939 at Rocquebrune, and his death had then passed almost unnoticed. In 1949 his body was brought back, to be buried, as he had desired, in Drumcliff Churchyard some miles to the north of Sligo. The citizens of Sligo had formed a small but representative and active Yeats Society, to assist visitors, providing maps and guides to the many places mentioned in the poetry and plays. At

Fall of the House 203

an early stage I was asked to give a lecture. But with the centenary of his birth coming into view in 1965, it seemed more fitting to consider a Summer School; as a memorial (rather than a statue of perhaps uncertain quality) and to offer something that would be valuable to the visitors and pilgrims. In previous years I had worked a little for Summer Schools at Stratford-upon-Avon and at Cambridge. I procured brochures of these and sent them to Sligo as possible patterns. Thus the International Summer School came into being, and took much of my concern for the next ten years.

There were many techincal problems. There was little accommodation in the town on the scale required, either for teaching or living. We were (and remain) tied to specific dates in the second half of August, during which two large schools, boys' and girls', could be made available for separate accommodation. There was, in addition to the hotels of varying grades, lodging to be had in various private houses, and this often proved an attraction for the American visitors, many of whom had Irish forbears. At the same time it seemed unlikely that the subject would stand up to very prolonged and intensive study, unless its catholic character were to be sacrificed in favour of a small community of selected scholars. Equally, it should not give 'credits' towards university graduation (there is a steady demand for this on the North American side) for that would involve a prolonged period of study, a large staff of tutors, and supervised essays or theses. What seemed necessary was a teaching organization covering a wide spectrum of students, ranging from scholars of the highest repute, or promise, to visitors who sought to 'fit in' the School as part of an Irish or even European tour. Nor did it seem practicable to publish the lectures, or some part of them, as an annual volume (this was also a steady demand); with distinguished lecturers working for purely nominal fees it was essential that they should retain the copyright of their work. A great many of these lectures were, in fact, published subsequently in learned journals, or incorporated in books, or set out in the papers of the admirable Dolmen Press.

The history of the school has yet to be written. The documentary material is already considerable and I have no intention of attempting such a task. In brief, it grew strongly from some twenty students in the first year to over two hundred in 1970. This last figure seemed to suggest the maximum which the town could accommodate; and, far more important, a number above which the sense of a community (however temporary) would be lost.

The two first directors were Oliver Edwards[1] and Denis Donoghue of University College, Dublin.[2] Then the Yeats Society invited me to take over; which I did until I retired in 1968, a year before I gave up my University Readership and College Fellowship. There were, perhaps, advantages in having one who was not only Irish but Sligo-born, but who was sufficiently distanced at Cambridge to be outside potential conflicts over nationalism, religion or politics. I was supremely fortunate in having many friends among Yeatsian scholars in many countries, who were good enough to accept invitations to come to the school. I like to think that they enjoyed a certain atmosphere of informality, the social aspects of their scholarship, the superb and historic scenery, and the warmth of the welcome which the people of Sligo gave them. For it was and is, upon these people that our success depended.

For my own part, I had always held that I was the servant of the Yeats Society; that I would undertake to organize the academic side – lectures, seminars, bibliographies and so forth. The society, under their very enterprising chairman, Frank Wynne, would be responsible for the administration, finance and the important 'recreational' aspects. These took many forms: plays, films, and concerts, dances in the evenings; archaeological expeditions in a countryside that was peculiarly rich in prehistoric remains, trips to two special places of pilgrimage, Lissadell and – far to the south in Co. Galway – Yeats's Tower and Coole Park. It seemed as if the little community developed quite rapidly a characteristic of its own, through the interplay of personalities concerned with mutual interests: and all, of course, free of the pressures of written papers, 'grades' or examinations. At the same time it seemed proper that the society and its work should remain autonomous rather than seek to place itself under the 'umbrella' of any particular university. There were recurrent approaches on these lines from North America. If we had accepted we should no doubt have solved many of our financial

---

[1] Then Reader in German at McGee College, Londonderry, and with an unrivalled knowledge both of Goethe and of Yeats.

[2] Sometime a Fellow of King's, afterwards Professor at U.C.D.

difficulties, but at the cost of sacrificing the character of the school, possibly at the expense of turning it into a kind of 'overseas annexe'. For somewhat similar reasons it seemed undesirable to forge any firm link with any one of the five Irish universities and university colleges, because of the significant rivalries among them. But all of them cooperated most generously in lending us the assistance of their scholars.

I have said that the students covered a wide spectrum. At one end, in the 'A' seminar, were scholars of reputation, or those writing doctorate theses on some subject connected with the course: for we gradually broadened it to include history, social history, and literary figures of the whole period besides Yeats. At the other end there were men and women who, on their application forms said, in effect: 'I don't know much about Yeats, or indeed about poetry; but I want to learn.' Sometimes they were people of middle age, husbands trailing reluctantly behind culture-minded wives, or the reverse; many schoolteachers from America; a fair sprinkling of nuns, superb people, wise and humorous; many poets in various stages of development, who found audiences in the social centre at night. Generally, fourteen or fifteen nationalities were represented, and their flags were flown over the building where the seminars were given. By 1968 there seemed to have developed, quite spontaneously, something like an ecumenical movement among the students themselves.

My memory dwells with delight on the personalities of those who came to teach and lecture. A list that would include them all would be far too long, but among them were Tom Parkinson of Berkeley, Richard Ellmann,[1] George Harper, the leading Neo-Platonist, Marian Witt; Donald Torchiana who wrote an impressive book on Georgian Ireland; Lawrence Lee, gentlest and most responsive of teachers; F. A. C. Wilson, once my pupil, who had written two controversial Yeatsian studies; Daniel Hoffmann; Cleanth Brooks, Northrop Frye, all names of power. Ann Saddlemyer, the editor of Synge, and Robin Skelton, came from British Columbia, where they had established a school in Anglo-Irish Studies. There was Russell Alspach, who with my pupil Peter Allt had edited the monumental *Variorum Edition of the Poems* (later, Alspach did the same alone for the plays). From Ireland we had the constant help, both in lectures and seminars,

---

[1] Now Professor at Oxford.

of Oliver Edwards, Kevin Nowlan, Francis Byrne, Robert O'Driscoll,[1] Brendan Kennelly from TCD[2] (to my mind one of the three leading poets of Ireland); with Denis Donoghue, whose immense reputation was in process of quick growth, and Roger McHugh from the same University College, Dublin.

It was in the nature of things that many of my friends should come from Cambridge to help. Among them was Muriel Bradbrook[3]; Graham Hough (author of an essay on Yeats, in his famous *The Last Romantics*), and Kathleen Raine, the poetess and the most eminent of Blake scholars; Francis Warner[4], John Kelly[5], and J. R. Mulryne[6], at different times my pupils. Raymond Lister came to talk on Calvert and Palmer: Mrs Yeats had given me the collection of slides by those artists, and some of Blake's, that the poet had collected for an American tour and that had formed part of a course that I had given at Cambridge called 'Poetry and Painting'. Edward Malins of Bath, an expert on landscape gardening and music as well as a dramatic producer, came several times from Bath, on one occasion bringing his own actors across for performances of *Plays for Dancers*. For the plays we often had companies from Dublin and Belfast, but gradually came to rely more and more on the very talented local drama company. Much the same happened with the Poetry Readings; these were initially given by professional actors, but we found two readers who far outshone them, and whose renderings were better (because of more understanding in the bone) than any I had heard, before or since. They were Mary Watson of Collooney, once a teacher of elocution, and Oliver Edwards.

The fortnight was a pleasant one, though not without its anxieties. For technical reasons the programme had to be composed in the previous autumn, and this involved a great deal of correspondence. It was published in January. Between then and the opening of the school in August frequent adjustments had to be made, because of lecturers being unable to meet commitments they had undertaken so far ahead. It was often necessary to extemporize, holding a balance between those who

---

[1] Now Professor at Toronto.
[2] Now Professor of that University.
[3] Professor; subsequently Mistress of Girton.
[4] Now Fellow of St. Peter's College, Oxford.
[5] Formerly of T.C.D.; now Fellow of St. John's College, Oxford.
[6] Reader at Edinburgh University.

Fall of the House 207

had famous names as scholars but whose ability to lecture was unknown, and those who would lecture but who were not so happy with seminars. One difficulty was to persuade lecturers to lecture rather than read learned papers; and not all realized the difference between lecturing and essay techniques. There was also the problem of voice-production in a badly designed Victorian Gothic hall, with an audience of between two and three hundred; so that on my retirement the Yeats Society were good enough (instead of a formal gift) to install a modern system of controllable amplifiers and speakers. Among those who showed that a lecture could be a work of art were Robert Speaight, and a Jesuit Priest, Father Bodkin; the latter, entirely blind, accomplished discourses of unexampled grace, fluency and control. The Yeats Society School continued to grow in scope and reputation. It was opened each year by a Minister of the Free State, or by an Ambassador from Dublin, or by some other notable. But by 1968 it was clear to me that many circumstances, chief among them the need for fresh blood and ideas, made it proper that I should give up the directorship. Another Anglo-Irishman, Professor Norman Jeffares, then of Leeds, took over for 1969, but I returned to give single lectures and some seminars in 1970 and 1971.

ii

The 'Sligo visits' thus fell into a kind of pattern: my wife and I went through Northern Ireland seeing friends; spent a fortnight in Sligo; and then went south to Connemara to rest and to fish at Delphi Lodge in Co Mayo. In all we went there for some ten years, usually sharing a boat with Hamish Blair-Cunynghame, once a Fellow of my own college, and later with H. J. Emeléus, professor of chemistry. Increasing stiffness made it difficult for me to fish any river, but the large and sturdy boats on the four lakes at Delphi Fishery made this kind of fishing still practicable. The lodge itself, holding a small number of keen fishermen, produced through the genius of W. A. Wallace something of the atmosphere of an Irish country house as I had known it. There was the unvarying peace of the water and of the great mountains of its setting; and at night, quiet of the hills; even in the western gales, and the rains that beat so constantly down the mountain

A Mountain Lake, near Delphi

passes and the oldest rocks in Ireland. So Robert Louis Stevenson:

> Grey deserted tombs of the dead in desert places,
>   Standing-stones on the vacant wine-red moor.
> Hills of sheep, and the homes of the silent vanished races,
>   And winds, austere and pure.

From the great fjord of the Killeary we cut across the mountains to Galway, and thence into North Clare; usually stopping at Ballylee to visit Yeats's Tower, which some of us had helped to hold against further decay, and arrest Yeats's prophetic verses.[1] The road went past what was left of Lady Gregory's home Coole Park, of which no trace remained; an example of destructive philistinism, for this house and the surrounding

---

[1] 'And may these characters remain
   When all is ruin once again.'
            ('To be Carved on a Stone at Thoor Ballylee')

district will one day become as important for the student of the Irish Literary Revival as the Lake District is for Wordsworthians.

From there we made an annual pilgrimage to Paradise: to go over the house in its new guise of German ownership, to talk with and bring gifts to the people who had served it. The 'Irish trip', with all its pleasures and perhaps usefulness, inevitably cut across many other things that I could have wished to do: journeys on the Continent, work for Terence Spencer at Stratford, conferences of different kinds. Only in 1970 was it possible to combine it with the newly founded International Society for the Study of Anglo-Irish Literature (IASAIL) at Trinity College, Dublin.

iii

On 29 December 1964 my son died. His story and his last diary has been recorded in a memoir written by my wife.[1] We have found that it has been of help to many who have suffered such losses, and for the understanding of the living in an age which is not easy when one is young.

iv

For a term in 1965 I was a supernumerary visiting Professor at Trinity College, Dublin, and then flew to British Columbia to receive an honorary degree at Victoria. It was now clear that retirement was pressing, and plans had to be made to dispose of my furniture and library in college, and for the clearing of the rooms in which I had lived for twenty-two years. It seemed just possible financially to continue to live in the house which we had built in 1926. But many lectures and papers had to be destroyed, and two-thirds of my books sold or given away. Clearly a new rhythm would begin on retirement.

But it was from about that date that Cambridge as I had known it began to change, and with some violence both physical and mental. Student revolt is a world-wide phenomenon. Much has been written about it; and I do not wish to attempt to com-

---

[1] *Desmond*, by Enid Henn, 1967.

ment on many admirable analyses. But I had written in the fifties when the plans for the new universities began to acquire momentum, that I did not believe that England could produce an unlimited quantity of men and women of high calibre to fill them: and that societies of this sort which grow too rapidly are subjected to all sorts of internal stresses. I had been attacked in Canada for saying that a university of more than 10,000 was an anomaly. Just before my retirement I had been asked to give a paper on the changes I had known in the English Faculty during my lifetime. A little later a society of Cambridge medical men invited me to give a paper on changes in undergraduate psychology as I had known it for nearly half a century[1]. These changes were clearly related to a world-picture of great complexity. Among the factors in my own experience is the emotional vacuum among young people, who are left without a core of belief in the whole Western tradition that they inherit, and who were turning, with fragmented mind and perceptions, to the East and to Russia. It seemed also as if young people of great intelligence, and usually of courtesy and charm, were in a situation in which emotional maturity had not kept pace with intelligence. Clutton Brock has an essay called 'Loose Emotion'. Recent events at Cambridge suggested that there is in fact such a whirlwind or vortex of emotion, moving arbitrarily from object to object; and any political or social event, however trivial, may offer a point round which the swarm may cohere and, for a moment, hang. These points exhibit no very clear order of values: the name of an obscure African politician, a Cuban brigand, a Chinese dictator, will serve equally as points of non-reference, or to generate some meaningless slogan. Robert Bridges put it concisely:

> The thicket of the people will take furtive fire
> From irresponsible catchwords of live ideas.[2]

The ideas are live, there is often courage, energy, altruism, and a great longing. One might despair were it not that it has happened many times before in history. But the danger is sharpened now from a multitude of causes. My own subject has

---

[1] Neither of these papers has been published. An earlier one, *The Causes of Failure in Examinations*, appeared in *The British Medical Journal for 1954*.

[2] *The Testament of Beauty*.

Fall of the House

become professionalized. Much of the delight has been taken from it by amateur Marxism on the part of those who teach it. The teaching done by the dons – that is, fellows of colleges and established university lecturers – has diminished in extent if not in quality. The numbers are too large. The week-end habit, of dons and undergraduates alike, has become general, and has diminished still further time and opportunity for teaching and for the much-vaunted communication. Because of the grants system, and some unwise propaganda by the schools, the university is perceived less as a place of learning than as a rubber-stamp for degrees. Over all hangs the black wing of the examination system.

An infinite amount of ink has been spilt on this topic. I have seen most of the alternatives, and taken part in certain experiments. At the end I return to certain propositions. No examination system is 'fair'; in addition to human error I am certain that there has been a five per cent error, plus or minus, for my pupils and my own assessment of their work over two years. From another point of view the undergraduate can see himself as handed over, bound hand and foot, to the judgement of seven or eight unknown examiners. He does not and cannot know the immense care that is taken in each case, nor the remarkable coincidences of judgement that the confidential mark-books reveal. He is too young to realize that he is in an existential situation which will remain for most of his lifetime; that is, he will be continually subjected to examinations in the form of judgements or reports on his work and prospects. The long series of examinations at school have taught him to regard the university examinations as a particularly formidable kind of hurdle, after which he will be released from all competition. This is a common illusion. The situation is wisely summed up in the following passage from Professor H. L. A. Hart's 'Report of the Committee on Relations with Junior Members' (Oxford 1969):

> 'Though student radicalism manifests in disturbances in universities, it is not primarily concerned with university reform or with education or with the conditions of student life; it does not arise from these conditions and is not to be allayed, though it may be contained, by their reform.'

At the same time the undergraduate is haunted by fears and uncertainties: for which one psychic relief is a retreat into drugs, or explosions into ill-considered violence. Here again the pretexts bear no relation to significant or logical events. Above all there is the fear of atomic annihilation; a central reason for rejecting the immortality of his soul, and of turning his back on the implications of death. There is a further most important result; a kind of psychic numbness, an insensitivity which (as in many literary movements of the past) can result in an attempt to simplify the art of living through drugs or some similar merging of reason into sensation. Huysman's *A Rebours* is almost a textbook here in this quest for essences of sensation.

At the same time I believe that the universities, including my own, are much to blame. Paper work and administration of every kind has multiplied, even since my own senior tutorship: and I remember that I saw SHAEF at Versailles drowned into ineffectiveness under the same paper flood. The administrative building at Berkeley, with its computer and stamped cards, the lectures relayed through loudspeakers, the virtual impossibility of a student arranging a quiet talk alone with any of his or her tutors, struck me as a kind of nightmare. Mere size is clearly an inhibitor of 'communication'; but effective and generous communication comes from teaching in very small groups, in the cultivation of friendship, and a most delicate balance between informality and ceremonial. The new generation of don (there are important exceptions) will approach his college teaching and the performance of college offices in a manner wholly different to that which obtained before the Second World War, and for perhaps a decade after. The university has of set policy placed restrictions on his college work and teaching. The new universities have opened out, at least in financial terms, a dazzling series of possible new promotions. And these promotions will depend, not on his reputation as a teacher or the *caritas* with which he may be regarded by his pupils, but solely on his published work. I have served on too many appointments committees, commissions for professorships, to believe otherwise. I am certain that the many protests and discontents – which always exist – were solved quietly and efficiently in the inter-war period by personal contacts. And there was, I think, an incidental product of this; the anticipation of many psychological troubles which now loom so large. The university student is too apt to regard the psychiatrist as a magician who will, somehow, relieve him from what he must know and suffer:

Endure that toil of growing up;
The ignominy of boyhood; the distress
Of boyhood changing into man;
The unfinished man and his pain
Brought face to face with his own clumsiness.[1]

Time, and talk with a wise and preferably silent man, who can occlude his personality at will, has seemed to me capable of healing many evils and perplexities.

Paradise aflame

v

Paradise was destroyed by fire on the morning of 6 October 1970. Next day the Irish papers carried photographs of its blackened ruin. By all official accounts it was an accident: the German owner, who had bought the house and a small portion of the demesne from my brother in 1960, had installed central heating and electric lighting. Old houses do not always tolerate these improvements. Others believe that the burning was deliberate; as seemingly of the same method and timing as the burning of houses in The Troubles and afterward, and in keeping with the

[1] Yeats, 'A Dialogue of Self and Soul'.

policy of the new Republican Movement which had pledged itself to direct action to prevent 'alien enterprises acquiring property in Ireland'.[1] When my wife and I visited the house a month before, there were some signs that the familiar process of erosion had begun; fences were being broken down, gates torn out, young timber 'hacked and wracked'. That September my wife had gone over all the house and told me that she found it informed by my Mother's presence, happy and fulfilled. For though my mother had been dead for thirty-six years, she had fought to save the house, much as Lady Gregory had done at Coole,[2] for the sake of her children and grandchildren, through the Troubles, the Civil War, and an aftermath of lawlessness in the late 1920s. We believed that she had succeeded by the strength of her personality, for she was greatly loved by the people; she had resisted both poverty and threats until, in old age, the fear of the burning returned to unsettle her mind. On my visits at Christmas I would find her wandering through the long corridors, candle in hand, obsessed with the fires that might have been begun by the raiders. It was ironical to recall all these events, in peacetime, and there was irony too in the contemplation of that blackened shell. For it was said that the fire had begun in the great oak Victorian sideboard in the dining room, where much liquor was kept by the new owner; there were armorial shields and devices, and overall the quotation from the 'Winchester' psalm:

Sit pax in domicilio tuo, et abundantia in turribus tuis.[3] And in the hall:

The Lord shall preserve thy going out and thy coming in.[4]

A few weeks earlier I had given a lecture in Sligo, called 'The Big House';[5] which took as a centre Yeats's play *Purgatory,* and, on the periphery, such poems as 'Nineteen Hundred and Nineteen', 'Ancestral Houses' and 'Upon a House Shaken by the Land Agitation'. I had not thought that foreboding would have been fulfilled so soon. It was a little short of 300 years old, but

---

[1] See, (*e.g.*) J. Bowyer Bell, *The Secret Army* (Blond, 1970), p. 361.
[2] Lennox Robinson (*ed.*) *Lady Gregory's Journals* 1916-1930, (Putnam, 1946).
[3] *Psalms* 122:7 'Peace be within thy walls, and plenteousness within thy palaces'.
[4] *Ibid.*
[5] Published in *Last Essays* (Smythe, 1976).

I imagine that, on such a superb site there were likely to have been previous settlements. One dream of brash youth had been to buy it, reafforest, clear the jungle that had grown up in shrubberies and orchards, restore the broken palisades of the garden, rebuild the greenhouses, make the cleared land fruitful again. The River too might yet be cleared of the rampant ash saplings, the stepping-stones renewed, dams built to deepen and cleanse the pools.

But it seemed to me as I wrote, that the Anglo-Irish race to which I belonged had been sliding downwards for a very long time. Writers have put various dates to this decay: The Act of Union of 1800, the Repeal of the Corn Laws, the Great Famine of 1848–9; the agricultural depression from 1870 onwards (which had involved England as well, as Hardy's novels show so clearly). There were the various Land Acts at the beginning of the century: I remember my Mother telling me that she had besought my Father to sell, to get rid, at any price, of the 'outside land'. So long as I could remember there had been agrarian troubles. When a ruined cottage beside the mail road was pulled down, a pistol and a pike were found concealed in the thatch.

Gradually the burning has swung into perspective. Whatever the wrongs of past history on either side, this civilization that I had known as a boy was founded on something approaching serfdom. So it had been with Greece and Rome, so with India, so had the whole saga of early Ireland of which the Romantic Nationalists make much. There might be, and was, friendship, great loyalty, an age-old concern with blood and race; but inescapably the Big House was built on wealth, privilege, and the large revolutions of politics and religions. I had known many men like Adam of *As You Like It*; the noblest of them, Martin Daly, who had been a constant companion, died a few weeks after the house was burnt. With him a long history of loyalties had come to an end:

'His fathers served their fathers before Christ was crucified.'

It was now clear that only by injections of foreign gold could such places be saved: and then, necessarily, by people who had been more 'foreign' than we who had come over (as it was said) with Strongbow. Those injections could be only temporary, and might be ignorant and ill-tempered. Those who bought such places, often derelict, and poured money into them, could never have the links that had come from slow labour, the building of what was, in effect, a family mythologem: woods named for men or women, the 'American Ground' set with shrubs brought from Florida; a springing well, where a girl had meditated; even a rustic bridge, named for a forgotten guest who, at the last drive on a winter's evening, had fallen through the handrail into the little stream below!

So the burning settled into the perspective of history. There was no need to hold to the strong imagination of two friends (who wrote to me independently in the same strain) that the ghosts of ancestors had come down that night from the graveyard on the hill, angry and revengeful at the stranger's occupation. Only it was clear that what remained of the tenants and old servants would suffer in mind and in body, and that I must do what I could for them. It was all part of such poetic destructions; Synge's

'I see the flames of Emain starting up on a dark night' . . .

Yeats's house in his play *Purgatory* that burnt as the ghosts dreamt through their sin; and, most vividly, 'The Curse of Cromwell', for the cycle might be thought to have completed that Ireland-wide destruction:

I came on a great house in the middle of the night,
Its open lighted doorway and its windows all alight,
And all my friends were there and made me welcome too;
But I woke in an old ruin that the winds howled through;
And when I pay attention I must out and walk
Among the dogs and horses that understand my talk.
                O what of that, O what of that,
                What is there left to say?

But more profound and noble, more relevant to one's mood, are Kathleen Raine's verses:

Essential fire is the unhindered spirit
That, laid upon the lips of prophecy
Frees all the shining elements of the soul;
Whose burning teaches love the way to die

And selves to undergo their ultimate destruction
Upon those flaming ramparts of the world
That rise between our fate, and the lost garden.[1]

vi

In the Library at Paradise I noticed but did not read a book of the early nineteenth century called *The Pleasures of Old Age*. Being young it was irrelevant. Nor did I read Cicero's *de Senectute* till a good deal later, being concerned to discover what book Yeats had in mind in that exquisite lyric, 'Mad as the Mist and Snow'. After a time of retirement I am thankful for still being able to live in Cambridge in the house which I built nearly half a century ago, and where the ashes of my son are scattered among the rose-trees.

I am above all grateful that there is still work to be done, friendships to be cherished, the pain of major surgery to be overcome. With those things comes the freedom from much that was tedious in chairmanships, committee work, the fog-drifted confrontations with the new and less courteous exponents of student discontent. Many things must be re-assessed in the time that may be granted for amendment of life. So – I wrote 'Attentions' on this theme.[2]

vii

I return to the Five Arches at Ballycorick, and the River above them with all its variety of meadows, woods, waterfalls and rocky glens. It is good to visit in dreams. It is a merciful provision that one never knows when one has done any one thing for the last time; shot a snipe, perhaps, on the gleaming silver-lighted bog, or walked the bracken slope crisp under frost, or thrown a line on some pool where every boulder and rock-shelf was known. It seems to me likely that the dead of a lifetime, and of three wars, crowd in upon one in friendship, the helpers of the end. This commerce of prayer and of thought is important. But nostalgia

[1] *Collected Poems* (1956) p. 77.
[2] See p. 300.

which can be destructive must be controlled. Six years ago this book indeed might have had its ending in such a mood; now, with more knowledge of tragedy, that too must be controlled. Again Kathleen Raine has put it infinitely more cogently than my own verses have done, and one of her stanzas seems the best epigraph:

> Not in overlong continuance see
> Of amulet or ghost, in wraith of what has been,
> Evidence of soul's immortality.
> The ghost that haunts, the haunting memory
> Is the continuance only of the dead.
> Such earthly-bound spirits, into soul's might unborn
> Miss the one way to that destination.
> From which the homing soul knows no return.

Graveyard Hill

PHILOCTETES
AND OTHER POEMS

Foreword

I have collected these poems in response to the wishes of some friends whose judgements I value. They include, among some newer ones, certain of those printed privately in 1958, and by The Golden Head Press in 1964. I have never attempted to publish any of them; one found its way by chance, in war-time, into a friend's book; another provided, I think, the germ of a poet's play. From the present collection I have excluded everything written (nearly enough) before my 'fortieth winter'; partly because those of earlier times seemed to me too personal, partly because the excitement in which they were written, or which they sought to express, now seems to be deficient in quality.

It is necessary to set out, as briefly as may be, something of the originating conditions. Most of the poems were written during the Second World War; the first a little before it in a manner that seemed to view the Spanish Civil War as a microcosm of the future. Similarly, *Urbs Beata Jerusalem* was written some months before the outbreak of the 1967 Arab–Israeli war, and perhaps contained some element of prophecy. A number of others were written during the invasion threat of 1940–41, when 'in a state of continuous excitement' the fundamental values seemed clearer, the 'Unity of Being' (I use Yeats's phrase) more apparent throughout England. And there was, perhaps, the stimulus, for a time at least, of putting into action de Vigny's words: 'If any man despair of being a poet, let him take his knapsack and march with the troops.'

That was followed, after many tasks arising out of Choice or Chance, by a period of bitter responsibility (in which personal death seemed less immediate, the tragedy of Europe more horrible), when the isolated and futile arbitration of war seemed to press for expression, in moods of anger and impotence: anger, I think, at the catastrophe of Yalta and its sequels, and at what seemed the indifference of post-war Cambridge to the destruction of a European tradition. Some later poems were, perhaps, the result of a prolongation of pain, and 'the energy that is reborn of a sudden blow', energy that afterwards may increase, or ebb, in obedience to some mysterious law; for whose operation we have many precedents, but no explanation.

I have added brief notes to some of the verses; since many of them are personal, concerned with experiences of boyhood, or war. For these some explanation seemed desirable. Allusion and allusiveness are inevitable when one has read much, and in particular when one has lived long without books, carrying (as in time of war) much traditional verse in memory; and therefore it has seemed best to give most of the less obvious references.

On the positive side, it becomes more easy to state, partly in notes, and partly in explanations which I have tried to make as objective as possible, the intention which I think underlay most of them. For too often in modern poetry the writer seems reluctant to reveal his intended meaning, and who shall blame him? The New Criticism will search for ambiguities, laminations of meaning, and so forth; its diligent exegesis may well reveal to the author excellences or deficiencies of which he was unaware. But here I have been able to use my verses as material to show the growth and operation of this form of expression, knowing that they are of the second, perhaps of the third, rank but aware at least of the circumstances which gave rise to each, the intention as it shaped and reshaped itself, the provenance and purpose of the symbols; the failure, and the intermittent success, of the attempts to close the eternal gap between the Image (I use the word in Abercrombie's sense) and its expression in the spoken word. I say spoken, for all these verses are meant to be read aloud.

As to the rhythms, and structure, few of these poems are traditional or of the closely-forged grain of rhyme; partly because the technique, which only comes from long apprenticeship and longer dedication, is lacking, partly because the tyranny of rhyme seems to me liable to reveal too clearly the joins in the welding. Instead, I have tried to allow rhythm to give a resonance to the words, the words to build a resonance into rhythm: with some use of cadences to mark the unities of the verse.

I do not think one need necessarily disparage the poem written at command, or on an occasion. Some verses belong to this category. It may well be that, from time to time, such pressures may set off something latent, half-prepared in the mind, but

Foreword

ready to expand and to combine, under stimulus, with stored and ripened experience. And there is abundant evidence in the notebooks of poets how a poem swells, reshapes itself, gathers to itself (through redraft upon redraft) the images that are conjured into its circle; though it may well start from a few lines of bald prose called *Notes for a Poem*.

Memory charged with emotion (perhaps what is commonly called nostalgia) seems to me important as enabling the individual mind to establish an essential connection through which it may attain harmony between past and present. But, from examples of the past, the use of memory in such a way seems to be open to certain dangers. It is, of all things, the most difficult to assess as to quality; perhaps because it is impossible to stand apart from it dispassionately, and to judge; or maybe because earlier memories, sincere beyond all question to oneself, can never (if only because of their woven complexity) be shared by others. For this reason I have used only sparingly subjects drawn from Ireland and my home; which are, on the surface, fitting things to remember as the happiest moments of childhood in a setting of indescribable beauty. The poetry of the hills, of mountain river or lake, of the wild and stony Burren in North Clare, have been celebrated too often and too well for me to attempt to match them; I think of Yeats's *The Fisherman,* and of *Coole Park and Ballylee* (1929), as touchstones. Perhaps, too, the lonely lake, the mountain waterfall, the sound of a snipe rising from the 'red ground', the sailing of a small boat alone in the Atlantic, are either too private to be imitated in verse or to demand a common experience (and so a sympathy) that, if it is lacking, brings failure or ridicule. And after 1922 political events became almost too painful to settle or combine in the memory, except under pressure of real or imagined death, for

'We too had many pretty toys when young'

– and against the perspectives of the war in Europe the killing of a house seemed no great matter. Some of the poems, especially those dealing with my boyhood days, form part of my autobiography, *Five Arches*, but as my poetry is appearing in the same volume, a number have been removed, and references to the pages on which they appear, given. One of them, 'Dark Journey', concerned the threat of the burning of my home, a threat which was not fulfilled – ironically in time of 'peace' – until half a century later.

I do not believe that literature is ever, in any sense that is as yet agreed, a substitute for religion or philosophy; though it may be 'philosophical', that is, something which predisposes us to attitudes which are, in kind and quality, proper to those final meditations; and can reveal intermittently, as the sun through clouds, the idea of the numinous, through which alone 'Unity of Being' may be achieved.

I do not believe that criticism, in so far as it sets out to be judicial rather than exegetical, can pretend to indicate a system of values that can over-ride those of religion or philosophy; I believe that when it attempts to do so it is capable, by its pretence and arrogance, of doing infinite harm to the living imagination. Indeed, of modern writing it has justly been said, 'The imagination has been laid in a great tomb of criticism.'

It seems possible that we have limited ourselves today by insisting on emotion which has no relation to any public interest. However personal may be the basic experience which one attempts to present, its implications must be, in some way or other, susceptible of recognition in a larger framework; it must have the depth which Yeats called 'multitude', even in a lyric. It is even possible that the constant attempt to explore, expose and weigh the individual psyche (for so we seem to have swung back, too often, to a vulgarized neo-romanticism) has been brought face to face with the end of that labyrinth; whether by the interest that we are induced to feel for the growth or regression of a poet's mind, or by the attempt to discover, in the darker woods of psychology, some common begetter of the human situation.

I do not believe (knowing something of the oscillations of judgement or taste and value in the history of literature) that the critic can or should attempt to pronounce *ex cathedra* upon what is or is not serious, *'sérieux'*, 'a significant gesture' or 'of moral concern', unless he is prepared to make clear to us, as precisely as possible, upon what tree his system of morality hangs. For the same reason I reject the position that literature is to be judged by a special or peculiar system of values, inherent in itself and discoverable by the critic, who alone can expound and assess them. I believe that much criticism today has grown too pontifical, too apt to set out subjective judgements under cover of alleged impartiality. It seems probable that we should become accustomed to scrutinize more closely the character of each critic; and his credentials to pronounce upon human relationships, including those that are loosely described as sexual, before we accept his judgements upon them.

It is for this reason that I find those critics most illuminating whose position as moralists is unequivocal, whether Marxist, or Neo-Platonist, or Christian, for they at least have a centre that can hold. It will be apparent that my own commitment is to Christianity. Part of the *apologia* for this is in the last chapter of a book called *The Bible as Literature*.

Cambridge, 1971–3

It has been said that the story of Philoctetes, the archer who was marooned on an island by his companions because a serpent-bite had produced an intolerable wound, is one of the more significant archetypal myths of modern man; as having great skill and power, yet helpless from one defect. (The other myths are perhaps those of Faust and of Orpheus and Eurydice.) The story is in Sophocles' play, though the action, it is hinted, has mysterious antecedents at Chrysê; it lends the title to Edmund Wilson's important critical work, The Wound and the Bow. *Here, the second movement owes something to Jung's* Memories, Dreams and Reflections, *where he describes a similar incident, with the making of a model harbour.*

PHILOCTETES

No harbour, no shelter in the island.
Only the dunes tossing anchorless
Under a white wind. The burning serpent-wound
(Searing spattering venom as it leapt fanged from the sand)
Reeked intolerably, feeding the flies.

Between the spasms of pain
He fondled childlike the weapon's intricate fashioning,
Remembered the touch of curved horn-tips, beauty of welded sinew,
That wax-moist string, honed steel of arrowheads
They needed before Troy.

                Now it was clear. He must build again his harbour:
Quayside with steep stairways to green sand-warmed water
Where cork boats veered to a thread mooring-line:
Bollards and rings and frames for the nets to dry,
Withes of a broken lobster-pot, a frayed coir hawser,
Long-line coiled in a box.
Set tavern brothel church behind the green
A golden castle on the guardian hillside.
– So lenses would grow clear, pain drown in delight,
Self-hood unravelled to knowledge.

Over and short came now
The first bracketing bursts on his hill.
He crouched by the gun, the breech he had laboured to close.
A spider filament moved with the gleaming glass,
Wavered and settled. They would come by that stony gulley,
The armoured men from the sea, spearhead and flankers,
Closing the range. Then into vision came
A crawling fly that raised its head emboldened:

And with the shot the ulcer shed its poison,
The blood flowed red again.

THRENODY IN TIME OF CIVIL WAR

(The words are for music, perhaps)

First Semi-Chorus
>So famine passes over the land
>(Yet the vines and the olives bear)
>So the dust and the smoke-pall lie heavily over the city
>(Yet the blossom is born in his season)
>And men make hunger in the fullness of the earth
>Burning the fullness of earth lest men should eat.

Second Semi-Chorus
>So fears are in the wayside
>And they are afraid of that which is high
>(Fiat, Dewoitine, Junkers,
>Guernica, Dessié, Teruel)
>Where the dead lie riven with fire
>Riven and torn with the injustice of fire
>And no wind stirs the valley of dry bones.

>*Speaketh the Spirit of Time:*

>Into what sorrowful ranks
>Shedding their tired light
>Form and re-form the planets that march in infinite space,
>Mending no evil, forsworn
>To that inconscient tread,
>Despairing their last dissolution
>   the merciful quenching of fire –
>These I know; and the rocks
>Stamped of the ice and the fire
>Endure for a knowledge of terror about man's feet.
>Slow as the glacier moves
>Slow as the granite is worn
>By the rain and the wind and the frost that hallow His name,
>So does He reckon His power
>His promises measured by these,
>And only once (He saith) is a stone unrolled.
>Dynasties hang like a cloud:

Pride and anger and blood
Swell for a moment, and break
At the white-hot lips of the guns.
But the birds return; and the showers
                             and sunshine distain the bodies
Cleansed of the flesh and the sinew. Starlight illumines the valleys,
The valleys filled with the bones that wait the breath of His word.

Questioneth the Philosopher, in his grief eternal:

                         Where turns the spindle of Plato?
– The barrels of the guns turn in the shining lathe
In all the immaculate conception of fire and steel:
The lathe is our symbol of power and death,
Of strength multiplied and exalted by the meshing wheels,
Returning on its pattern, unswerving, without pity or haste.
Shell and bomb and engine are born of the matrix of earth,
Torn and milled and shaped by the teeth of the lathe
Racked and pierced and smoothed by the teeth of the lathe.
Till shining rings are oil-tempered to priesthood of death:
Steel and fire endlessly shaped to destroy.
      Only on the lathe does the spindle of destiny turn.

Crieth the Spirit of Man:

    The years march on, the drums and the conquests pass.
The people cry from captivity to the suffering of God.
From the captivity of Babylon to the captivity of Rome
From the martyrdom of Niemoeller to the martyrdom of Paul.

Yet we have blessed Thee in all thy attributes,
We have cried on Thee by the Hundred Names,
But the temples are empty, and no wind stirs
In the dry valley, in the branches of the oak-tree.
           And still we cry:
By those who have died with a curse on the mercy of
 God,
By those who die shrunken with hunger,
By those who die in the gas-cloud, on the barricade,
By those who die torn with the fruit of the lathe,
By the promise of redemption of hunger, and of
 remission of pain,
What of Thy justice, Lord?

Answereth Wisdom, the spirit of knowledge in man:

 Ye have looked for a coming
In flame and justice of flame
Lifting the eyes of the people to see
        fall'n in fire from heaven
(As the guns search the starlight) that Enemy
 freighted with death.
Or to a simpler thought, when the judge sits
 even-handed
Weighting his scales with mercy: and all the pleasures
 of sense
Are stabilized and perfected to balance that
 knowledge of hell.
Aware of terror beyond conception
Of injustice beyond endurance
That are redeemed only in the circles of fire and ice:
Only redeemed in a world where the tyrant dies
As Zeus and Jahveh die: in the desert, on a hill,
And the dark cavern shows light for an instant
 beyond.
So the heart pays that reckoning, for the infinite years,
For the scroll written with blood, written in hunger,
Scored in the clay of Babylon, in the stone of Egypt,
So ye are redeemed by the breath of a poet or of a
 prophet,

Redeemed for a little moment by the image-making
   of man –
By the breath of the wind that passes through the
   valley of dry bones.

Speaketh the Spirit of God:

   How long is neither a prayer nor a promise, nor
      their shadow:
For no man knoweth how long.

It is the cry of battle, the cry of defeat,
To call spirit to hold when sense, shattered and torn,
Flees from the last emplacements, and the cloud
   comes on.
Only he knoweth, in a garden, on a hill,
That dark and bitter wine that strengthens the soul
The vinegar mingled with gall that steels for an
   instant the soul
When the shadows fall on the spearmen, and the
   eyes harden and glaze.
So that hope is the image of My thought, as the
   broken flesh of My flesh,
That the crooked should be made straight and the
   rough places plain
Lest that infinite pain should be too terrible
The steel and flame too searing to be borne:
So I have thought that the rock sets free the fettered
   god,
I have given the vision of bone joined to his bone,
(The splinters of bone scattered in the little valleys)
That pain might be borne.
What should I know save that the heavens declare
My glory, and My creation of firmamental fire
Where night certifieth unto night of My own
   forebeing?
So, I am pain and despair: I am famine, and the
   dying king:
Knowing no praise in the grave: nor forgiveness from
   the pit.
Ware only in that complexity, in the lift of that
   sky-torn sea,

> That learning bound fast to suffering waiteth on man:
> That only in Plato's vision,
> Only in a dream on an island or on a hill,
> Are the valleys exalted, and the high places brought low:
> For an instant the light breaks –

Chorus of boys' voices

> Breaks as the blossom springs, and bird and beast are rejoicing,
> Breaks as the sea that laughs in its waves beyond telling,
> Breaks as the wind comes clean through the smoke of the cities,
> As the sun tells forth for a moment the infinite goodness of God.
> So grows the heart in His gladness to sea and blossom and sunshine,
> Lifted to hope and redemption in the vineyards and valleys of corn;

Men's voices

> Yet of His wisdom again the night and the storm come darkling,
> And the valleys fill with the bones of despair and of knowledge,

> > So long Thy knowing, O God.

TO WILTON HOUSE

So Donne and Yeats and Landor were left in the quiet room
With the gentle ghost that had fellowed me so long.
And I passed to the sunlit bay, and the laughing waves
To site the guns in the heather, and reckon the battered odds
Of the first war shamefully ended, and the second unbegun
(For the thorns were not yet ripe on the sands
      nor the dragons' teeth sprung on the beaches)
And we could talk on the terrace at night, drinking the wine,
Letting the mind flow easy between us four.

          My friends were there:
Dick, the gallant, the courteous, carefree and angry,
A thousand years of England grown into his side,
Who went to stand between his village and the sea
Asking only that he might be placed in the front of the battle to come.
And the Guardsman, grey-haired and lean, blue-tanned from the desert sun,
Steel-straight, laughter in the grey eyes: who followed me
To the stone house by the River, and kept my mirth alive.
John Dain from his school desk: Patrick who spoke all tongues:
And all that gallant company – Norway Poland Holland
 Flanders, from the torn beaches,
Re-tempering after defeat.

         Then in a moment flung
To the high room where the Van Dycks watch the maps
(Half a million rifles guarding King Charles' country)
And the beaches marked blood-red.
Above, the winged horse, and the maiden bound to the rock,
Watch us and wonder from the curved ceiling.
And I lie awake on a mattress, reckoning it all.
– All the folly and waste of the sunlit empty beaches, and the torn roof-trees,
– All the horror that follows the dark keel at night
– All the monuments broken with fire
– All my beautiful dead men.
The winged horse snorts above, and the planes move,

Engine calling to engine, declaring His power, through the
stabbing lights.

                                          (Whose invisible worm?)
But the Palladian Bridge guards the River
   and the gun-pit guards the Bridge
   and the trout hang poised in the shallows above the weir
   and the moon lights up the River to guide the enemy home.
Whom do I sup with tonight? (The Pleiades are gone.)
Yeats and Donne and Landor – three races and three men –
Guard me from the terror by night, and my own thoughts worst
   of all
In the blankness of the night.

                                        What do new friends avail?
What mask do I wear? (Ophelia's mind o'erthrown)
What valediction forbids mourning?
                          There's no constancy in the compasses:
The iron turns not west for any stone.

Only Inigo Jones, and the shadowed lines that he drew
And Sidney's tales of Shepherdesses as he walks outside
(Zutphen far off) – that white flame still a-fire –
And Touchstone jesting on the lawn outside.

                                      Only the Epitaph stands.

But the moonlight's still on the River, and the engines overhead.
In this great room where all the past looks on
Can I not match an elegy to show
That dust grows angry with its blood and state
And all futilities dissolve again?

                                        Arithmeticians, we?

Come, my Captains, for the blossoming night
Grows red and angry, and the worm's abroad.
Wheels mesh in the machine.

CHRISTMAS EVE, 1940

There are no bells tonight for the Child's birthday vigil,
   Never a welcoming candle or homestead fire:
Only by the manger the sweet-breath'd cattle are waiting –
                         Watching the door of the byre.

There are no bells in the morning from the blackened torn city
   To toll the merciful hiding of broken things:
Too few the steeples now for that brazen pity,
                         Too distant the Three Kings.

No birth, nor death, may wake them to our comfort:
   Greater the message in their mouths they bear.
For on the hills the shepherds wait the signal:
                         A falling star, a flare.

REFLECTIONS BEFORE JERICHO

Night after night our watchfires lit the land:
We patched our tattered gear and torn feet,
Whom that unreasoned pitiless command
Had doomed to countermarch in the white heat

That He might see, borne in His litter there,
What stronger devils manned that shining wall;
Or mask His helplessness, and our despair,
In that ineptitude of ritual.

Six times we carried Him before His foes:
Their battlements gave back His sorcery.
He had no answer to the taunts that rose
From men-at-arms that seemed to choke the sky,

Secure in pride no power of His could tame.
Our hatred's swelled; but two that stood aloof
Thought of their hospitality of shame,
And flax-stalks laid upon a sheltering roof.

Dawn brought the bitter sea-wind from the south.
We stood to arms, and our sun rose dismayed;
For through the host there ran from mouth to mouth
The seven-fold torment of the day's parade.

At the ninth hour the dust-choked murmur died.
We gripped our spears, and with incurious scorn,
Saw where the priests, to soothe His avid pride,
Raised to their lips the trumpets of ram's horn.

ON CATTISTOCK HILL

Here by the empty barrow
   We laid and cocked the Bren,
And mimic warfare wakened
   The prehistoric men.

The hard light turf lies yellowed
   From winter's burning snow,
And starveling cattle trample
   The muddied meads below.

Here we had climbed the hillside
   Under a sickened dawn
To see the cratered sheep-fold
   And the dead lambs unborn.

Beyond the Roman villas,
   Across the fairy ring,
Wakens an English county
   To greet the cruel spring:

And on the terraced hillside
   The faint and tortured sun
Struck on a flint-man's arrow
   That lay beside the gun.

MARCH MOON

The Scotch firs stand scale-barked against the skyline:
The river-lake in the park
Harbours no ripple.
       The swans on the reed-grown point
Are motionless, she on her nest, her mate
Placid beside her, unheeding the siren's wail.

There are no lights tonight, for the full moon
Has lit all quiet space, and the stabbing yellow shafts
Break on no cloud. Tired eyes strain at the stars
For the black shadow among them. Far to the south
Red flashes light the sky, and the distant guns
Thud a little, and cease.
       The trees by the water's edge
(Three of them side by side, branches outstretched)
Are mirrored beside the swans.
       But what darkness may cover
The earth at this ninth hour, to hide the merciless moon?
What veil is rent by the guns?
       A wild duck moves uneasily in the reeds,
And the owl floats over the grass, seeking the mice that quaver
Among the stems; and the earth shakes to a bomb.
The swan lifts her head.
       But the tomb is sealed.
Quem quaeritis in sepulchro, O Christicolae?
– Among the twisted girders, the shelter wreckage,
The choking dust of the plaster, glare of the fires.
The air is heavy with the smell of death
And the sound of falling water.
       The rock is split.
But there are no linen clothes for the mangled children
That men gather in the dawn, while the daffodils still sleep
Beside the lake, and the mousing owl sweeps on
Into the softness of the woods.

RETURN TO THE DAYE HOUSE

The trees were bare in the moonlight, and the paths
Soft underfoot, and no fish rose in the stream,
In the remembered eddies, on the rippling summer shallows.
So I came back weary and sickened at heart,
To the grey stone house in the trees.

Nine short weeks, and the cold came down upon me:
Cold bred first of knowledge, and the sight of the skeins to unravel
Before the guns should cease – and after men ordered their ceasing –
The skeins that will be heavy, and stain the hands
That fumble for the crossed threads: thereafter rising
From my own empty heart   and a world of streets and roof-tops
And the hands slow to a new task.

Wraiths drift in the river mist: I call on the place and hour.

The maps of Europe rise in torment, shuddering on their pins
As the storm blows up from the East.
                            The ants crawl inward:
Yellow and brown, from the steppes, from the desert: the tribes
Drift to the west, and vanish.
                            The slopes of the sea-shore change.
The ants turn back the rivers, and level the great spine-mountains.
Pickt and whitened bones are set for landmarks
And race and creed must plough and harrow the soil.
                            But a crown's awry –
(Holbein's pin through the skull: poison that tears the entrails,
Or a spear-point in the side) and the sluices break.
Stained water mounts in the meadows.

What pattern is this   I have seen shifting and turning
In the firelight of my room with the shadows dancing
(And my friends moving in the shadows.)
                            A Polish soldier
– Four wars behind his voice – talks in even tones
Of his torn land, and his dead. Rognes the Norwegian

With the great set rugged face, and pale eyes filled with hatred:
Bodley, Thompson, Threlfall: O'Rorke and Roman the Belgian
With his gentle laughter, all pain behind the tones:
(Half-soldiers, poets, scholars – what's the tag?
Does Sidney walk in Wilton Park tonight?)

Why have they brought us here to watch the pageant unfolding,
Famine and fire across the fluttering maps?
The slow oxen plod on, and the corn springs in the rain.
Why must the great guns swing in their turrets, across the Straits,
   and the sunk ships guard the mole?
(Because the cattle starved in a drought on the Steppes
Because the lumps of amber must ring the neck of a queen
Because a Nativity ikon burnt blue and gold at Kiev)
                              But tonight the air's a-whisper
Hate and lust and intrigue   pity and lies and fear
Brood on the Palace of Atreus.

A message falls on my desk.
A ship founders or a bomb falls or a cry goes out
To flutter the souls that crowd in the fetid shelters
(Coveys crouching in stubble, under the hawk's shadow)
To close the breech of the gun, or send the ammonal skywards,
Or twist bridge-girders in torture.
                              The pendulum ticks on.
Bombs in the soft night on Pearl Harbour
Bombs on the cruisers at Brest, on the Baltic trawlers,
On the Shwé Dagôn at Rangoon, on the steaming Perlis jungle.
And the limbs sprawl in the creepers for ant-folk and rat to
   whiten
Or the polyp to turn to coral, or crab to tear.
And in the beginning were words, and the soft-voiced diplomats
   talking
For the ant-folk must have room   on the coral islands on the
                              sands of Eritrea
Corn and wine and oil for their larger breeding
Copper and rubber and oil for their swifter killing
(And the desert thorn's aflame.)
                              Snow falls on the steppes.
Shells plunge and the diamond diapered patterns rise
To cover the creaking bodies. There's snow on the pinned maps

That weights them against rising in the winds of the world
                                      The frontiers have gone.

Here's the grey house: stones laid on kindness and laughter,
And the long generous breeding of this place. Firelight and
  books again.
And a wise loved voice in greeting.
                                  But what shuts out the cold?
The mist's about the warm and sheltering pines,
Skein upon skein, my serpent coils of cold.
Maybe the old and the wise, who have turned the wheel,
Can break the charm about me.
                                                I will go in.

FRAGMENTS OF A TESTAMENT

I

'For I have dreamed a weary dream
Beyond the land of Skye.'

– Another's words, but why should they not hold true,
Since my dreams for others have been true of late?
But yet not weary; for God could not be greater in goodness
Than that the cycle of sixty years come round and the name
    untarnisht
(Behind the dead horses, in the white Afghan sun)
Ending light-hearted, hand on stock or tiller.
Therefore I summon up my testament, my ghosts,
To match in this clumsy verse the thoughts that fight
Through the long hours, waiting for the dawn, in the
    Double Cube,
Or in the Park, when the bird-song breaks from the trees.
'Beyond the land of Skye' – whether from that grim island
(Do you remember the night in the dinghy, pollack-fishing, when
    the storm came up from Mull
And we edged her through the seaway, light-hearted under the
    shadow?)
Or from my own west coast, where the great tides flow
Up from the Shannon, and I learnt to handle sheet and oar:
The oak-tree roots clutch at the cliff, so near to falling
(The tree that falls with the House) and the redshanks cry on the
    mudflats.
And plover flight in the dusk, lost flickering ghosts:
I call upon those days, and on my empty home.

II

The long sweet days by the river, above the five-arched bridge,
And white-trout leaping in the sea-weed pool,
Or where the water raced by the white-thorn hedge
And wrist and eye were timed to drop the flies.
The snipe drum overhead: and the small soft rain in my face,
Glad that the rain should stir the river to life
Leaping over the fall at Clondagad.
By a score of waters that happiness came back –

The stream at Linton: the salmon-river at Voss:
The lakes in the Björndalsvand: and now, most loved of all
(Since love was sharpened by want, and the need to forget all else)
The broad bright shallows below the Palladian Bridge
And the mayfly swirling down.

III

They were good days too on the marshes, flighting duck in the dusk:
Walking the hills, the red ground and the mires,
The peace of the hidden valley by Lough Lomàun:
Laurel and rhododendron that sheltered the woodcock in frosts,
Brake bracken pool throughout that countryside.
And while the gun lay light still in the hand
The crisp Fen stubbles in the October morning
The evening light golden on Brandon woods.

IV

Perhaps it is good that men should worship the gun
As I saw them worship it once in the jungle near Chandergore
(A twelve-pounder buried in the living tree, for seed and fruit,
The clay horse on the muzzle, the garland round the breech).
The gun makes each St Peter, holding the keys,
Bright and beautiful, pressed home in the magazine,
Power and dominion over the Kings
                                        and at the temple
Swifter than asp at breast when the bolt goes home,
Accident shackled at last.
                        But its own clean beauty is constant
Hammer and scear and bent in a Chilton lock:
The breech-block of the Bren, and the delicate shining plunger:
The intricate Vickers, the lightness and grace of the Browning,
And the friendly feel of walnut in the hand.

V

Why must the dead go down into water, and the snowflakes
Melt on the coffin-lid?
O but the empty house, and the rusting gun,
And all that wisdom gone when I needed it so.

VI

Good days in the white fives-courts, when hand and eye were quick
And the volleys rattled through the long match;
Or standing in the deep, when there was leisure to watch
The ball soaring in its long perfect curves.
                                          Days in the gym
Dripping with sweat, when the gloves seemed lead, and legs went numb,
And Knight, the patient and kindly, had striven to show me
Something of ringcraft, and the joy of blow gone home.
But maybe best of all, by Ditton in the light ships,
With the great blades swinging, and the hiss of the water passing
As the bows strode on through the dusk.
                                     Lost now, but caught for a moment.
On the Canal in Calcutta, sculling in my last race.

VII

I have loved all craftsman's work, and the tools of the craftsman:
The bite of chisel and plane: the grain renewing its beauty
And the feel of the thumb on the edge new-made from the oilstone.
Greenheart growing smooth with glass-edge and paper:
Strakes taking curve and bevel under the draw-knife
As the boat grew on her frames: concrete new-mixed and setting:
Lead poured into moulds, clear-silvered and kindly:
Mending and working of lines and nets and ropes.
It is good that skill should renew the book-dimmed eyes.

(I name the last simplification   and counter-weight to care.)

VIII

But the grooves ran crooked, and a cracked mirror threw back
(Mirrors of others' eyes, and a careless word)
Self against Soul, each at war with other.
A stammering tongue, and sleep so long denied
To the room above the courtyard; the pistol beneath the pillow
In a land of civil war, brought bitterness and mistrust
For the life's plan broken at twenty, and light gone from the eyes.
Only Tillyard's wisdom to help me through

Half-drunk with poetry, raw and eager and restless:
Ignorant, fearful of women, and driven to hide my fear
In a dim worship of their power and strength and comfort:
Killing desire in work and the strength of my body.

IX

Perhaps it is good that the body grow slower, as bringing to play
New mind-muscles developed to balance the loss.
In war I have found companions, men and women,
Who took me, not knowing or caring what name I bore
In another world: and seeming content enough
With what I could give. Yet all the while
I have stood a little apart, half-dreaming, but eager
To learn new war-craft.

X

It is strange that again one must speak, in this new trade.
Why should not two tongues speak together, neither hindering
  other?
I taught men once to love Hogarth: the clean swift line of Blake:
Constable's evening peace: and Gainsborough's loved women:
The intricate figures of Donne: tragedy's grandeur and sweep:
Phantastic learning of Browne: made living the thought of the
  dead.

XI

The Park is sunlit: the planes roar overhead –
The grayling play in the shallows, and the garden's a-glow with
  bloom.
I know not which of the Three be nearest now
To order the tangled threads, or kill the ache
At the heart's root.
                          Van Dyck's women face me –
Stiff drapery and necks beringed with pearls –
The Wilsons glow on the stone walls outside;
And caravan work proclaims its heraldry.

The dusty maps stand, crucified with pins.

There is no fear of the morrow, and I think
Perhaps I shall one day wake.

ANTIPHON: AFTER BATTLE

i

The doors of the dovecotes opened one by one
And the half-moulted birds blinked for a while at the light,
Looking for the withered olives we had made ready for them.
The delegates fawned in our tents, in the Palaces

                                              and the scraps of paper were signed
And all the Americans shot off their pistols, and the RAF their flares.
At the Headquarters, they started to throw the files out of the windows
(So we had fought, four hundred miles from the battle)
– But that was wrong, for the Chief had to write his dispatches,
                                so they threw out toilet paper instead.

Sit back on the ridge above Actaeon's fountain.
Sit back and watch the lights come on in Europe –
Lights in Turin, with thirty murders a night,
Lights in Klagenfurt, with the Jug patrols in the streets,
Lights in Macedonia, where the gold and the Stens are hidden,
Lights in the Val d'Aosta, where Allies chaffer for honour
(To gild Pétain's surrender, or raise the sunk ships at Oran?)
Lights in Damascus, from the bursting seventy-fives.

And a lady MP visited Buchenwald.

So we moved the tanks to Udine, and the guns to Monfalcone,
And held our conferences, and printed more paper money,
And saw the weasels settle to wait on the river lines,
Wondering which teeth should be sharpened or drawn that peace might come.

ii

Terraced the vines and lemons drop to this moonlit sea
Concrete emplacements, skull-smooth, watch the Sorrento headlands,
Where the cruisers came to Salerno, in the cere-cloth misting of dawn.

                              Tired and slashed and seamed
Cross-hatched with the quivering olive, and the flaunting twisted
    brushwood,
Scored with the wedged gapped draw-knife of the ice
Mountains menace the white towns; grapes ripen in the dust.

                              iii

'Seek out reality: leave things that seem.'
We lie in the blue water; sunlight deadens the brain.
A murmur comes from England, where the great men
Sling mud against the moon, or claim their due
Naked, for Corioli.
                              What limb is set by honour?
In the hospital ward flies swarm on moist flesh
And Italian girls scrub the floors, thinking of the evening's lover.
Ether drifts through the balconies.
                              There's no reality here
Or in the stone graveyard of the Acropolis, or among the gardens
    at Versailles:
No answer from Cumae, where Virgil's lines are cut
White marble, gold-lettered, smeared and defaced
With pencil signatures of pilgrims.
                              (Si quid mea carmina possunt!)
The Roman nobility sit in the night-clubs, at cards,
Measuring out their lives with Allied lire and dice,
To a braying saxophone, against the sea-blue night.

                              iv

Berkeley was wrong. There is no refuge in the brain.
Only the hand is right: mattock and spade and knife:
Masons dust-grey and sweating to square the stone
That bridge and aqueduct may carry again.
But most, I think reality's in the sea
And the sea-farer's gear. Nets drying on quays
The strong brown smell of barking: new coir swangs:
The bright craft beached on their rollers, or loading at Trieste
The slaves set free for Venice and the parched eastern towns.
Still in the little shipyards the schooners grow
Dark-ribbed against the sky: oak hewn and scarphed and bolted
Before the lovely woman-curves grow on
From the steamed strakes of pine.

v

Here's full night on the sea.
The fishing boats with their flares disperse and cluster again.
Prow-lights that call fish up from their woven depths
To pattern in silver at the last the net.
Stars move, wave-dimmed on the waters.

THE RIVER

i

This is the River, the windless rippled tide,
The pale foot-trampled sand of the nearer shore,
And the black splintered wharf. We wait beside,
Mouths dry, and the vapoured airy unquiet hearts
Clutch at new rhythms.

                        Into the Cavern's dark
Black waves slide and eddy against rock walls;
Vaulted, receding, till the River's winding course
Sheds its last waves to silence.

                        We wait the returning Ship.

Soon we shall see her labour up-stream, hear the grunt of the oars,
Watch her turn and swing, and nuzzle the weed-grown piers,
Making fast for us.

                        But now we wait for the ferry.

There is time to remember our valediction:

The needles that stitched soft vestments against our pain,
The fight for the twice-caught breath, the slow malignant scalding,
The hemlock-coldness creeping up to the loins,
The gush of blood to the throat
                        limbs scuffling against the linen.
And we stare at the Cavern's mouth, remembering that confusion,
Our own reluctant wheeling above the crumpled body,
Summoning composure for the dark.

                        We wait for the ferry.
Those are the first memories: needle or knife,
The surrogate for breath, hissing gently from the black cylinder,
The alien blood dripped into the shrunk veins
That could not thicken the ghost.

                                                        Then we recall
The specious gloss of the hearse, the deceitful sinking platform
In the meticulously neutral chapel with its varnished pine,
And as the shell drew nearer to the flame
Our oaken boards salvaged for bookshelves.
We remember the sprinkled ashes, the gleaming crumbled bone

That nourished the Grass or the Rose.
Or the new-trampled mud, the green-lined grave in the rain
Three handfuls of earth. No matter now.
This is the River.   The wharf is lonely and cold.

                              ii

Here is the Ship treading the tide with her fore-foot. White
    shapes
With shrunken corded muscles and hidden faces
Crouch over the oars.
In the stern-sheets sits the Woman, the Harlot,
Child-faced, small rounded breasts, clutching her breasts
Her hair stirred by the wind coming up the Cavern,
A jar of honey on her knees. She gives no sign.
Wharf-piles grate on the planks; the oars edge her outwards,
We drift to the black archways, towards the images of fear,
Images we have made.

                              For now we must return
Through death-in-life to what is stored against us,
Images of what we have thought.

                              They will come at us now
Out of the niches in the rocky walls
Out of the unthreaded caves behind each arch
Out of the dripping holy wells of the rock:
They are our thoughts, images of our own begetting,
Nourished in soft warm womb-cells of the brain

Sped to the nerves and battlements of body
Forcing lilies from the sour clay.
Now, as we back through the Cavern, we must seize and repel
    them,

For they are our life, our only living, our enemies,
And we must meet them, in the horror of the Cavern,
Unravel action to innocence under the eyes of the Woman,

We on the white, bone-white Ship.

iii

This is their first assault: small eager thoughts like bats
That fasten with hooked claws on wrists and fingers,
Or stir the hair.   Echoes of the oars have waked them
In the dripping roof.
Now along keel and gunwale, slide white studded arms
Clutching towards us. And here are phantasms of our three
    slayers
Scorpion Archer and Crab   descended from the Zodiac,
Shining in the rock-vaults. A fish leaps, obscene, phosphorescent,
The blinded fish of the Cavern. And here is a butterfly
Strayed from our last light, begging its passage on the Ship,
That settles on the Woman's hair. Wings rustle in the dripping
    roof.
These are the hazards we have made:
These we must live again while the Woman-Harlot watches
This is thought-in-image ineluctable
Transmigration irreversible yet reversed
Drifting to innocence.
And only with thought-in-fire can we meet them
Thought that we now invoke, in this frenzied face of terror
Nursing the little fire against the moist winds of the Cavern
To singe the white assaulting tendrils, the black-ribbed wings,
The spiders that walk the waters.
We drift downwards still, fighting the images
Wingd finnd clawed bristled swollen
Burning them back   lest they settle to weight us to sinking

Or tear us from the bone-white Ship.

iv

Always the Woman-Harlot watches our warfare, unmoving,
The honey at her knees.   For she is our symbol
Of desire thinned to a shadow, desire nursing the flame,
Seeing our sins thicken about us.

                                                  We swing in the eddies.
The images hiss and rustle. This is the time to pray:
Pray that the fire may endure, the cleansing coal on the lips
Fire in the bone-white soul: fire of the intellect
Fire that we must nurse in this passage of the Cavern
Fire half-quenched by the wind of the moist images
Fire that can shrivel the enmities of air

Fire from Heaven.

                                  v

The winding course grows lighter: very far overhead
There is a cleft in the rock. Miasma breaks to mist.
And now is the Pool, and the Three Statues that we must pass
Grey, unmoving, carved in the rock face.
                        We are swung to their feet by an eddy,
And linger there.
      Now the rustle of black wings has died: there is only silence
Silence, and the smell of fire from the bone-white Ship.
As we wait in the half-light for the Statues
The Woman's eyes fixed upon us.
But today there is no judgment
No answer from the stone no gesture from the impassive hands.

The eddy snatches again, and now we feel
The first push of the sea-tide against the River, the quickening of
    the waters,
Chattering on strakes. Now comes marsh-land,
Grey-green sea-holly and marram and thyme of the saltings
And the curlews boding the day.
Here are the first gulls on the water
And a salmon like a great silver ingot leaping
In praise of the sea. The Ship lifts to wave-laughter,
And the rowers raise their heads.
Here is our quay: stone masonry ascending
A rivulet of clear water falling beside it
From a spring by the olive trees.

                              Now the Woman, the Harlot, rises
   And in that light of morning her robe is blue

The deep blue of the Maiden. She has traversed the Cavern
   with us.
We desire the honey no longer.

                                                      And now her fellows
Throng the stone stairs to greet her, and go before us
To the trees, and the singing birds.

BUDDHA AND THE FISH

As on the wall of Plato's Cave
   He saw a shadow drift before,
And, breaking the rhymed surface-wave,
   The circled dipping of an oar.

Safe in the coffined limestone cleft
   His muscled tail and steel-strung bone
Watched the green-misted world about
   His vision's geometric cone.

Freed of seine-fear by cloven rock,
   Fed by snail shrimp and schooling fry,
Ravening the amber nymphs that climbed
   Steep ladders to transfiguring sky;

Above his world of shadowed light
   Wrenched by the wind in flashing bars
Sat Buddha with a palsied wrist,
   Lord of ichthonic avatars;

And drew across the lighted gyre
   Some fibred tinselled dancing thing:
The riven water rose and swirled
   To that destructive water-spring

And feigned life and instinct death
   Met in the whirlpool. Buddha stirred.
A slender thread and bending twig
   Compassed compassion of His word.

God drew his lashing eidolon
   Free from the matrix of the flesh:
Rounded the bridging arc to meet
   The valediction of the mesh,

Till quivering in angelic air
   Love to the grassy margent bore
Second of fishes to the feast
   Beside a Galilean shore.

SHOOTING A BAT

Sound of late bees, and the wind in the hazel-coppice,
Autumn falling, and long
Glory of rhododendrons gone,
Ere the October Moon brings in the snipe.
Here to the right the begonia greenhouse stood:
Now cracked red tiles on which the briar creeps
And edges towards the bitter hazel-trees.

Yet through the wrought scrolls of the garden gate
I see that centre walk, still flower-bright,
That drops to the East Shrubbery and the stream,
Its flanking roses in last autumn's strength.
'Forsaken Garden'? No casual visitors
Image loved shadows warring in despair
Against the smothering coltsfoot and couch-grass,
And rotting palisades where the peach-trees cling.

Now I must wrench free from that sentiment:
The funeral-windowed house, the leprous plaster,
Half-kept – against what?
                                        Shall I still cut
Shafts for my arrows from the hazel grove,
Choose once again the smooth unfruiting rods,
Steel-ring them patiently lest splinter wreck,
Season and head and fletch them?
                         But there's no strength for the bow.

Why must I think in symbols, being over-read?
To focus childhood's speed of hand and eye
And outface age and its indignity?

Invenit destructum: extructum reliquit.
(Victorian Gothic carving over the doorway)
Two hundred years to ruin; then rebuilt;
Bred its young life a century to fame,
And all's to naught again.   We had served history's turn.
A swarm of bees was trapped in a shuttered room
And dead dried dusty litter the window-sills.

Perhaps it is all my doing.

                        For once, on a summer's night,
The grown-ups at coffee, on the balustrade,
Beside those red geranium-heavy urns
Talked gaily, looking on the great sweep of the River –
Deer Island, Thrummeragh, Coney and Rosscliff,
That float on the bright moon-path of the springs;
And east and south beyond the Elm Field
The screen of fire that keeps our Burial Ground.

                            Bats flickered across the sky
Between the quiet beeches and the lawns
Hawking for the last soundless gnats of dusk.

                                   That I, ten years,
Arrogant, lonely, angry at neglect,
said:
    'I could shoot one of those.'

                                There was a roar of laughter.

'What nonsense! No one could!'
                                     'Shilling if you do!'

Stubborn-dismayed I fetched the tiny gun –
Thirty pellets of shot in the paper cartridge –
Fired, and a bat fell.
'That was sheer luck.   You couldn't do it again'.
I lifted and closed the breech-block: the smoking case
Gave its faint brimstone smell.

                                  I fired at a shadow
And another dropped.
                The party was silent
                        It's bad to flatter the young.

Next morning in the sunlight the furred bodies
Lay on the ground, fingers clenched, teeth bare.

I did not read my Homer till next year.

EBB TIDE

Look for a stone as big as your strength can roll it:
Not one that's bedded in sand or gravel or mud
But raised on shingle, clear stranded water around it,
Curtained with weed at the mouth   limpet and barnacle starred,
Hiding a cave.
                              Brace fingers, shoulders, thighs,
Turn it (no wing will start) and you have cracked
Fortress and citadel to light and fear.
The green crab sidles backward, right claw on guard,
Grinding full armour.
                              Ridiculous flutters the nine-eyes,
And a little exquisite olive-backed silver eel
Slides to his proper dark.
                              Tiny translucent fry
Flurry a moment in climacteric of light
And sink to rest in the pebbles, taking new tints from the sun.
The noise and the troubled water settle.   Only the crabs
Grate as they back to their new defensible rock-wall.
Balefully they watch the disturber of the cave.

And that is I, the tyrant, the resurrector,
Prometheus or Theseus? No; a lewd ignorant spy
That rolled the rock for power, for clumsy arrogance,
For greed of curiosity.
                              So, let me watch beside them,
Lest oyster-catcher or turnstone or curlew comb the beach
Or that most terrible cloaked and hooded crow
Shatter this courteous armistice they give me.
Watch till the healing tide creeps up the ledges
Lifting its grey slow veil above the mud-flats,
The veil to cover what my shame has rent
And give them their cave re-born.

SLUICE-GATE

No more than a loosened stone above the sluice-way,
A pivot rusted and jammed. So our great clanging shield
Sagged sideways   the lockt line of the wall broken.

A hundred years it withstood
The searching groping fingers of each flood,
The battering undertow of the Harvest Springs,
With a south-west gale behind.
                                        Closing iron crushed
Delicate swelling wrack, the smooth silk ribbon-weed,
Repelled the red crab's armour, the thrusting prawn.

                     Only a trickle ever went past the shield's rim
Half-filling reeded dykes in the meadows behind
Lifting moisture to grass-roots   salt-healing the cattle.

Now the sea-wall's pierced where my Scotch Firs stood nobly,
Where the weasel-pack came out on summer evenings
To play and chitter before their screaming kill.
Briar and laurel alike die round the white poisoned tree roots:
All we had won is squandered in the grey slow flux of the tide.

My race might have watched the sluice-gate:
Cleared the black gravel the waves wash over the boat-slip:
Brought the clean heat of the forge to shape and rivet
Between two tides' respite . . .
                if we'd had courage and faith to cherish the wall.
– Sold a picture maybe: or the empty silver cups
Gathered by *Galatea, Gertrude*: Clyde, Nova Scotia, Marblehead;
The great sparred yachts that anchored off the sluice-gate
Flying the Squadron Flag; ancestral folly
A dying sailor watched from a turreted room.

There was nothing to sell, at the end, but trees and a little honour,
And a roof-tree ready to fall.
                            The tide creeps up to the orchard
Lips the grey lichened apples, the slender feathered bamboo,
The proud-set rhododendrons.
                         Word, name, ghost, all failed
Before the embittered meadows, the merciful rising mudflats
Where the redshank probes and cries.

ACCOMPLICE

This is the place for our rites: this cedar-shaded hollow
Cool and dry-scented, where orchard-slope drops sharply
And burrows cluster at random.
Here we must harrow the Underworld, drive up the ghosts,
We who are hungry for them.

White messengers are ready; tumbling, sharp-set, in a canvas bag.

First we must net this Underworld; hang them on sliding cords,
Fair them over the runner-mouths. Drive the pegs deep, but
 gently,
Lest the ghosts hear our foot-falls.

Take up our messengers. First we must master and arm them.
Cunningly tie the neck, loop the pink weaving muzzle;
Spit in the hand, smooth muzzle and fur to his liking;

Fasten the clue for this labyrinth, coil it loosely above,
Lift a net clear.
                    The messenger of the gods hesitates,
Sniffs the still hot air; shivers a little, catches
Some faint known scent that spells ancestral blood.
The death-line snakes out slowly, grating on dry earth.
We stand waiting for those who are summoned.

                    Suddenly there is thunder in this Underworld:
Rushes of stamping feet: silence: a rush again.
The clay-stained line whips faster
And thudding feet grow louder: noise nears to burst into
 daylight.
A net leaps out of the hillside. Inside the drawn purse
He kicks and screams in the net-toils.
                                        Move quickly to this ghost.
Clutch kicking legs, teaze out the meshes, and hold it an instant
Where the quiet light through the cedars touches brown eyes.
Hand-edge falls on the neckbone.

Out of the burrow comes Theseus, dusty, red-eyed
Weaving his nostrils bewildered   a little angry maybe.
Does he catch the scent of the slack grey bundle beside us?
But others wait below.

Wipe hands in the grass, caress him, and turn him downwards
To drive grey spirits again.

THE TOWER REVISITED

Drive your cart and your plough –
                              said that fierce William Blake.
(And there they are, the plough and the cart, in the great square lower room,
Rusting, rotting in dung; the scratched initials above,
The plaster chipped for souvenirs.
                              – over the bones of the dead.
So it should be; and I turn from their dark corner
To staring windows, rain-starved river, weed-stalking moorhen,
Idly glance at his arrogant bad verses set in slate on the wall.
Someone has scrawled them with charcoal.

                              'Sure wasn't that fella Yeats
A great imposther always?'
                              But they carted no stones of the Tower
To Galway housing estates. The Norman mortar too hard?
Coole's nothing; a threshold stone uncovered of mould,
That gaping tourists may see how a house is killed.

Yeats drove nor plough nor horse: rode but an imaged one
(Though envying always the riders, mounted men or women)
Voices of hounds and drumming of hoofs on Benbulben,
Horses of fire, of shadow, Blake or Homer or Spenser,
Tamers of horses from Troy   nightly over Drumcliff.

Ridden or riven the tomb by angel or engine or plough?

Thick-sown the graveyards of Ireland lie to grey weather
Nettle and briar and elder, and frost-cracked limestone.
Yet no man ploughs them to corn, or trenches for footings.
This is the holy ground; the dead are above the living:
Scatter Synge's skulls and the coffin boarding to mark it,
Only cram with more dead.

That is Blake's challenge: processional symbols some farmer
Lazily left with the Tower. Now let us take them from it.
The plough to tear, the cart to carry, the graveyard walls to break.
Scour, sharpen, yoke, harness: rend the encircling briar,
And honour the dead with truth above the stone.

'ODE POUR L'ELECTION'

One   Shot-in-the-lungs goes upward in the tower:
Shot-in-the-brain lies twitching, claws scrabble earth:
Shot-in-the-bowels goes on, winced in the pillar of fire,
To die rat-ringed at evening, in rime-white bracken.

These Images, do they return at D less ten?

– When the vulture-nurses crowd the stilted bed
Black-White   gloating in power over half-infant again.
Are shadows of triumph on smooth professional faces
Smiling their nightingale comfort: a woman's smile,
Maternal pride in ignominy of unloved doll?

The smiles set like glazed sugar: paper chains
Sway in the noisy Christmas corridor.

Two   He could not face the seventh, better to turn
To blackthorn brake beside an autumn stubble.
('We feel the safety of a hawthorn glade')
And the twice-rooted briar that snares the grass
Tripped, to fall cleverly.
Or to the rock-fanged lake, and a quick western storm.

Either would do, for cover.
                                Better, perhaps, the lake.
To feel the boat riding lonely, light by the forefoot,
Engine live to the flames that bite on the screw,
Kind waves baring breast-whiteness.
He would deny them at first, the women's part,
So they'd grow fiercer, whiter, hiding the shore line,
Crest upon crest feigning to hunt him down.

Ahead, as he crouched by the tiller, the up-flung prow
Shows stem-piece to keel-mortise: the useless rope
Chattering on ring-bolt. Strakes slam: ribs groan on
  nail-roves.
So he would hold her into the eye of the weather
To his last exaltation of wind and spray,
Till wave laid bare the limestone and the larch splintered
Falln upon rock. And after that were kindness of green
  waters
Six feet below, great fishes nosing his hair.

One Folly of rhetoric, words spun to self-pity.
That's the land's curse; word weighing down deed.
The neutrons nowhere, everywhere: emptiness
Of our past mock-heroics, mud-flats of the ebbed tide.

Two But might one roll the dice below the cross
And let God choose? For I have read
That those who tire of pain may play, and the sixes fall
For an unrent garment?

One There's no certainty but next dawn.
Nothing but light's intensity, and God
In all places like the neutrons.
Gamble no moment, the stumble, the mistimed wave,
Lest cowardice cheat his pain, and find at last
A skull in a gold box.

This is the dialogue with no last term.

PRELUDE FOR 1962

Maybe a nightmare, but certified once in action.

A rabbit scrambles slipping falling back
On that smooth-tilted limestone quarry-face
(We might have carved a poet's death-name there)

                                      Grey burning haildrops
Splashed rock around him. He screams and climbs
Seeking the wood's shelter from this quick laughing thunder,
Till god's sight measured angle and pace the better
And he fell kicking in thorns.

Tonight there's snow on the apple-trees, ice on training wires,
Shell-pink light on the roof-tops.

                                In snow the cripple's unmanned:
Labour and care and falling-fear together
To hold a little life for the last premiums
At the quarry's edge, or in laurel-thicket beyond?
Shall he gather, to shore tradition, memories
That once seemed strong or gracious, reneging self-pity,
Moments of magnanimity on water, mountain, fire?
Clouded then childhood's sin, the sensual touch,
Probings of the cleft rock, flesh swollen or shrunk with desire
(So the ganched conger writhes and threshes in sea-pool)
Mind's hot imaginings no moist warmth had healed.

Limbs too sprawled for the boat; no thigh braced to plate-casing
Against black mountain squall.   Lean vainly, watch the water
Spill the lee gunwale.   He cannot move
Thwartships to tiller, bite blade, fling muscle to stretcher
(And who sheets home the foresail or the shroud?)

Now the snow's fallen   what meaning?

We have to kill to know satisfactorily whether
There is moisture for us in the well, or nucleic acid
At centre of foetus cell. Are they stored, communicable
These patterns in the small elvers of the loins?
What do we spill to the river in night's November flood?

Burn low the enveloping gas-jets. Bearings labour in bone.
Yes, but let it come quickly, the gun's lead on the rock-face,
Spasm of riddled heart.

                                                                           Spare only
God's seventh wave of pain: or give once more but once
Heather in sunlight, the bright lifting wave, the swift-stabbing
    heron
Patient in lake.

DARK JOURNEY, 1919

i

I do not think that we can know the woods.

Perhaps in winter daylight   hoar-frost on bramble and cobweb,
Crisp dying grass underfoot.   Then we can tell
Where the hare will break in her soft leaping terror,
Woodcock clatter from laurel, pigeon from matted ivy.

We reckoned a boyhood by larch-growth
                                          man's life by a silver fir,
Joy by our apple leafage.   But that was by day.

Now it is changed. Night's down. I must leave lamplight,
Cold with three fears, to walk the woodland.
                                                 Why, then?
Feign guard against world of fire
                               of petrol and straw and looting,
Broken stained glass and charred wet wood in the morning?
A muddied pit in the lawn, his dog shot into it first?
Last night they burned Fort Fergus across the valley
Into the smoky dawn.

                         I must walk the sorcerer's wood.

Three fears on me this night.   Armed men
Who'd ring the house in the woods before the lorries came:
Laughing, a little drunk   their rifles blessed from the altar
To pay three conquests, hunger of the hill fields.
The second's my own; are they friends or enemies now?

Roosting pheasant in spinney, owl in the grey beech:
Finches and thrushes in warmth of rhododendrons
That burst in fluttering if a twig is stirred:
The ghost of a red-jawed collie I'd shot when he harried
    our ewes:
Some cat gone wild from the village. And always the soft winged
    woodcock
That probe their marshy hollows, flitting from water to rushes
Through their marked lanes in the trees.

The third I cannot know, though I have made this fear
Between a boy's pride and folly and half-belief
Of stories nailed to bridge and stream and coppice
Garden and orchard and boathouse   stone and shade
Kinsmen who made the woods. Do they walk the paths in winter?

Will something happen to stop me?
Take (binding thong tighter) comfort in the hand
Two rounds (no more, and one must not load it
For private honour). Soft shoes to match the dark.

ii

Cross the gravel, the lawn by the sundial.
                                            We must go clockwise.
(Our rites are useless, but we keep them still:
Carry a fir-cone, perhaps: but no light or fire).
Skirt the garden, down to the shrubbery stream.
Pass the apple-house, sweet with hay and the Ribstones:
Down rough steps in trees' tunnel to the East Screen,
To the river talking quietly on the rocks.

                                            Now turn seawards,
Cross foot by foot the little split-log bridge
Feel its chill iron rail, lashed to the rotting uprights.
Stop for a moment, listening. Here one stands for the drive.
Hands slippy now with sweat, lock-plates burn in coldness.
Finger tells pin and screw and scroll-work: just to be sure.

It's lighter now; I can see the slopes of the orchard,
Mist on the lichened trees. Feathered clumps of bamboo
Grate on stems quietly in a wind from the sea.
Across the dyke-slashed meadow
Curlew, redshank, widgeon cry softly, without fear,
Restless low music along the dying tide.
For a little the going is fairer. Black gravelled path. Hedge-roots
    eaten by water.
A rat drops into the reeds. Now the trees close again.
An iron gate: the quiet wreck by the quay-side,

Ribs thrusting black from her kelson. The boathouse in
  lighter air.
I have startled a feeding curlew. Stop, frozen: and listen.

Feel (so foolish) the clean brass rims of power.
Charm against ghost, or raider.
Look in the half-tide creek. *They* might have landed there
(And all things come from the sea). But only an islander's boat
Swings to her painter, complaining.

iii

Turn now to the great wood, the hardest and darkest,
On the long slope of the hill that lifts to the fir-screened
  graveyard.
Blood quickens. The paths are secret and steep
Clogged with dead leaves that stir.
                            Our slate-lipped well from the rock
Glimmers whitely with lime.
Bend to the water. It has not failed us in drouth.
Cup the right hand for the iron-chill sweetness. This too is a rite
(But do not lay down the gun). Take a steep way
Where paths cross and wander. Bear from the stream on the right
Noisy in the listening laurels. This is the utmost fear
For all things use the middle path on the hill.
Now my roots swell and cross to trip me:
They have struggled against the iron shale, they are beaten
  upwards,
No safety from gale in their splayed foothold.
Crush a soft laurel branch for the bitter cyanide smell:
Hold twig as sprouting fingers (myth may ward off the wood)
Here is a cork-tree, half-dead, we brought from France:
A moss-grown pineapple stone, cut as Hogarth had planned it,
Beauty's geometry so alien here. An ammonite too from the
  limestone.
Landmarks that were removed. Stop and take breath.

Two gunshots from the end. Light grows with the path's
  steepness.
Do not go faster, for then the trees will move,
Briar snake outwards, hazel cut and lash.

Even the stream grows louder: is it going to break before me?
Cup-rounded, dry-lipped.   Thought is a chalice of fear
Dull, like a polished coconut.   That's what he told me
One who had seen the Grail in a family safe
In the Welsh Hills.
        Now move again. A rabbit thumps
At the edge of the Elm Field. Good that he's feeding. This is the end.

No light in the white turret. Glass sheds no shot-blast
Between window and desk-lamp. But I have finished.

Gun by the bedside, though.
      We may load it, now.

TWO PICTURES

i

Between the ox's skull, garlanded, ribboned for marriage,
And the five-spoked wheel of his life
Cupid stood, puzzled   pushing at the wheel's rim.
Was the skull (as they said) for patience, dumb labour resting in death?

Better the dolphin-emblem, twined about anchor-stock:
Swift sinuous gay body of rescued rescuer:
Fluke-fastened now to the sand.

         So my sea's images rove in the blood, and stir it:
Who taught Pythagoras to splice a rope,
To serve against the lay? Tarred canvas settles to shape
To hide my shameful joining. But the short splice will not render
Through mast-head block when I turn seaward, when
The mainsail lifts to stir the lazy keel.
Halyards, words, jam in the throat.

ii

Surely he came to that grave woman in woodland,
Riding a stumbling donkey on stony path,
A crook on his shoulders. Whole hands are soft from the fleeces.
No prophet spoke of that. Dogma flutters, wounded,
A dove in a steel gin.
There is no love they call immaculate, no new man from the womb.
But everywhere the white birds of the ghost, in lake or on headland,
That come if we are still.

iii

God rest him from all offence, in the lanes, beside the fall;
Send the white birds, their wings salt-flecked from the sea.
God send him strength to draw from his groin the arrow
That strikes below the armour's scalloped rim,
God send him patience, ox's skull or anchor,
And woman waiting in the thatched hidden hut
Where woodland falls to the sea.

29 DECEMBER 1964

I

I do not know what wrong was done in Chrysê,
What false turn taken on the Corinth road.
– Some lane that shouldered the mountain, rutted and stony,
Clogged with unflowering gorse and shark-tooth briar.
Mandrake and foxglove rooted in the banks.
No woman-flowers. Only the mind's harsh drugs
Distilled in many countries.
We only guessed the intolerable pain of the journey
Without knife for the briar, without armour against thorn,
Without hope that the high banks would fall at last to sight,
And, over some crest, the sea.

We only know that he jested to us, to his friends:
Gay, bitter, courteous, loving; pouring help outwards, lest any
    should see;
But this love growing, swelling, as he turned back on his road,
Knowing it was too late to win the crossroads below.
Back, then, to interminable peace; but with a catch at the throat
At a boy's voice in King's: at his long-lit Christmas tree.
All peace and kindness; to us who did not know.
Kindness and peace, now that his net was closing
(Each mesh drawn tight, tested beyond failure)
And he could beg no mercy from himself.

II

The dead bear gifts in their hands.
So young the giver, so old the hands that take them.
Take them in shame, in love, in memory: tear-blinded eyes.
But what is this gift showered on his friends, on ours,
This returning rain?
Memory indeed.   Memory of bright air.
Of water and summer gardens. Of jests snatched lightly
As a swallow flashing on water: effortless, gay.
But – this other gift? the deep pools stirred to love
In all this host: men, women who turned in compassion
To us who are left. Prayer and compassion undreamed of.

Was it that horror had breached some dam in their minds,
Some depthless questioning of their own selves?
– As if each one's shadow had cleared and vanished
Because he had faced the utmost hidden fear,
And this was all mens'.
      Now that the body lay
Between the glass and the flowers had he cleared the
 account for us all?

URBS BEATA JERUSALEM

I

This was the strong city
This was our God's salvation in wall and bulwark
In the watch-towers and the archers
In rock-hewn tunnel and tomb

We had remembered her in captivity:
The star-gazers, the magicians, the daughters of music,
Masters of the carven work, of the Seven Lights,
The line of prophets that cursed, wept, entreated,
Proclaimed their visions of famine, or plenty, or destruction,
Called her Harlot or Bride.
They brought creation to adorn her, in the Lovers' Garden, in the laughing valleys,
Tamed the birds for her symbols   pelican, eagle, dove,
Lifted her brazen serpent.

But was there ghost or soul?

II

How blessed the City!
We have seen her desolate
Temples of intricate symbol, the carvings broken with axes,
Roofed again from the timbers of the high snows,
Plated with gold from idols, from breast-warmed jewels,
That many-times melted gold.

There were poets who set us in their battle-songs
Songs of nostalgia, despair, hatred, revenge,
Battles past or desired.
We dreamed of great battles, in Esdraelon, in some valley of decision.
We had always looked for a battle, that we might be blessed and bless
Among the burning chariots, the hamstrung screaming horses,
Finding our feet in blood.

                       For always the enemies ringed us
From the deserts of the south, from the Great River, from the dark-ribbed ships of the coast
Chariots and horses, monsters of fear from the sea.

We had seen great armies that scourged us to south or north,
Armies that stormed our walls, that slew us as unbelievers,
Armies that cried we were blessed in the City for ever
In a God we did not know.
They brought the living waters from the Great River,
Wrenched off the neck-fetters that bound us, forged them anew.
They rode or walked through the gates.

III

There were inns in the City
And rubbish-heaps outside the holy walls
Where prophets might be stoned:
The small resounding cruel city and the jostling streets
Dark, and the secret houses on the wall.

IV

Punishment in the desert, punishment
That wove the web of the golden builders of temples,
That scourged us as slaves along the dusty roads,
That brought back our remnant, in the darkened ships
From the seven-times-heated furnace.
We had called on Jahweh for fire, on the altar, between the cherubims,
On the hornéd altars of Gentiles. Now he has sent us new fire
In gun and land-mine, in the bellies of the aircraft,
Scourges in the thorns of the wire.
For we are the City, the divided, the unblessed City
Stripped of the Wall to lament at, stripped of Kedron's streams:
Watching behind the guns, the desert thorns
Scattered abroad, hating and loving the City,
Knowing the Veil that is rent for ever behind us.

V

The den of the dragons, the den of the machine-guns
Sited on our divided landmarks, the narrow crossings; guns that yearn
Eastward to Jordan. New prophecy shouted from Sinai
While the coiled horned vipers lie ready to strike from the sand.

VI

Yet we are the world: its pattern of evil,
Of repentance and strength, nobility, courage, corruption.
Its image is our patience, its banner our persistence.
We have known too many prophets to heed their promises.
We know that the cities about us are manned to our destruction:
Always, we speak with them, watch them, the gun by the ploughshare.
The gun, the ploughshare, the wealth poured out of the waters
That our desert may blossom, the green fir grow in the desert,
We have turned the living waters into our garden,
Though the jackals fringe the farms.

VII

There have been too many prophets. The old men know the Words,
They bow to the Scrolls: brightness of blood on the lintels,
Blood of our cruel and beautiful holiness,
And bitter herbs of the Law,
But we are young, and we have taken the blessing,
By guile and strength we hold to the young men's blessing:
We have learnt to speak with cunning in the gates.

God spoke thrice to the City: but now we have forgotten
The pillar of fire, the bells on the dancers' feet.
We listen now for the whirlwind, the going in the mulberry trees,
The unstilled whispers in the air.
We know that blessing is wisdom; that we must travel
By Mazzaroth in his seasons, by Arcturus,
By Orion whom He chained.

So the golden sands are drawn to the little broken City
Blessed to our salvation   in our kindred under the Law.
They have taught us the cutting of stone, the power of red-lipped steel,
The traffic in bitter waters.
This is the Covenant without promise, our handiwork that we have prospered.
Our hands take that rough Blessing.   But not the Peace.

ON A DYING LADY

Red brick glows in spring sunlight: a blind and blinded street
That ends in a yew-dark garden, unknowing sea or mountain
(So near to us who are free).　　Grey pitted tarmac
Gives on prim gravel, starved rose-beds. The visiting Morris
   Minors
Throng driveway; go gladly; flowers fruit left on their altars.

There are two and twenty very old ladies
Waiting here for death.　　Most can afford to die slowly.
They have many stories to tell.
　　　　　　　　　　　Strokes twitch the shrunken muscles.
Toothless they mumble on kindly-spooned food.
Most of the day is sleep. Cheerfully nurse announces
A Visit. A little recognition flickers
On the apple-red empty tight-lipped face.
She cannot move hands or feet. Only the head jerks ceaselessly
To some secret effort of nerve; the puppet wire-tugged.

How does the soul fare with these, the half-living?
　　　　　　　　　　　　It has thinned for four years now.
Does it fear or desire its flight, make any preparation?
Communion by injection.　　Wine cannot comfort again
From smooth kind clerical visit.
　　　　　　　　　　　Every meal's an event,
Spurned like a child, or greedy for nurse's treat.
A moment of living, between the drugs and the sleep.

　I think that memory flickers like light, erratic, beyond
　　　　　　　　　　　　　　　　　　prediction,
Thrown back from some circling satellite, fifty years distant,
Breaking through cloud-layer.
Yet retreats, sometimes to names: people, places, a white pony
(His hoof among the unseen photographs, beside the
   temperature-chart)
Her special garden to cry in, wrested from the wood's edge,
Now rock and briar, john's-wort and rotting logs.
So children, grandchildren, come for dutiful visits.
Their names, their doings, merge and blur in sound.

                              I sit and talk,
Searching for this reflecting layer above her,
Of fifty years ago; of an older servant who loved her,
Of woods run wild, replanted: a wrecked boathouse: the River
In unimaginable beauty of light.

What rays break through? radiance of memory
Beyond expression of the half-formed sounds?
I think that she would join the past with gladness
But drug or needle tear her back to dying.

Will the merciless blind healers never let her go?

FIRST ANNIVERSARY

Now Rose keeps winter house
Below the scattered bone-dust, the rich dark dung:
Sheds rotted petals from October blooms,
(Yet freed by autumn air from the winged worm's probing)
So her strong urgent tap-root, small-threaded tendrils
Grope now in sleep; as lovers turn
Their searching fingers, looking for safety,
Warmth in this moist abundance.

I have cleared and sown this ground, changed it from grass to pool,
From pool again to rose-plot, without foreknowledge
Of that bright morning in the New Year's light.

Now through long summer we and they have fed
On this most strange conversion of the dead.

I have uprooted two unfruiting trees,
Limbs gnarled and lichened, the shrinking leaf gone silver.

Is this the garden of the defeated old
Who face the longer unhonoured sickness
In yet uncalcined bone?

     Or have we found
Signs in the sere stems that grate and whisper
Of new buds thrusting when the knife cuts back;

Movement, voices (so faint) in the swept house?

St Lucies' Day comes nearer, and after that
Eight days of life. End of a long name so soon?
Yet we have heard the whispers
And our friends for us. But no presence in dream.
Dead petals, sodden grasses, mask our sleep,
And night's returning pain.

IN THE BEGINNING ...

i

But for us there is no beginning.
No words to match the layered aeons, the imagined bursts of fire,
Air water wave an ascending mist
From yet untroubled pool.
For the mists were pure, unfitted yet to inform
The shapes of angels. All is abstraction, like the terrible words of
   poets,

Spiralling in time.

ii

There is no beginning.
For we dare not shape with our lips the vowels of the Name.
No sound can compass images to mediate them to mind.
We may not trust the emblems of fire or forge,
The hot silver, the gold; the anvils of creation that sent
Fierce shining metallic forms to harbour in brushwood of Jordan,
The plated monsters of the reed-fringed rivers,
The sea-beasts seen among the creeping ships.

iii

Or did the flying wheels
Circle the waters (in that silence before the rocks)
To scatter the word from their rims;
Or mesh inexorably, turning as in lathe,
Spindle of the new creation; to tie the concentric whorls,
That fire-shod shafting to fix the two great Lights?

It did not return from the void, unprospering.
                                                Perhaps
Mind failed in that first silence of beginning.
Mouths dry with fear   unable to praise or to bless
In horror of the slow-lifting dark.
That is why (they said) they dared not   fling a poet to space
Lest he should strive, above the crackle of thorns,

For words to measure perfection of number and starlight
And so mind fail.
                     But the turning wheels (they say)
Record half-speech. We do not know them yet.

iv

What was the word, single or triune,
God lockt in the ark, God in the dome's mosaic,
That which broke the ice-floes,   or split the rock or the veil?
That stored the hail in granaries   snow in the racks of cloud
That which would not command the stones to bread
(Only the wine from the water),
Was it then indivisible, unfruiting?   As yet the trees are seeds:
Dormant, yet ready for breath   as in new planted pine
The tendrils stir so slowly, to the world's heart
Quickening: ravening life from the sediment of the rocks
While God watched through the broken floor of heaven.

v

Did Adam rise, drawn up by the hand of the potter
From the red mire of Eden, from the banks of the waters of
    comfort,
While the beasts of the five days fed incurious in the meadows?
Is this our parable of that unnumbered dust
Compacted, caught from the heavy air
Into rocks' laminate?
Dust drifting; to become the pitcher of the fountain, the
    sepulchral urn,
That symbol beyond the beginning: raised out of mire or tomb?

Or did he lie prone, maybe, while the arrow fell to his heart
Among the first scanty flowers: and the Tree grew out of his
    loins?
Star or word: arrow or breath: breath that forced life
Into that white tortured figure   crucified on the rock
                                                      while God
Pressed Himself upon Adam: agony of God's exhalation,

And the snake, like a coiled ammonite, loosened on Adam's
    thigh.

vi

What blessed the waters before they broke on the rock-shore?
Did they hold in their grey sediment of being
Diatoms, beauty of plankton, the small star-life
To serve the sky for models; fecund beyond imagining:
Mirrors in the thickened waters?
                    Now come paired fins for benediction of hands.
Lungs for new spirit (but the heart still cold)
Will crawl between the tide-line and the foam.

vii

And now I do not know the words
Of beginning, or of time, or the death from the Garden.

I do not know what pulses throb, moment by moment, from the arteries of starlight.

Only I know
That the Second Word, now and in the beginning
Has named the Shapes of creation, manifest in image:
Unity drawn from the molten furnace.

I know the return of bone to clay among the rose-trees.
I know in their death and life the mystery of the waters
The concentric rings that spread, dying, in the pool; dispersion
To the new Forms.
I believe in salvation by fire, by dissolution and dispersion,
I think that after the fire may be the dust-cloud (that thickens and drifts to kill)
That the word and the world be renewed in the new forms
At the Voice.   But the words are hidden from me still.
As in the beginning, in the closing waters.

FOR SHOTARO OSHIMA

On his Seventieth Birthday

I do not know the link first forged between us.

Perhaps that ancient sword, the grace and ghosts of the Nöh;
Swordsman, saint or sage: or, seen against the sunset
A twisted thorn-tree, a bamboo leaf, a scroll
Of the ancient wisdoms: formal beauty of women:
Spirit distilled to its essence of lofty things.

We have shared delight, the lifting heart, understanding in
    marrow of bone.
We have shared, in this dark turbulence of our times,
Courage, high breeding, strength of the full-made Poet:
The quiet passion of emblems: white birds against the sea,
Antiquity of immemorial stone,
Ancient stories of battles, of lovers, of tombs,
That image a world's wisdom into verse.

I do not doubt that what you have made endures.
Your scholars to tell of the healing words, declaiming
Against the gathering storm-cloud, his strange high joy.
And on this anniversary, you have taught
Among two ancient peoples, courtesy.

LIVING IMAGES

i

Once they commended my summers and clear November frosts
On the high moorlands   on the tide-flats   in the warm
   laurel coverts:

Heron at siege in the trout-pool: a Northern Diver
Monstrously lovely, mysterious, startled from a hill-tarn:

Plover that dipped wings in salute to the west
Flickering over the Graveyard Hill.

The altar-grove of firs by the tide's edge
Where dark birds came in the dusk.

Small birds of thicket or brake   under the hawk's shadow.
                        Mousing owls in the heather
Sinewed stoat in dried bracken, laired in cut stones of the
                                                    sea-wall:
Grey lashing enemy congers under the Coffin Rocks.

There, too, I knew
The wayward careless kindness of our horses
Smell of sacrificial hoof and hair   hot iron
                             wet slack of the forge
Slow breathing creaking bellows
                        bell-clanging rhythms of anvil:
So also
The finger quick on trigger, bow-string,
The puff of stricken plumage where shot or talons strike
Wing-tipped mallard in sedges   enewed in mercy of water
Movement at dawn and cockshut light, end and beginning.
This was my mystery of a boy's world
And its unstudied pain.

This was Shakespeare's too.

ii

So I recall it in the woods of Charlecote, on Cotswold Downs,
All warfare: dog hawk arrow parables of death.

                    But never I think in nightmare
Unless imagination riot with untamed emotion
Before the light forgiving ghosts that pass at nightfall
Processionally over the memory and the gun's muzzle.

He pitied hare, wounded deer, dogs in the storm
(Or storm-starved at the gate)
Would pity (but in horror as I today)
Mangled bird beast, strewn after night hunting –
Pulp ground, dispersion to fouled dust, by the wheels:
That know nor chase nor hunter nor burial in the leaves
Nor transformation in carrion.
                    Only the horror of the wheels.

iii

Urn Buriall knew better, and in that thought mind mounts
Above the clanging smoking wheels, that beat the brain
By their steel shapes of horror, this mad wrecking progress.

Do not sustain hatred of this bloodied feathered road.

All is dispersion, and all dispersion is one:
 In tomb   in furnace   among the studded teeth.
This imagination is my own betrayal.

No Form survives the fox's teeth, no nestling the black backed
                                                          gull
(Bodies of royal children, children of royal parents).
No matter dust's grain and nature: sunlight and rain are kind
Ripening new shapes.

THE HARROWING OF HELL

*'Being put to death in the flesh, but quickened
by the Spirit: by which also he went and preached
unto the spirits in prison.'* (I Peter 3: 18, 19)

I

It had always been three days
So men reported from Rome   Alexandria   Cloyne
Egypt   India   Thibet
And Er who saw the spindle, in his first sleep after battle:
Three days of indecision, of that first dreaming:
Loosening of silver threads from spine or loins,
The image taking shape above the body.
It is (they tell) opaque at first. Then seemingly more solid:
Face downwards, watching the body. Then stands upright
(Life shrunk to the bed's foot)   taking colours of spirit
As the tide ebbs from the fore-shores of the body.
Round it, maybe, are kindred. And those who pray.

II

But at Calvary there was no need for this first trance or dreaming.
That day was the thief's radiance in Paradise.
For spear-point had set free   for baptism and atonement
Blood and water commingled as in a chalice
That He should descend in light to this last ministry
As He had promised.

III

There were so many dead:
The disobedient, the ignorant,
Dante had known them, drawn their faces as masks
For parables, exemplars; all sin recorded for judgement.
Some were bound by their own minds in flame,

Some foundered in black mire, in the pits of Solfatera,
Ranked in the circles of their still-living thought,
Dyed in the colours taken down from earth:
For some were red or grey, from their dens in the earth:
Some tinged with blue, from some memory of the sky.
Some dark like chrysalids, the cracked skin of old men,
In whom were sealed the butterflies, *l'angelica farfalla,*
For they did not know they were dead.
But most, I think, had been given wings in death, and so
They were restless   turbulent   flitting in this grey underworld,
Wheeling like marsh-birds at some sudden signal
Clustering for a moment at a seeming shaft of sunlight
That struggled through Hell's roof.
Then wheeled again, seeking the cave's recesses
Among the darkened elder souls in likeness of bats
That hung, torpid, hooked to the dripping rocks.
The wheeling souls yearned for the sunlight, probing dry twisted roots
For crevices; for blood that would quench thirst, thicken for a moment their forms.
Some sought awareness of death, the second death,
The completed destruction of the husk that bound them
(Fire's resolution incomplete, withheld the third handful of dust)
Valediction to peace.

IV

Into the grey world came
Through the lowest of those rent earth-veils some cleft opened by earthquake
Spirit in His new whiteness.

                       The dead thronged round Him, complaining
In high thin voices, the twittering of small birds
Yet inarticulate, confused with the whirring of wings.
They murmured of long injustice, of the empty words in the
                                                       scrolls
That had echoed, and died in the roof, among the twisted
                                        tree-roots, in the fibred clay
From beyond time.
They remembered prophets of salvation, of stones for Covenant
Rainbows over black water

For momentary hope. And some remembered
That they had been called for questioning, by name, to a cave,
To the pool of the seers, to the blood-filled trench,
To a burning ship on a headland:
Questioned in mockery, bidden to fall again
By witch or foam-mouthed prophetess, beside the cleft in the rock.
'Try the spirits, whether they be of God.'
But how can we try them – in the medium's mouth?
In the slow-turning wheels that whisper voices on the borders of sound?
Only the Light can try them   part them one from another.

V

We do not know what the Word Incarnate
Preached in the underworld: what He proclaimed
Of some New Law or hope. They tell us that the spirits had
                                                     been imprisoned
Since the beginnings.
How long the roll-call?
Perhaps the saint had seen, or drawn from some scroll,
That He took into baptism the Eight, and so mankind
That remembered the tossing waters, raven and olive,
Before the world was replenished.
                        From them, man's priesthood descending,
Grace might spread through Hell?

Three days from the ninth hour. The wings grew quiet, listening,
And Spirit drew slowly upwards towards the folded grave clothes
To walk the paths in the morning.

BURNING OF A HOUSE
(6 October 1970)

I

The grey west rain slakes ashes: turns carven oak to mire.
Journalists, casual visitors,
Come to wonder
At this fallen house: the broken roof-trees: gravel that smells
of fire.
Rafters will stand for a while, like the dark ribs
Of the Galway Hooker sunk at the creek's mouth.
The urns on the balustrade have been stolen for souvenirs.
Once they had been
Heavy with geraniums, bright with lobelia.   And slowly
Bushes, rare climbing shrubs, the johnswort that edges the drive
Will sidle outwards, fighting, choking each other
In new raw life from the bone-dust of the house.
Pernettias cloak the sundial
(But its bronze dial was stolen.)

Small birds roost secure in the rhododendron thickets
By the walk to the locked garden.
Only the jackdaws, companionable, compassionate,
Fly puzzled round a single crumbling stack
That gives no warmth for the nest.

II

We never know when we have done some act:
Walked that bracken edge, crisped with hail-stones,
Splashed through a rushy spring
Felt the soft gracious air on Lough Lomaùn,
Pushed through the saplings to the trout-pool's margin,
Walked by foot-touch – eyes far ahead – on the bog-lands
For the last time.

III

Here they have done more evil than fire or crowning bramble.
Torn gravel from the ancient rivers:

Uprooted the bones of the Roman and of the mammoth
Hollowed the chalk downs whose springs gave life to the
                                                    grass-lands.
Sealed for ever the small life beneath us:
Worm and questing ant and the groping grass roots:
They have sealed them under the tortured slabs of concrete
That quiver and tremble under the thudding pistons.

IV

Who am I that should blame
Greed   treachery   malice
Thievery in God's many names
Commandment to root out the heretic
As snouts of pig or badger tear a meadow:
Wrench out the iron palings, oak from mortice:
So we had once thought of destruction that hemmed us,
Yet planned that it would not fail.
But that was high ancestral arrogance
Of power and race and price.
It is better that these cracked stones sink into history's footings
And that I remember actions of the last time.

WATERFALL
(Klondagad)

Here is the Mist of the First Day
Rainbow'd, life-dealing   aspersion rising from the rock-pool.
In sunlight the veins of water show brown from the hill-streams
Runnels out of gorse bracken briar   beside grey limestone.
Obedient to the night's storm   the greater or the latter rain.

The water-song changes its pitch from moment to moment:
Flings out its mist-curtain as the Rock shatters the Flood.
Beyond this wall of water
Is a Holy Well.   No pilgrims reach it:
But – sanctity out of the mist?

Once in high drought I edged my way by the rock-rim:
Finding a little hollow part rock-spring, part brimmed from the
    Mist,
Holy (may be) from the cliff-hung rowan above it.

There are two other cascades.   One, today, is slender:
Miniature of the main fall, a foam-flecked pool at the foot.
The other a dripping cleft, overarched with rowans,
Root-hungry on the rock.

Once, when the land prospered, this was the leat for the mill
Morticed to rock-platform, drawing life from the clamorous fall.
Now there is only a trickle
Where, at hawthorn-time, the elvers from the Atlantic
(Three years their journey from the Sargasso Sea)
Drive upwards in their birth-stream. White threads of
    protoplasm:
Consciousness, fierce and delicate, in a black mote in the head.
Inch by inch they struggle   over the wet rock-face
In the benediction of the mist:
Rest by trickling pools or green-starred mosses,
Beckoned by brown waters of ancestral birth.

              For only they can scale
The Fall that holds back the Leapers, the Wise Ones
From the Nuts of Knowledge in hazel thickets above.

Now climb this tunnel: hear the sounds grow fainter:
Hand-hold on ash saplings   clumsy with rod and gear
To a new quiet world, still-edged with the rainbow.
Here is my river in laughter and peace again
Pool upon pool in sunlight   rock-steps in the brown water,
Each, mystery and joy: renewed nightly to harvest of the
  unknown.

I have turned the flank of the Fall.

NINE O'CLOCK

There are two betrayals of body.

First the thorn-prick: poison sheds part of mind's turmoil.
We are aware of, but do not hear, the turning wheels,
Man's bright new sun above us.
                      Angels move white-robed in the shadows of vision,
Mouths bound as for the dead.   We try to greet them;
But words will not form: are the lips poisoned too?

Now comes a second spear-thrust.
                      Blades have been washed in the rivers.
The sun goes out, and all the tendrils of mind
Shrink crushed within brain's white anemone.
Some part of it must be living, but
I do not know where.   Is soul, too, lost in the wood
Beyond or below vision?   Even the dream is dead.
(Dream of an empty strand, and the Atlantic rollers on shingle,
Running to meet the gale and the white surf.)

While from the side
As in the lonely Garden, bone must be racked away,
Muscle crucified to rebirth, for a new companion.
                                  I do not know its shape.
There is blood on the shining floor, and linen.

Blood of the bride-sleep, spilt among the grasses?

Now they give new blood.   It trickles slowly
Into the tributaries of body.   Blood of strangers, anonymous;
Will the sacrifice be accepted, the ghost thicken, below
These sterile tubes?   What dreams will they bring with them?

Wake to pain's kindness, and the oozing side:
The healers have killed the dream,

CONVALESCENT

On the long dark corridors, above the strident mosaics,
Are ill-kept varnished pictures; Landseers, dogs,
   deer innumerable,
All that could glorify a German prince,
Delight an adoring girl
                   – they are here for our rest.

Men do not die just now. They only come crippled,
   or bewildered,
From slow erosion of bodies' engine; some shattered fuse in the
   brain:
Evils of services rendered.
                   We come to rid ourselves
Of memories of the room where the bright walls closed about us,
Where the bedside flowers, the sterile furnishings,
Have seen (file upon file) the indignities of body,
The cheerfulness of those that tend us: the spy-hole in the door.
But where is the heart-ache healed?
Life will grow easy on these lawns, among the aged trees.
Italian terraces, dolphins and riding cherubs,
In sight of the laughing sea; till we are returned
To the more potent drug, the greater helplessness,
To the wheeled chair: the daily dressing of the oozing wound:
To our fear of that which is high.   We have not heard
The whispered consultations in the corridor,
Seen the night-sister's journal.

Ships various as those that pass seawards threading the Solent.
               Reefs are taken in
To match for a little longer the spreading crack at the mast-step,
The cordage racked to weakness.
We pass on the corridors, speak in the dusk of the cedars,
Signal to each other with flags that lift and fall limp:
   gather weight again
Borne – by what currents?
We are lapped about with kindliness. We know – with what
   selfish hope –
The crews more stricken than we, or bound for colder fog-banks.
But – we too make ready to cross the ferry.
               Their riding lights dim behind us.

WAVE

All that I know is my breaking:

In creamy smother at the cliff's foot
Upflung to my slow warfare on the rock
Torn back to lavish new energy of life
On gaping barnacle, steadfast limpet, brown bladder-wrack.

Now I have lipped the half-tide pool, to make its creatures
Stir with new wine of plankton   fresh tinctures of metals
Leached from all rivers, from the grinding mills of pebbles –
The small foods of my bounty.

I cannot know the colours I have taken
In sunlight or rainstorm
From the bright kelps of the rock-creeks.
But surely I have worn
All glory of secret dyes: indigo purple violet
                              clear green of the sand shallows
Wine darknesses of Homer's sea: I bear witness
Of olive bed of pollack   striped splendour of mackerel-shoal
Caught in sun's prisms.

Now I too gather broken beyond reef's shelter
On cliff-face, trapped in rolling shingle
Drawn back into tide's wantonness
To take my Proteus' shapes from a new-loosed storm
To Resurrection.

Exercise for the Seatonian Prize, 1973

APOCALYPSE

One becomes, to self and to all else, at once Seen and Seer: identical with Being and Intellectual Principle and the entire living all, we no longer see the Supreme as an external; we are near now, the next is That and it is close to us, radiant above the Intellectual.
                                              Plotinus, *Enneads*, VI.7.36

i

Island of exile: a Roman guardship
At anchor in the Bay.   Rocks in the heat, and very faint
The goat-bells tinkled.   From close-cropped grass
The cliff-edge fell to green water.
Only to the East
There was a cloud like a Scroll, tight-sealed and threatening.
But nearing the Island.
                    Listen to the wave-ripples on the beach,
And to this menace of thunder.

ii

When body's tides, in their intricate restless channels,
Set free the mind to dream or vision or ecstasy
The images swirl and spiral like changing cloud-shapes:
They come from within, are sent from Powers within us.
Some are born of our memory, voices in the Synagogue, from the scrolls:
Of a healing tree and a garden; of serpents in the dust or on a cross:
Images that we had known in the blood-streams of our people:
From the desert, from the great rivers, from beasts of the
    sea-depths.
Some we had made (layer upon layer) in our visions
As voice failed before sight.
There were beasts that pressed upon angels,
    Horns   eyes   wings
             in the multiplicity of emblem, in tumult of air:

Women with streaming tresses and lion-faces,
Scorpions of destruction,
Angels between beasts and men and spined dragons
Fallen in fire.
These were mind's artefacts to stand before a throne
To glorify the Name that may not be spoken.

Below, like the curled lip of the storm that hid the scroll
There was the terror and loveliness of the sacred colours,
Stones of the Breastplate, stones of the Tribes,
And of the wheeling Zodiac.   Woven in that tapestry,
Wheeling in arcs like eagles in mind's heaven,
The holy feasts and seasons: with all their emblems.
They governed our sowing and reaping,
Season of threshing and the trodden winepress,
Plague and sickness: walls built against our foemen,
Walls built to shelter Him in Glory.
So the incense of our prayer eddied about the Tabernacle
And stirred the purple veil.

iii

Whom shall we send, and who will go for us?
Who is worthy to open the book, to break the seal
Of the thunder scroll?
    Only I, in my vision.   All visions are one.
I have seen the living creatures, the cherubims by Chebar:
Colour of the terrible crystal, of amber, of sapphire stone:
I have heard the rushing of the overflowing Word.

Yet the shapes, the lights, change swiftly, molten, merging
To the cut jewels of the breastplate:
Light-in-the-word, the words from the beginning;
They move in numbers, in triads
(There are three that testify); four orders of earth:
Four Rivers and their angels.
They flame in the Seven Lights, the flowing Vials of plague.

iv

The blood spoke better than Abel.

Spilt blood as it dries
Cracks, curls into flakes at the edges

As its light dims.
There must be blood: in the field, on the altar,
For the Lamb stands as slaughtered: the throat is cut:
He stands in the blood.
Yet as I looked my vision clouded and changed
And He rode on a white horse, and was named the Word
Written on thigh, on vesture dipped in blood:
There followed heaven's armed men.
Whom shall we send?
– Send against the locust-hordes that have taken the likeness of
horses?

– Send against the Parthians? the chariots of the sea-tribes?
– Send against Rome? the harlot of the sea-borne cities?

Vultures or eagles wheel above our warfare,
And a third of the earth shall die.

v

Now Ezekiel's fire-chariot has drawn to the height.
Words have fled before vision.   There is only
A descending city, a rainbow over a throne,
A Bride
And fire in molten stillness.

Set Him above the Cherubim.   The seals are loosened
The images and the forms   move swiftly across the storm-cloud.
Angels that guard the three doors of Creation
Uplift their hands.
Now there is silence, a silence of transition,
A preparation of knowledge.

vi

It is finished.   The height and the depth,
The mountain-cliff that reached to the depths of the dried sea
Have ceased to separate.
Height and depth are no more, and the reed that measures the
  City

Moves forward beyond vision, beyond the abstraction of mind.

Now to the City come
The standing delivered dead
Beings of light, translucent in whiteness of fire,
Before the walls that glowed with the jewels,
Stones of the Tribes: yet all tinctures merging
To a single Light beyond.   There is no shadow or shelter.
                                                          Only consummation
In the Light.

ATTENTIONS

I

Here in old age
There must be a new kind of attention:
Not to books, for mind cannot carry
Long arguments (only some poems)
And literature has become
Not ecstasy, but a meticulous intricate game
Of the professional manipulators
Who have forgotten Sidney and *Chevy Chase*
And the rising of the hair.
       — A new kind of attention
To grass-stems, and to the dawn-chorus,
To earth crumbled in the hand,
Softness of small rain; the glow
Of a caged fire, and the ultimate bone of the ash.
I have gentler enemies that cringe before me
Bind-weed and yarrow, and the small flying worlds
That I may not let live: where once I hated
The carrion-birds, the weasel, the black-backed pirate gull
Or an aircraft over a gun-sight.

II

A new kind of attention:
Not (now) to words, or curves
Of wood or sailcloth or flesh,
The greater artefacts.
     No more than a file or scraper
Silk feather hook steel finger-light.
And I cannot master
The marsh of the lakeside, the quickset thorn,
The briar that caught a life-line.
For death may come – how better? – at some small thing
Setting a seedling, tightening a bolt,
Or watching a new moon.

III

There is a new kind of attention
For every season, day,

Greeted with joy in the delicate pain of dawn.
Each hour can lock at will
To eager memories: lore of the high places*
Wood river and lake
All waters that heal thirst.

IV

Temptation is not quiet
(As Yeats at such age had sung)
Rather a subtle pressure of images
That once were solid, now are brain-spun phantoms
Of old loves: of friendships half-decayed:
Of strength and quickness of eye.

Yet phantoms gracious in the end
As the circle of helpers closes.

---

* The Irish *Dindshenchas* (The Lore of the High Places).

Notes

THRENODY . . . This was written, in sickness, in the South of France at the time of the Spanish Civil War. I could not foresee that I should help to release Niemoeller from Dobbiacco Prison, in 1945.

TO WILTON HOUSE. Wilton became Headquarters, Southern Command, about the time of Dunkirk. The Double Cube was the Operations Room. On a one-inch map of the Command the Beaches were marked with red strips, of width varying according to their vulnerability to invasion. My wife and children were then on the Atlantic crossing to America. A single useless Lewis gun – the only weapon available to guard the HQ – was sited by the Palladian Bridge. 'The Epitaph' is William Browne's, on The Countess of Pembroke. *Arcadia* is said to have been written at Wilton. German bombers returning from the Midlands picked up the Avon as a navigation mark.

CHRISTMAS EVE, 1940. The ringing of church bells was kept for a signal that the invasion had begun. A children's hospital had been hit in one of the big cities during a particularly heavy raid; fragments of bodies were gathered and buried in gardeners' baskets. (See 'March Moon'.)

REFLECTIONS BEFORE JERICHO. This concerns (on the surface) the stupidity and waste of any military planning, its apparent pointlessness.

ON CATTISTOCK HILL. During a battalion exercise my company occupied a hill topped by a prehistoric earthwork. In the valley below a casual bomb landed in a sheep-fold.

MARCH MOON. The burning of Southampton made the sky red for great distances. A children's hospital was hit. The latin is from the medieval Resurrection Play.

FRAGMENTS OF A TESTAMENT. *Afghan Sun:* Thomas Rice Henn, killed at the Battle of Maiwand, 1881. There are monuments in St Patrick's and Rochester Cathedrals. *the dead/go down into water:* My father died on my fourteenth birthday, and was buried on a day of great storm. *Bristol:* the raid of 4 December 1940, in which there was a direct hit on the HQ where I was working. *Wilsons:* a series of Richard Wilson's landscapes of Wilton used to hang in the cloisters.

RETURN TO THE DAYE HOUSE. The Daye House, once the dairy of Wilton House, was the home of Edith Olivier, where I had been billeted. She was then Mayor of Wilton. Her wisdom, gaiety and genius for friendship will be remembered by many. I had returned from a Politico-Military Course, ostensibly training for work in post-war Europe.

ANTIPHON: AFTER BATTLE. The Palace of Caserta, once Allied Forces Headquarters for the Mediterranean Theatre, is a pretentious imitation of Versailles. The cease-fire in Europe was succeeded by endless political complications and tensions. On at least two occasions Allies had their guns trained ready to fire on each other. The Partisans took the opportunity to pay off old scores, often with great cruelty, on the collaborators; in France, Italy, Jugoslavia, Greece.

THE RIVER. This has some reference to John Armstrong's picture, *The River of the Dead.* The episode of the salvaged coffin-wood is authentic. There are echoes of Dante and Blake; and, at the end, of Blake's picture known as *Regeneration* or *The Sea of Space and Time.* Kathleen Raine has shown its relation to an episode in *The Odyssey.*

BUDDHA AND THE FISH. There is an ikon of Buddha fishing: unusual, because He may not kill. He must therefore be drawing the Fish – the Christian symbol – from one life to another. The scene is Lough Mask, where the trout live in clefts eroded in the limestone. Fishermen will perhaps recognize other meanings in depth.

SHOOTING A BAT. This was an episode at my home, which memory threw up after many years. It may have been awakened by a horror of killing, born of experiences in the war. Hazels are a Celtic symbol of wisdom, bitter, because nothing will grow under them. Bees stand for wisdom, co-operation; honey for sexual desire. My home looked out on what we called The Big River, some seventeen miles across, where Fergus and Shannon meet. Deer Island was the deer park for the House in the eighteenth century. The gun was a Belgian saloon gun: a boy would naturally pull a cartridge to pieces and count the silver grains. Two of those then present have confirmed the episode.

EBB TIDE. A boy's pleasure was to turn over the big rocks on the foreshore to see what they concealed. 'Turn but a stone, you start a wing'; the borrowing is inverted. The nine-eyes is a flat eel-like creature with spectacle markings; the young of the ling? I had a perpetual feud with the hooded or scald-crows, which in spring pecked out the eyes of the lambs. The turnstone is a wading bird.

SLUICE-GATE. This is of the big meadows, known as 'corcass' lands, which drained into the creek by an iron shutter. This closed automatically on the flood tide, and opened to drain on the ebb. When it broke down, the meadow became perpetually flooded, and the surrounding trees were killed. The squared 'dry' stones of the wall formed lairs for many stoats, known by us as weasels. They play and hunt in packs. 'Briar and laurel' carry (perhaps) the usual symbolism. *Galatea* was a steel ninety-tonner, much over-sparred and over-canvassed, thrice beaten by *Mayflower* for America's Cup, 1880–83. *Gertrude* was a fifty-ton ocean-racing yawl. The meadows are 'embittered' because of the excess of salt (which once, drawn up into the grass-lands, was good for the store cattle), and may be a memory of Meroz: 'Curse ye bitterly the inhabitants thereof'.

ACCOMPLICE. The title is taken from Wilfred Scawen Blunt's 'cold distich':

'Assassins find accomplices: man's merit
Has found him three: the hawk, the hound, the ferret.'

During the First World War it was often impossible to get cartridges; and as a boy of sixteen or so I used to borrow ferrets and nets to provide food for the house. Muzzling a ferret is a peculiar technique. A piece of fine waxed twine is doubled, knotted over the neck, then under it: led along under the chin, knotted below and above the muzzle, and led back to the neck. A ferret so muzzled will not work until you spit upon your hand, and smooth down muzzle and fur till he ceases to claw the twine. There are perhaps some emblems – Theseus, Ariadne; as well as that of blood on the hands, and a scene in the *Odyssey* which occurs in 'The River'.

THE TOWER REVISITED. This was an experience at Thoor Ballylee. Irish farmers are casual about their possessions, particularly ploughs and rakes: which often remain out all winter to 'stop a gap' in a hedge. Yeats, who edited Blake, would have known and perhaps caught up the fortuitous symbols. 'Arrogant bad verses':

'I the poet William Yeats
With old mill-boards and sea-green slates . . . '

Coole was taken down, stone by stone, to save rates. Another breed of men would have seen that it, and the Tower, were preserved as memorials of the Irish Renaissance. Thus was Yeats's prophecy ('Upon a House Shaken by the Land Agitation') fulfilled. The threshold-stone has been stripped so that the caretaker may be able to show visitors something of the house. Tamers of horses from Troy: this relates to a letter from Yeats to Grierson, describing how the Black and Tans took two young men, tied them by the heels to a lorry, and dragged them on metalled roads till the heads came off. Yeats did not make a poem out of that; but he might well have thought of Hector. Synge's skulls: see his account of a funeral in The Aran Islands. But the Elizabethan habit of breaking up old graves for the new tenant is everywhere; because of the sanctity of the old burial grounds. Above the stone: I had in mind the sentimentality which was then seeking to erect a statue either in Sligo or Ballylee.

ODE POUR L'ELECTION. *Shot-in-the lungs:* a partridge (and occasionally other birds) will often go away apparently unhurt for a considerable distance. Then it rises almost vertically, turns over at the top of its flight, and will be picked up dead, breast upwards. This is because the lungs have been punctured by the shot, and the bird is trying to keep the blood out of its wind-pipe. Such are called 'towered' birds. *Winced in the pillar of fire:* a bird wounded can be seen to tremble as the rear of the shot-column (which is visible to a trained eye) strikes it. There is also some Biblical reference. The three wounds are meant to suggest three types of cancer. *Rat-ringed:* after a shoot there are, inevitably, a greater or lesser number of wounded birds and beasts, according to the quality of the markmanship. One thinks of such creeping into bracken or briar thickets as night falls (like Shakespeare's 'Poor hurt fowls creep into sedges'): and the rats closing in upon them. *Seventh:* an operation, but also of the seventh, and traditionally longest, wave of the sea. '*We feel the safety* . . . . ': the quotation is from Keats:

'And when a tale is beautifully stay'd
We feel the safety of a hawthorn glade.'

I had in mind such a brake, with open space in it: of great security and shelter because of the close-knit stems and branches, the armour of the thorns. *Ahead, as he crouched* . . . : a lake-boat (usually built of larch) behaves in a special manner in rough water under an outboard, if one is driving her alone. The bows rise high, showing much of the keel as the boat rides to the waves. The oak stem-piece is mortised into the keel with a traditional and beautiful joint. Strakes are the planks of a clinker-built boat. Nail roves are discs of copper through which the ends of nails pass before they are cut short and clenched. *Fall'n upon rock* recalls the seaman's precise description of the shipwreck of *Acts*, XXVII: 29.

PRELUDE FOR 1962. When Tennyson heard of Byron's death, he carved the words 'Byron is dead' on such a rock-face at Somersby. *Ganched conger:* ganching was a common medieval punishment, impaling on iron hooks attached to castle walls. We used to hunt conger-eels on the reefs at low water, with a cod-hook lashed on a garden bamboo. On being disturbed the great eel would sometimes come out and attack one; or be dragged out by the hook. They were four or five feet long, sometimes as thick as a man's thigh. There is some projection of the image into the *small elvers* following. Night's November flood: the mature eels run to the ocean (and thence to their breeding grounds in the Sargasso Sea) in the first floods of November, and in the dark of the moon. Seventh wave: as in notes to *Ode Pour L'Election.* Enveloping gas-jets: of a crematorium furnace.

DARK JOURNEY. This is of 'The Troubles', 1918-21. My home was 'under sentence' for burning. The walk round the woods and shrubberies was a mile or more. Larch-growth: I used to cut them for spars for boats. Silver-fir: a tree planted at the gate-lodge when my Father was born: it was some seventy feet high when he died. The sorcerers' wood is, perhaps, from Dante, three fears from 'St. Patrick's Breastplate'. The soil contained much iron-bearing shale. Sprouting fingers are a memory of Daphne turned to a laurel. The pineapple stone (perhaps from the pillar of some eighteenth-century entrance gate) was cut into lozenges in accordance with Hogarth's 'Line of Beauty'. The house was burned to the ground, whether by accident or design on 6 October 1970: see 'Burning of a House'.

TWO PICTURES. This is, I think, 'about' a Titian, reproduced by Edgar Wind, of the symbols of Patience, Love and Chance. Near it is an emblem, also of Patience, and perhaps also of Hope and Salvation, of a dolphin twined round an anchor. The second picture is by Calvert, called 'The Return': the Christ-like figure rides towards the woman who waits for him in the shepherd's hut. The white birds stand for the Spirit. The short splice is easy, but clumsy, and will not pass through a block. A proper long splice in a rope is first 'wormed' and 'parcelled' to fill up the strands, then served *against* the run or lay of the rope's twisting. 'O Pythagoras, so good, so wise, so eloquent, before my last voyage I taught thee, a soft lad, to splice a rope.' (*cit.* W. B. Yeats).

Urbs Beata Jerusalem. This was completed a month or two before the outbreak of the Israeli-Arab War. In the 1914-18 War the British laid a pipeline from Egypt. Allenby walked, not rode, into Jerusalem. There was an extensive and illegal traffic in

Notes to the Poems 309

Jewish refugees from the concentration camps in 1945: from the Adriatic ports to Haifa and elsewhere. The 'fiery serpents' of *Numbers*, XXI. 6 and *Deuteronomy*, VIII. 15 are thought to have been horned vipers. Here they become sprengminen of the frontier-zones; anti-personnel mines which leap into the air before exploding: as in *Philoctetes*. The 'going in the mulberry trees': 2 *Samuel*, V.24. Bitter waters: the wealth of the Dead Sea, but also perhaps, *Revelation*, 8.11: 'and many men died of the waters, because they were made bitter'.

FIRST ANNIVERSARY. There are precedents for poems on the anniversary of a death. In the first line there is some debt to a poem by George Herbert.

IN THE BEGINNING. See Donne's *Aire and Angels;* of the 'informing' of angels by 'condensation' of the air. AEIOU: the Name that must not be spoken? Fire or forge: Blake's *Tyger*; monsters, *Job* 40.21. Flying wheels: *Ezekiel* 1.15ff. Mesh . . . : Blake's *Jerusalem*: the Mills of Mind. Shafting . . . : Plato's spindle, and *Genesis*, 1.16. From a commentary on the flight of the spacecraft Apollo 12, November 1969; in spite of the computer-foretold track, certain 'fixes' were also taken by sextant from stars. Crackle of thorns: perhaps the static in the broadcasts, perhaps *Ecclesiastes*, 7.6. Ice-floes: *Psalms*, 147.18. Broken floor: as in Blake's illustration to Job: 'Behold now Behemoth' . . . (*Job*, 40.15). The potter: as in the Nuremburg picture of Creation. (*v*. Jung, *Psychology and Alchemy* p. 139), fig. 71. According to the Midrash, the clay was red. Unnumbered dust . . . laminate: one theory of the Beginning, put forward as a result of lunar exploration. Pitcher: *Ecclesiastes* 11. Sepulchral urn: *v*. Browne's *Urne-Buriall*. Prone . . . arrow: the mystical picture reproduced by Jung, *op. cit.* p. 243, fig. 131. (14). Snake . . . ammonite: Blake's *The Elohim Creating Adam*. Arteries of starlight: the signals from the 'pulsars'? Seed of the Word: the *spermatokoi logoi*; Plotinus, *Enneads* I.6. Salvation by fire: the Hymn *Dies Irae*? Drifts to kill: perhaps the atomic fall-out?

SHOTARO OSHIMA was President of The Yeats Society of Japan.

LIVING IMAGES. As in some other poems, this begins with memories of my boyhood. It arose out of a long journey on a motorway: and is related to a book which I was then writing, called *The Living Image*; and concerned Shakespeare's use of imagery drawn from the created world. Some of the terms are technical, and Shakespeare's: hence, Heron at siege: standing motionless in the water, waiting for the fish to come within range of its bill. Coffin Rocks: a reef, stripped at lowest tides, but also near to smooth domed rocks on the foreshore on which the islanders rested coffins when they brought them to the mainland. Sacrificial hoof and hair: a memory, I think, of prehistoric man sacrificing horses to his gods. Wing-tipped: there were then professional punt-gunners on the Shannon Estuary. Each shot inevitably wounded many birds that were not gathered. Cockshut: a brief time on a winter's evening, just before it is too dark to aim, when the woodcock begin to move. He pitied Hare: 'Poor Wat' of *Venus and Adonis*. Wounded deer: *As You Like It*. Dogs in the storm: *King Lear*. *Urne Buriall*: Sir Thomas Browne. The book generally: but in particular, 'Life is a pure flame, and we live by an invisible sun within us.' Bodies of royal children . . . 'When these bodies that have been the children of royal parents, and the parents of royal children, must say with Job "Corruption thou art my father . . . " . ' (Donne, *Death's Duell*).

THE HARROWING OF HELL. Cloyne: Bishop Berkeley is said to have given orders that his body should lie undisturbed for three days: presumably so that the spirit might disengage itself. Many races hold similar beliefs. Bed's foot: Donne's 'Nocturnall'. No shadows: *v. Purgatorio*. Blood: Odysseus' raising of Tiresias for questioning. The Eight: it is said that the preaching was to those of the Ark: and hence descend through creation.

THE BURNING OF A HOUSE. This concerns the burning of my home in Clare, on 6 October 1970. The threat to it in 'The Troubles', 1917-21, is described in 'Dark Journey'. Waterfall: the great fall at Klondagad, not far from a most ancient church and churchyard, divided what we knew as the Upper and Lower Rivers; or, on the maps, the Ballycorick and the Owenmore. It takes its source in Lough Acrow, ten miles up in the mountains, and flows ultimately into the River Fergus, just above where it meets the Shannon. The left-hand channel is clearly the remains of a mill-stream. There are traces of a leat above, leading to a large deep pool. The 'smaller and the latter rain' is Biblical. The Fall bars the migratory fish – the Salmon (Salar, the Leaper) and the sea-trout. Hazel is the emblem of wisdom. In Celtic legend the magic salmon goes up the river to the pool in Glen Cagny, eats the nuts of the hazel, and goes back to the rivers of the world to spread his knowledge.

NINE O'CLOCK. The turning wheels: *Ezekiel*, Blake, the wheels on the hospital trolley. Bright sun: the theatre-lights that throw no shadow. Spear-thrust: for final anaesthesia. Washed in the rivers: the Zulus before battle; and sterilization. Anemone: as in a sea-pool. The wood: perhaps from Dante, *Inferno*. Arnold's *Dover Beach*: perhaps the roaring of blood in the ears in anaesthesia. The creation of Eve? 'And the bride-sleep fell upon Adam.' Floor . . . lines: *Revelation,* and the tomb of the Resurrection. Ghost thickens: as in the raising of Tiresias by Odysseus. Side, spear: a crucifixion.

CONVALESCENT. This was at Osborne House, in the King Edward VII Convalescent Home for Officers August 1972 and again in November 1973. In that setting, and within sight and sound of the shipping in the Solent, it was natural that the sea-voyage imagery should suggest itself.

WAVE. I have read somewhere 'All a wave knows is that it breaks. The setting is, I think, at Mullaghmore, near Sligo. The colours suggested have been caught in certain paintings by Jack B. Yeats.

APOCALYPSE. There may be some debt to Austin Farrer's *A Rebirth of Images* in the interpretation of the colour-jewel symbolism.

ATTENTIONS. Clearly there is the underlying memory of Yeats's 'An Acre of Grass':

> My temptation is quiet
> Here at life's end
> Neither loose imagination
> Nor the mill of the mind
> Consuming its rag and bone
> Can make the truth known.

Its theme is (in part) what seemed to me to have been the loss, to the study of poetry, of its freshness and joy, of which one expression was Sidney's of Chevy Chase: 'Certainly I must confess mine own barbarousness, but I never heard the old song of Percy and Douglas that I felt not my heart stirred more than with a trumpet.' The Lore of the high places: the Irish *Dindshenchas*. . . . 'the circle of helpers': the shades of ancestors and friends gather to help the passing.

GENEALOGY
(limited to the persons concerned in the narrative)

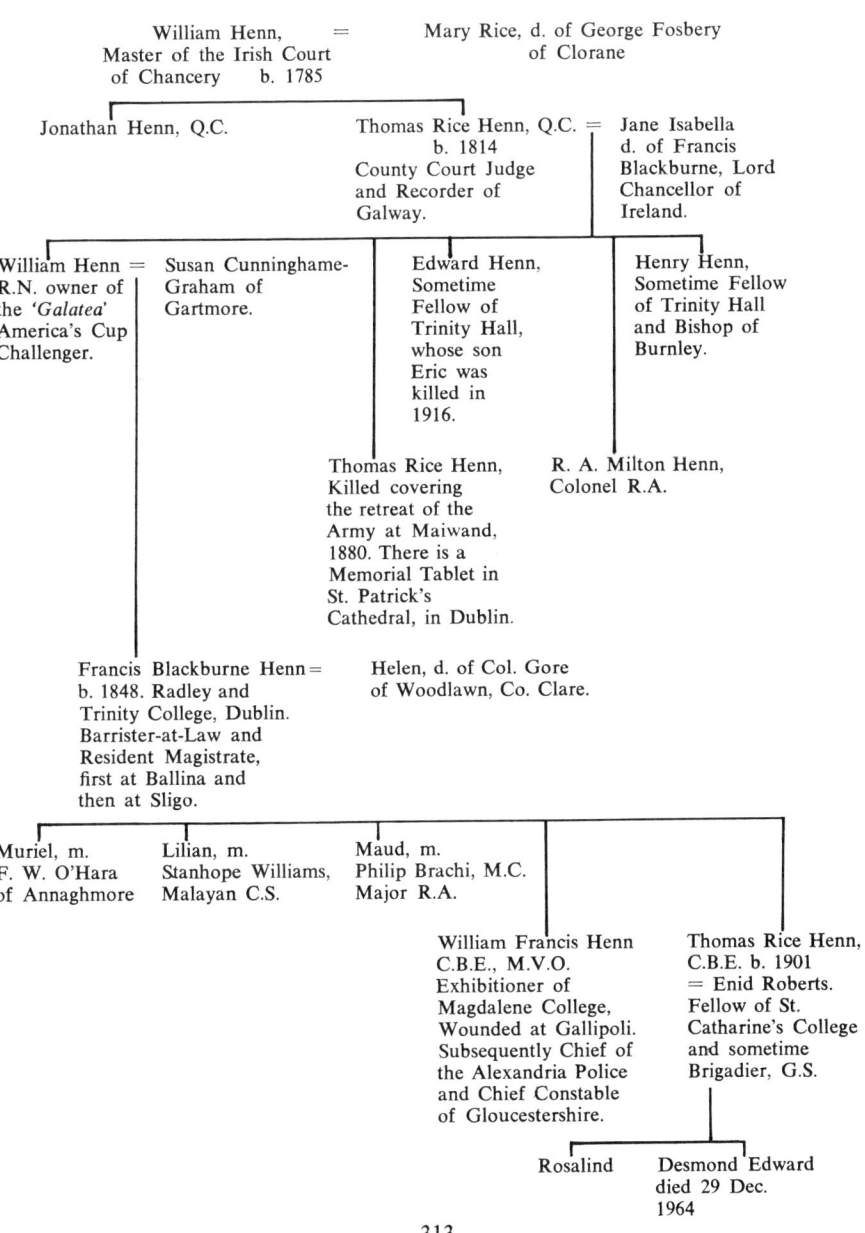

Henn of Paradise.

Henn, Thomas Rice Esq. of Paradise, Co. Clare, barrister at law, Q.C. m. October 1845 Jane Isabella 2nd daughter of the Right Hon. Francis Blackburne, late Lord Chancellor of Ireland, now Lord Justice of the Court of Appeal in Chancery in that country, and has

    1 William
    2 Francis Blackburne and other issue.

Lineage. The family of Henn, one of English origin, has been settled in the County of Clare for nearly two centuries. The name was originally Hene, subsequently Henne, and lastly, about the year 1685 the final 'e' was dropped, leaving the name as it is spelt at the present day. Henry Hene, a distinguished Englishman, was Lord Chief Baron of Ireland in the reign of Charles II and James II and a commissioner of forfeited estates for the counties of Clare and Galway. The Lord Chief Baron was descended from an English line as ancient as any of which there are authentic records. The name is to be found in Doomsday Book Vol. I p.28. Title Subsexe XIII. Tena Willide Braisse in Birbece hynd Rodulf ten de Willo Hene, and to this family belonged a baronetcy, now extinct, created by James I, anno 1642. Henry Hene, Lord Chief Baron of the Irish Court of Exchequer, is stated to have been nephew to Sir Henry Hene the 1st Baronet, being the son of his elder brother William, who was himself the eldest son of Henry Hene Esq of Barking in Surrey. The history of this baronetcy may be read in Burke's Extinct Peerage, p. 256. It is sufficient to state here that the 2nd baronet Sir Henry spelt his name Henne, and that at the time of the 3rd and last bart, Sir Richard,[1] the name became what it is at present. Richard Henn settled at Paradise anno 1685, having in that year obtained a grant of 'Paradise Hill' from the then Earl of Thomond. He married May 6th 1701 Mrs. Barbara Lewin and dying without issue in the year 1717 devised his estates to his brother Thomas who in 1708 m. Miss Barbara Darby and had issue by her Richard, William, Thomas, Mary, Eliza, Anne and Catherine. Thomas (the father) died in 1735 and was succeeded by his son Richard who m. in 1731 Bridget Hickman by whom he had issue Thomas who d. young: William who succeeded to his property: Mary who m. Donagh O'Brien and Anne who died

---

[1] A portrait was in the dining-room at Paradise, it went with the burning.

Appendix

unmarried. William Henn married Bridget Browne and had issue by her:

1. Richard Henn who m. Miss Mary Arthur of Glenomera,
2. William who died without issue,
3. Edmund who m. Miss Gennys (an English heiress of Devonshire) whose name he took becoming Ed. Henn-Gennys.
4. Thomas who married Miss Blakeney but had no issue,
5. Poole who m. Miss Pentland by whom he left issue William Poole: Jane who married John Hunt: Eliza who m. Bolton Waller Esq of Shannon Grove Co. Limerick and Anne who m. – Gubbins Esq: Richard Henn Esq who m. Miss Arthur and who on the death of his father s. to the estates, had issue William, Thomas and Lucy who all died without issue and he devised the lands of Paradise to his wife Mary, who in turn devised them to her own brother the late Thomas Arthur of Glenomera Co. Clare.

This beautiful property, after remaining in the possession of Mrs. Arthur for about thirty years has been recently restored to the name of the ancient proprietors, having been repurchased from Mrs. Arthur's younger children by Thomas Rice Henn Esq, whose descent from the original grantee of the estate is derived as follows: William Henn 2nd son of Thomas Henn, the brother and devisee of Richard the grantee, was called to the Irish Bar and created a judge of the King's Bench in 1768. In his will which bears the date July 20th 1784 and was proved 9th June 1796 he names his 3 eldest daughters: Mary m. to Francis Casiy of Leafield: Susanna m. to William Daxon, of Ennis and to Frances and an only son.

William Henn, who became a Master of the Irish Court of Chancery 10 July 1793 and m. July 1782 Susanna, sister of the late Sir Jonathan Lovett Bart of Lipscombe Parks in Bucks, by whom he left issue: *1* William of whom presently: *2* Jonathan the celebrated Q.C.: *3* Richard of Herbert St. Dublin m. in July 1841 Maria dau. of – Atkinson Esq of Upper Mount Street Dublin.

1 Susanna m. April 1813 Charles Mayne of Stephens Green: *2* Eliza m. Jan. 1810 Edward Mayne of Stephens Green: *3* Eleanor unmarried: *4* Jane m. May 1826 to Walter

Hussey-Griffith of Clare Street Dublin: *5* Frances m. Jan. 1831 to Stephen Collins Esq. Q.C. of Merrion Square Dublin.

The eldest son William Henn Senior Master in Chancery in Ireland m. 1809 Mary Rice eldest daughter of George Fosberry of Clorane Co. Limerick by Christiana his wife dau. of Thomas Rice of Mount Trenchard in the same county by whom he has issue:

1 William who died unm. *2* Thomas Rice the present proprietor of the Paradise Estate, *3* Jonathan Lovett and five daughters: Christiana, Susanna, Mary m. to John Stanford, Ellen, Jane m. to Robert Holmes.

The Paradise Estate is situated on the river Fergus at its present junction with the Shannon and is described by Lloyd in his Survey of the Co. Clare published in the year 1760 as being one of the most beautiful in this kingdom.

It is an interesting fact connected with this distinguished family that Henry Hene, the Lord Chief Baron, a man of known attachment to the protestant faith was removed from his high office by King James II in order to make way for Mr. Henn's maternal ancestor, Sir Stephen Rice, created Lord Chief Baron A.D. 1686 upon whom the same sovereign afterwards bestowed the Barony of Mounteagle. The title of Mounteagle denied by Parliament to Sir Stephen Rice has been recently restored as is well known, in the person of his patriotic and gifted descendant the present Lord Monteagle of Brandon.[1]

Crest – on a mount vert. a hen-pheasant p.p.n.
Motto – Gloria deo
Seat: Paradise, Killadysart, Co. Clare.

---

[1] Mount Trenchard, near Foynes and within a mornings' sail of Paradise, is now a monastery.

Extract from: A Genealogical and Heraldic Dictionary of the Landed Gentry of Gt. Britain and Ireland by Sir Bernard Burke, Ulster King of Arms, 1868.

INDEX

INDEX

Abbey Theatre, Dublin, 71
Abercrombie, Lascelles, 150
Adami, G. C., 96
Airey, Terence, 175, 179
Aldenham School, 70, 73, 78, 83, 84, 87, 95, 120
Alexander of Tunis, Earl, 137, 153, 165, 170, 172, 185
Alexander the Great, 142
Ali, Syed Amir, *The Spirit of Islam*, 108
Ali, Torick Ameer, 108
Allingham, William, 60
Allison, C. R., 111
Allt, Peter, 205
Alms, Colonel, 161
Alspach, Brig. General Russell K., 205
Andrew, John, 10
Angelin, Maître Nicholas, 121
Annan, Noel, *Leslie Stephen*, 97
Aristotle, *Poetics*, 89
Armstrong, E. A., *The Folklore of Birds*, 14
Arnold, Matthew, 99
Attwater, Aubrey, 94, 99, 113
Auchinleck, General Sir Claude Eyre, 137
Austin, J. L., 99

Balgarnie, Mr, 99
Ballylee, Thoor, *see* Thoor Ballylee,
Banks, Mr, 102
Barker, Sir Ernest, 150, 152
Barling, Ivan, 100
Battle of Britain, 136, 144, 145
Beck, E. A., 119
Beck, Millicent, 119
Beerbohm, Max, *Zuleika Dobson*, 95
Beevor, Mr, 84
Belloc, Hilaire, 90
Bennett, Joan, 91

Bennett, Stanley, 91, 114
Beresford, Mr, 102
Bernstein, Col., 167
Bickerdyke, John, *Wild Sports in Ireland*, 11
Bickersteth, G. L., 88
Blair-Cunynghame, Hamish, 207
Blake, William, 88, 92, 177, 194, 195, 201, 206; *Milton*, 46
Bodkin, Fr M., S.J., 207
Bosnia and Herzegovina, Archbishop of, 175
Boyer-Bell, J., *The Secret Army*, 79, 214
Bradbrook, Muriel, 206
Bridges, Robert, *The Testament of Beauty*, 210
British Irregulars, Black and Tans, 74, 81, 82
Brock, Clutton, 'Loose Emotion', 210
Brooke, Rupert, *The Soldier*, 88
Brooks, Cleanth, 205
Browne, Leonard, 124, 125, 126, 140
Browne, Sir Thomas, *Urne Buriall*, 67, 125; 143
Buchan, John, *Memory Hold the Door*, 31, 32
Burrows, R. A., 186
Buxton, John, 133
Byrne, Francis, 206
Byron, George Gordon, Lord, 24

Calcutta, 101, 103, 104, 106, 107, 120, 188
Calcutta Rowing Club, 107
Calvert, Edward, 206
Cambridge, 33, 41, 47, 55, 58, 59, 87, 93, 111, 114, 123, 127, 157, 186, 187, 203
Cambridge Colleges,
  Clare College, 89, 91, 93, 111, 151
  Corpus Christi College, 109, 130
  Downing College, 127, 132

Girton College, 91, 110, 206
Gonville and Caius College, 73, 86, 87, 88, 96
Jesus College, 89, 95, 96
King's College, 88, 91, 196, 204, 206
Magdalene College, 22, 28, 73, 94, 111
Newnham College, 99, 110, 196
Pembroke College, 73, 87, 94, 95, 98, 117
Peterhouse, 111, 116, 118, 131, 138, 161
Queen's College, 87, 113
St. Catharine's College, 73, 74, 91, 111, 118, 119, 123, 131, 150, 204
St. John's College, 73, 90, 118, 151
Sidney Sussex College, 111
Trinity College, 73, 93, 99, 111, 113
Trinity Hall College,11, 40, 73, 74, 96, 111, 113, 119
Cambridge University, 74, 86, 87, 93, 95, 110, 114, 130, 131, 135, 147, 190
  Cambridge and Oxford Joint Board, 114; Cambridge local examinations, 114; English Tripos, 87; Expenditure on Officer's careers, 86; General Board of Faculties, 190; Lecturing in Arts Faculty,110; Library of, 93; status of, 74; University Press, 95; University Press, Secretary of, 95
Cambridgeshire Rowing Association, 196
Cameron, Donald, 117
Cammaerts, Francis, 170
Campbell, Roy, *The Flaming Terrapin*, 200
Carson, Lord, 57
Cecil, Lord David, 149
Chadwick, James, 87
Chapman, George, 142
Chaucer, Godfrey, 90
Chaytor, H. J., 118, 119, 131, 189
Chesterton, G. K., 90
Church, Richard, *Over the Bridge*, 9, 68
Churchill, Sir Winston, 175

Chutter, J. B., *Captivity Captive*, 111
Cicero, Marcus Tullius, *de Senectute*, 217
Clancy, Father, 196
Clark, General George, 171
Clift, Rupert, 84, 88, 98; *Leonard the Cox*, 88
Clinton-Baddeley, V. C., *Festival Review*, 93
Coleman, Lt. General Cyril, 156
Coleridge, Samuel Taylor, 106, 199
Columbia University, New York, 197
Conrad, Joseph, *Youth*, 101
Cooke, A. H., 73, 83
Coole Park, Gort, Co. Galway, 29, 58, 194, 204, 208, 214
C O S S A C Headquarters, Chief of the Staff to the Supreme Allied Command, 160, 161
Coulton, G. G., 74, 90-1; *Four Score Years*, 90
Coulton, Mrs Joan, 91

Daly, Martin, 194, 215
Day-Lewis, Cecil, 'The Stand-To', 145
de la Mare, Walter, 199
de Grey, Dick, 148
de Lattre de Tassigny, M., 170
Delphi Lodge, and Fishery, Co. Mayo, 207
Dickins, Bruce, 152
Dickson, Macneile, 89
Donne, John, 88, 137, 139, 143, *Twickenham Gardens*, 147
Donoghue, Denis, 204, 206
Dorman-Smith, Brigadier Eric, 156
Drury, Rt. Rev. T. W., 118, 119
Drury, Miss, 118
Dunsany, Lord, *The Curse of the Wise Woman*, 33; 'On a Surrealist Picture', 200

Eccleshare, Colin, 91
Edwards, Oliver, 204
Eisenhower, General D. D., 164, 165, 167, 168, 171
Eliot, T. S., 88; *Sweeney Agonistes*, 199
Ellmann, Richard, 205

Index

Elvin, H. L., 113
Emeléus, H. J., 207
Empson, William, 94
Encyclopaedia of Sport, 25
English, F. H., 84
Epstein, Jacob, 'Genesis', 92
Euripides, 180

Fairbairn, Steve, 96
Festival *Review*, 93
Festival Theatre, Cambridge, 92
'Festung-Europa', 161
First World War, 35, 64, 91, 95, 119, 121, 132, 150, 154, 189, 190
Flecker, James Elroy, *Hassan*, 88; *To a Poet a Thousand Years Hence*, 88
Fleming, Mr, 102, 105
Fleming, Lionel, *Head or Harp*, 62, 69
Forbes, Mansfield, 89, 91, 92, 93, 94, 113
Forbes, Dorothea, 94
Fortesque, Lady, *Perfume from Provence*, 121
Frye, C. Northrop, 205
Fyfe, David, 104

Garden House Hotel, Cambridge, 197
Garibaldi, Giuseppe, 198
George, D. Lloyd, 57
General Strike, (1926), 111
Gilbert, Mr, 84
Goethe, Johann Wolfgang von, 204
Gogarty, Oliver St. John, 71
Golden Head Press, The, 11, 223
Gonne, Maud, 58
Gore-Booth, Eva, *Breffney*, 60
Gore-Booth, Eva, 18
Gore, Colonel, 21
Graves, Nancy, 149
Graves, Robert, *Goodbye To All That*, 94
Gregory, I. A., Lady, in quotation from 'Beautiful Lofty Things', 20; *Visions and Beliefs of the West of Ireland*, 32; *Lady Gregory's Journals* (ed. D. Murphy), 70; *Lady Gregory's Journals, 1916-1930*, (ed. L. Robinson), 214

Gregory, Major Robert, 74
Grierson, Sir Herbert, 75, 88, 89
Grumbold, Robert, 151
Grundy, J. B. C., *Five Windows*, 11

Hallward, Bertrand, 116, 118, 131, 138
Harding, Sir John, 172, 176
Hardy, Thomas, 215
Harper, George Mills, 205
Hart, Professor H. L.A., 'Report of the Committee on Relations with Junior Members', 211
Heaton-Armstrong, Jack, 147
Henn, Desmond, (son), 116, 130, 196
Henn, Edward, (uncle), 73
Henn, Eric Lovett, (cousin), 64, 73
Henn, Francis Blackburne, (father), 16, 17, 18, 19, 20, 21, 23, 25, 29, 41, 45, 46, 51, 55, 57, 59, 62, 63, 65, 66, 67, 68, 69, 70, 77, 125, 215
Henn, Helen, (mother), 13, 16, 17, 19, 21, 48, 50, 55, 65, 66, 67, 68, 69, 70, 71, 74, 77, 81, 83, 100, 123, 192, 195, 214, 215
Henn, Rt. Rev. Henry, Bp. of Burnley, (uncle), 73, 74
Henn, Jane Isabella (grandmother), 49
Henn, Jonathan, (great-uncle), 58
Henn, Maud, (sister), 22
Henn, Muriel, (sister), 22
Henn, Rosalind, (daughter), 116, 130, 196
Henn, Chief Justice Thomas Rice, Q.C., (grandfather), 22, 29, 58, 80
Henn, T. R.,
  as a young man at Cambridge, 57; family background, 58; father's death, effect of, 66; friends going to Cambridge, 71; possibility of going to Cambridge, 73; further educational possibilities, and March examinations, 73; home for the holidays, and contrast of life with Co. Clare, 81, 86; Director of Studies at Clare, Magdalene, Peterhouse, Sidney Sussex, Trinity, and Trinity Colleges, 87, 111; career at Cambridge, 99, 123; Indian interlude, 103; return to

Cambridge after India, 109; 'Original Evenings', 113; duration of University appointments, 115; life at Cambridge, 119, 126; special Pro-proctor, 139; return to Cambridge after War Office interview, 132, 134; home at Cambridge, 132, 217; rooms at St. Catharine's College, 150; Officer's Course, 150; War service as Deputy Assistant Chief of Staff, 171; return to Italy, 172; Cambridge post-War, 185; Chairman of English Board, 191; President of Cambridge Rowing Association, 196; relinquishing of Fellowship, 204; Director of Yeats Society, political advantages of, 204; Course given, 'Poetry and Painting', 206; Visiting Professor at Trinity College, Dublin, 209; paper by him on changes in undergraduates psychology, 210; thoughts on retirement, 217.

Henn, T. R., *works*:
'Attentions', 215; 'The Big House', published in *Last Esays*, 214; 'The Causes of Failure in Examinations', 127, 210; 'Dark Journey', 82, 225; 'Ebb Tide', 43; 'Fall of the House', 213; 'Graveyard Hill', 218; *The Lonely Tower*, 192, 196; *Shooting a Bat*, 57; 'Sluice Gate', 44; 'Waterfall', 32· Warton Lecture on Poetry, 76.

Henn, Wiliam Francis, (brother), 22, 73
Henn, William, (uncle), 16, 24, 43, 44
Herbert, George, 139, 140
Herklots, Hugh, 113
Heyman, G. D. H., 185
Hillary, Richard, *The Last Enemy*, 145
Hinchingbrooke, Viscount, 151
Hirseli, Charles, 153
Hitler, Adolf, 123, 125, 135
Ho Chi-Minh, 198
Hoffman, Daniel, 205
Holbein, Hans 'Pageant', 141
Holmes, Martin, 154
Home Guard, 134, 136, 137, 138, 149, 152

Hopkins, G. M., *Binsey Poplars*, 50
Hough, Graham, 206
Housman, A. E., 38, 113, 131
Hunter, Colin, 98, 117
Huysmans, C., *À Rebours*, 212

International Association for the Study of Anglo-Irish Literature, (IASAIL), 209
Irish Agricultural Organization Society, (IAOS), 57
Irish Civil War, 100, 214
Irish Free State Treaty, 80
Irish Literary Revival, 58, 209
I.R.A., 48, 66, 71, 72, 79, 80, 81, 82, 88

Jack, A. A., 89
James, William, *Varieties of Religious Experience*, 123
Jeffares, A. N., 207
Jefferies, Richard, *The Amateur Poacher*, 25
John, St. of the Cross, 200
Johns, Dr. W. E., 118
John, St., 14
Johnson, Mary, 25
Joint Intelligence Committee (London), 163
Jones, W. H. S., 87
Joyce, James, *Ulysses*, 61
Jukes, J. E., *Loved River*, 27
Jung, Carl Gustav, *Memories, Dreams and Reflections*, 228

Kearton, Cherry, 93
Keats, John 92
Kelly, John, 206
Kennedy, John, 83
Kennelly, Brendan, 206
Khan, Abdul Habib, 105, 106
Kingsley, Charles, *The Water Babies*, 24; *Gods and Heroes*, 25
Kipling, Rudyard, 11, 24; *MacAndrew's Hymn*, 15; *Captains Courageous*, 61, 86, 88, 101

Lamb, Charles, *Tales of Shakespear*, 25
S.S. 'Lancashire', 101
Landor, W. S., 137

Index

Langland, William, *Piers Plowman*, 90
Larkin, James, 57
Lawrence, T. E., 111
Lee, Austin, 113
Lee, Lawrence, 205
Lemnitzer, General Lyman C., 175, 179
Lendrai, Maria, 131
Lewis, C. S., 140
Lewis, Percy Wyndham, 92
Leys School, The, 99
Lister, Raymond, 206
Literature, Royal Society of, 95
Loti, Pièrre, 61
Lucas de Here, 140
Lucas, F. L., *Journal under the Terror*, 91; 96, 113, 200
Lukacz, George, 198
Lumley, Sir Roger, Earl of Scarborough, 164
Lush, Maurice, 175

Macaulay, Lord Thomas, Babington, *Lays of Ancient Rome*, 24
Macklin, David, 118
Macklin, Hilary, 118
McGrath, Raymond, 92
McHugh, Roger, 206
McLean, Kenneth, 163
MacManus, D. A., *The Middle Kingdom*, 32
Macmillan, The Rt. Hon. Harold, 173
MacNab, Colin, 154
McNeill, J. G. Swift, 71
Malinowski, Bronislav, 201
Malins, Edward, 11, 206
Markham, John, 46, 47
Markiewicz, Countess, Constance, née Gore Booth, 18, 58
Markiewicz, Maeve de, 15
Marlowe Society, the, 99
Martin, Sir Leslie, 191
Marvell, A., 142
Masefield, John, 88
Masterman, John, 133
Matthewson, Mr, 102
Mazzini, Giuseppe, 198
Mead, G. C. E., 84
Mitchiner, P. H., 120

Montgomery of Alamein, Viscount, 154, 172
Moore, George, 15, 58, 60; *The Brook Kerith*, 94
Moore, Thomas, 24
Morgan, W. G., 163, 168, 183
Morgenthau, Henry, Jr., 167
Mosley, Oswald, 123
Mudie-Cooke, Miss, 95
Muggeridge, Malcolm, 122
Muir, Edwin, 201
Mulryne, J. R., 206
Munthe, Axel, *The Story of San Michele*, 56
Murphy, Richard, *The Last Galway Hooker*, 40
Murray, Gilbert, 89
Mussolini, Benito, 123

Niemöller, Martin, 182
Nock, A. D., 93
Norman, Monty, 176
Nowlan, Kevin, 206
Nuttall, Neville, *Proud River*, 27

O'Brien, J. Ed., *The Vanishing Irish*, 196
O'Casey, Sean, 19, 59, 199
O'Connell, Daniel, 58
O'Driscoll, Robert, 206
O'Duffy, General Eoin, 123
Olivier, Edith, *Night Thoughts of a Country Landlady*, 148· *Without Meeting, Mr. Walkley*, 148
Owen, Sir Richard, 25
Oxford and Cambridge Joint Board, 114
Oxford Colleges
  Christ Church College, 108, 118, 123
  Worcester College, 133, 149, 150
Oxford University Press, 150

Pages, the, 157
Palmer, Samuel, 206
Paradise, Co. Clare, 19, 20, 22, 23, 26, 27, 28, 32, 40, 44, 46, 50, 53, 54, 55, 65, 66, 71, 72, 80, 82, 100, 110, 116, 123, 125, 209, 213, 217
Parkinson, Tom, 205
Parnell, Charles Stewart, 54

Parsons, Ian, 113
Pater, Walter, 88
Paull, Mr, 84
Paul St., 201
Peard, Walter, 31
Pearl Harbour, 151, 153
Pembroke, Lord, 147
Petain, Field Marshal Henri Phillippe, 180
Pius XII, Pope, 175
Plato, 201
The Pleasures of Old Age, 217
Plotinus, 29, 201, *Enneads VI*, 296
Plutarch, 32
Poetry Society, The, 149
Pope, Alexander, *Homer*, 25
Porphyry, 29
Portway, D. P., *Militant Don, Old Contemptible*, 131; President of Selection Board in India, 188
Potts, Leonard, 96, 114
Powell, Enoch, 99
Preparatory Schools Rifle Association, The, 63
Punch, 159

Quayle, Anthony, 175
Quiller Couch, Sir A., 'Q', 87, 88, 89, 90, 111

Raine, Kathleen, *Collected Poems*, 11; *Defending Ancient Springs*, 201, 206, verses by, 216, stanzas by, 218
Raleigh, Sir Walter, 88.
Rankin 'A' (later Operation Overlord), 161
Rankin, Colonel, 121
Redpath, R. T. H., 99
Rennell, Lord, 176
Richards, I. A., 'Practical Criticism' lectures, 89; *Practical Criticism*, 94; *Science and Poetry*, 94; *Mencius on the Mind*, 94
Richards, Ivor, 96
Richardson, A. E., 150, 151
Richmond, Admiral Sir Herbert, 132
Ridgeway, Sir William, 142
Rilke, Rainer Maria, 183
Rising, the (1916), 76, 77
Roberts, S. C., 95

Robertson, Lt. General, Sir Brian, 172, 176, 181, 183, 185
Roehm, Ernst, 123
Ronsard, Pièrre de, 73, 140
Roosevelt, President F. D., 175
Ross, David, 60
Rossiter, A. P., 111
Ross-Lewin, Tom, 32
Rowe, Nicholas, 'Horror', 'Terror', 142
Royal Society, The, 142
Rushmore, F. M., 118, 119
Russell, G. W., (A.E.), 57, 71
Rylands, George, 99, 114

Saddlemyer, Ann, 205
St. Thomas' Hospital, 151
Sassoon, Siegfried, 88
Scott, Sir Walter, 24
Second World War, 91, 99, 105, 115, 120, 127, 128, 212
Shakespeare, William, comparison with Yeats, 17; *Cymbeline* 59; *Taming of the Shrew*, 87; *Othello*, 130; *As You Like It*, 137, 215; *Hamlet*, 139; *Romeo and Juliet*, 140; *Henry IV*, 148; quotation from, as pass-word, 154
Shaw, George Bernard, 58, 59, 88; *John Bull's Other Island*, 71
Shelley, Percy Bysshe, 24
Sinker, Paul, 96
Skelton, Robin, 205
Skues, G. E. M., 147
Smythe, Colin, 32, 214
Snow, C. P., *The Masters*, 115, 197
Somerville and Ross, 53, 55; *Experiences of an Irish R.M.*, 25
Sophocles, 228
Speaight, Robert, 207
Spencer, Terence, 209
Spens, Sir Will, 109, 113
Spencer, Edmund, 62, 195
Spofford, General Charles, 170, 172, 173
Spring-Rice, Tom, 98
Statesman and Nation, 91
Stephens, James, 200; *The Crock of Gold*, 25
Stephenson, Alfred, 89
Stevenson, Robert Louis, 208

Index

Stewart, H. F., 87
Stoddart, T. T., *Angling Songs,* 29
Stratford-upon-Avon Summer School, 203
Stratford, conferences, 209
Street, A. G., 136, 149
Strong, L. A. G., 199
Supreme Headquarters Allied Expeditionary Force (S H A E F) 160, 164, 171, 185, 212
The Swan and Her Crew, 51
Swift, Dean Jonathan, *The Counter Scuffle,* 22; 81, 143
Sydney, Sir Philip, *Arcadia,* 137
Synge, J. M., 16, 47, 58, 139, 143; *The Aran Islands,* 195; 'Danny', 20; *Deirdre of the Sorrows,* 59; *Riders to the Sea,* 60, 61
Tait, André, 131
Tait, Margaret, 118
Taylor, H. M., 190
Tennyson, Alfred, 1st Baron, 'Ulysses', 9
Things to Make, 51
Thoor Ballylee, 29, 193, 194, 204, 208
Tillyard, E. M. W., *The Muse Unchained,* 87; 95, 99, 113, 192
Tito, Josif Broz, 181
Torchiana, Donald, *Georgian Ireland,* 205
Tracy, Honor, *The Straight and Narrow Path,* 14
Trench, W. S., *Memoirs of a Land Agent,* 21
Trinity College, Dublin, 16, 70, 71, 72, 209
'Troubles', The, 9, 22, 26, 28, 70, 76, 81, 82, 86, 88, 100, 125, 188, 213, 214
'Twa Corbies, The', 45

Union, Act of, 1808, 215
University of California, Berkeley, 197, 212
University College, Dublin, 204
University of Columbia, New York, 197
U N R R A, 186

Vernon, Sir Richard, 148

Verrall, A. W., 88
Villon, François, 73

Wallace, W. A., 207
Walney, Nathaniel, 139, 140, 141, 142, 143
Warner, Francis, 206
Watson, Mary, 206
Webb-Peploe, Godfrey, 89
Webster, John, *Duchess of Malfi,* 99; 140, 142
Wells, H. G., 58, 59
Westcott, Rt. Rev. Foss, Bishop of Calcutta, 108
Whalley, Phillip, 96
Whistler, Rex, 149
Whitby, Sir Lionel, 127
White, Gilbert, 146
White, Milner, 152
White, T. H., *The Elephant and the Kangaroo,* 113; *England Have My Bones,* 49; *The Sword in the Stone,* 113
Wilde, Oscar, 59
Wilkinson, C. H., 150
Willey, Basil, 96
Williams, Prof. W. M., 99
Wilson, Edmund, *The Wound and the Bow,* 228
Wilson, F. A. C., 205
Wilson, Field Marshal, H. M. W., First Baron, 170, 171, 172
Wilson, Mona, 149
Wilson, Richard, 173
Wilton House, 93, 134, 136, 147, 148, 149, 151, 152, 156, 159
Wintour, Charles, 161
Witt, Marian, 205
Wolff, Fraulein, 23
Wood-Martin, W. G., *Traces of the Elder Faiths in Ireland,* 25
Woolley, Sir Leonard, 149
World Conference on Medical Education, 127
Wynne, Rt. Rev. Edward (Bp. of Ely), 95
Wynne, Frank, 204

'X' Pit affair, 182

Yale University, 135

Yeats, J. B., the elder, 15
Yeats, Jack B., 24, 47
Yeats, W. B., 10, 13, 17, 18, 24, 29, 32, 53, 54, 73, 75, 77, 88, 122, 123, 137, 192, 194, 201, 202, 223, 226
Works: 'Ancestral Houses', 214; 'Beautiful Lofty Things', 20, 192; 'The Curse of Cromwell', 57, 78, 216; 'A Dialogue of Self and Soul', 213; 'The Fisherman', 225; 'Innisfree', 60; 'The Irish Airman forsees his Death', 74; 'Mad as the Mist and Snow', 217; 'The New Faces', 194; 'Nineteen Hundred and Nineteen', 82, 214; *On the Boiler*, 15; *Reveries Over Childhood and Youth*, 15; *Purgatory*, 214, 216; 'The Stare's Nest by My Window', 76; 'The Statues', 57; 'Three Movements', 42; 'To be carved on a Stone at Thoor Ballylee', 194, 208; 'Upon a House Shaken by the Land Agitation', 214; *Variorum Edition of the Poems* (eds. P. Allt & Russell K. Alspach), 205

Yeats, Mrs W. B., (George), 193, 206

Yeats International Summer School, Sligo, 202, 204, 207

The Yeats Society, 202, 204, 207

Young, E., *Night Thoughts*, 140

Young, Brett, 60

Young, G. M., 149